❖ Gender and Welfare State Regimes

Gender and Politics represents the most recent scholarship in the areas of women, gender, and politics, and is explicitly cross-national in its organization and orientation. Recognizing the contribution of women's studies to gendered political analysis, the goal of *Gender and Politics* is to develop, and to publish, frontier analysis, the empirical research exemplary of the intersection between political studies and women's studies.

The series is edited by Professor Karen Beckwith at the Department of Political Science, College of Wooster and Professor Joni Lovenduski, Department of Politics, University of Southampton.

Gender and Welfare State Regimes

edited by
DIANE SAINSBURY

OXFORD
UNIVERSITY PRESS

OXFORD
UNIVERSITY PRESS

Great Clarendon Street, Oxford OX2 6DP

Oxford University Press is a department of the University of Oxford.
It furthers the University's objective of excellence in research, scholarship,
and education by publishing worldwide in

Oxford New York

Athens Auckland Bangkok Bogotá Buenos Aires Calcutta
Cape Town Chennai Dar es Salaam Delhi Florence Hong Kong Istanbul
Karachi Kuala Lumpur Madrid Melbourne Mexico City Mumbai
Nairobi Paris São Paulo Singapore Taipei Tokyo Toronto Warsaw

and associated companies in Berlin Ibadan

Oxford is a registered trade mark of Oxford University Press
in the UK and certain other countries

Published in the United States
by Oxford University Press Inc., New York

British Library Cataloguing in Publication Data

Data available

Library of Congress Cataloging in Publication Data

Gender and welfare state regimes / edited by Diane Sainsbury.
(Gender and politics)
Includes bibliographical references and index.
1. Women–Government policy. 2. Welfare state. 3. Social policy.
4. Comparative government. 5. Sexual division of labor.
I. Sainsbury, Diane. II. Series.
HQ1236.G4613 1999 361.6'5–dc21 99-13231
ISBN 0-19-829417-4.   ISBN 0-19-829416-6 (Pbk.)

1 3 5 7 9 10 8 6 4 2

Typeset by Best-set Typesetter Ltd., Hong Kong
Printed in Great Britain
on acid-free paper by
Biddles Ltd
Guildford and King's Lynn

❖ Acknowledgements

This book grew out of a set of papers presented at a panel on 'Gender Inequality across Welfare State Regimes' at the 1996 Annual Meeting of the American Political Science Association. The editor and authors of the first four chapters are grateful to the two panel discussants, Wendy Sarvasy and Tim Tilton, for their comments. We would also like to thank the two series editors, Karen Beckwith and Joni Lovenduski, for their strong support of this project. At a formative stage of the volume, the referees of Oxford University Press offered useful comments that strengthened the design of the book. In particular, the editor is thankful to Leslie Eliason for her constructive suggestions. A final word of thanks is owed to Robert Brewster for technical assistance and moral support.

❖ Contents

❖ Part One
Gender Inequality and Welfare State Regimes

❖ Part Two
The Gendered Impact of Policies across Welfare State Regimes

❖ List of Figures

❖ List of Tables

❖ Abbreviations

ABS	Australian Bureau of Statistics
ATP	Allmän tilläggspension (General Supplementary Pension)
AWBZ	Algemene Wet Bijondere Ziektekosten (Exceptional Medical Expenses Act)
CPSI	Central Pension Security Institution
DIR	Department of Industrial Relations
EEOC	Equal Employment Opportunities Commission
EOC	Equal Opportunites Commission
EU	European Union
ILO	International Labour Organization
Istat	Istituto Nazionale di Statistica
LIS	Luxembourg Income Study
NOSOSKO	Nordic Committee of Social Statistics
NWO	Netherlands Organization for Scientific Research
OECD	Organization of Economic Cooperation and Development
OLS	ordinary least squares
PPPS	Purchasing Power parties
REOB	Foundation for Law and Government
RFV	National Social Insurance Board (Stockholm)
SCIP	Social Citizenship Indicator Program
SD	Statistics Denmark
SII	Social Insurance Institution
SYF	*Statistical Yearbook of Finland*
TAFE	technical and further education
UN	United Nations
WLS	weighted least squares

❖ Notes on Contributors

JONATHAN BRADSHAW is Professor of Social Policy at the University of York. He is Director of the Institute for Research in the Social Sciences, Associate Director of the Social Policy Research Unit, and Co-Director of the European Observatory on National Family Policies. He has written numerous publications on single-parent families. Among his most recent are *The Employment of Lone Parents: A Comparison of Policy in 20 Countries* (1996) and 'International Comparisons of Support for Lone Parents', in Reuben Ford and Jane Millar (eds.), *Private Lives and Public Responses: Lone Parenthood and Future Policy in the UK* (1998).

JET BUSSEMAKER is Lecturer in Women's Studies, Department of Political Science and Public Administration, Free University, Amsterdam. She is co-author of 'Gender and Welfare States: Some Theoretical Reflections', in Diane Sainsbury (ed.) *Gendering Welfare States* (1994), and co-editor of *Gender, Participation, and Citizenship in the Netherlands* (1998).

JANET C. GORNICK is Associate Professor of Political Science at Baruch College, City University of New York (CUNY). Her most recent publications include 'Public Policies and the Employment of Mothers: A Cross-National Study', *Social Science Quarterly* (1998), and 'Gender, the Welfare State, and Public Employment: A Comparative Study of Seven Industrialized Countries', *American Sociological Review* (1998).

MAJELLA KILKEY is Lecturer in Social Policy at the School of Comparative and Applied Social Sciences, University of Hull, and a doctoral candidate at the University of York. She is co-author of *The Employment of Lone Parents: A Comparison of Policy in 20 Countries* (1996) and *A Synthesis of National Family Policies 1996* (1998).

MARCIA K. MEYERS is Associate Professor of Social Work at Columbia University and Associate Director of the New York City Social Indicators Survey Center. Her most recent publications include 'Child Care in

Welfare Reform: Are We Targeting Too Narrowly?', *Child Welfare* (1995), and 'Supporting the Employment of Mothers: Policy Variation across Fourteen Welfare States', *Journal of European Social Policy* (1997).

JULIA S. O'CONNOR is Director of the National Economic and Social Council in Dublin. Up to September 1996 she was Associate Professor of Sociology with cross appointments in the political science doctoral programme in public policy and in the School of Social Work at McMaster University, Hamilton, Ontario, Canada. She is author of 'From Women in the Welfare State to Gendering Welfare State Regimes', *Current Sociology* (1996), and co-author of *States, Markets, Families: Gender, Liberalism and Social Policy in Australia, Great Britain, Canada and the United States* (1999).

KATHERIN E. ROSS is a Ph.D. candidate in the Social Science Program at Syracuse University (USA) and staff associate of the Luxembourg Income Study. She is co-author of 'Supporting the Employment of Mothers: Policy Variation across Fourteen Welfare States', *Journal of European Social Policy* (1997), and 'Public Policies and the Employment of Mothers: A Cross-National Study', LIS Working Paper No. 140 (1996).

DIANE SAINSBURY is Acting Professor of Political Science, University of Stockholm. She is editor of *Gendering Welfare States* (1994) and author of *Gender, Equality and Welfare States* (1996).

KEES VAN KERSBERGEN is Lecturer in Political Science, School of Public Affairs, University of Nijmegen. He is co-author of 'Gender and Welfare States: Some Theoretical Reflections', in Diane Sainsbury (ed.) *Gendering Welfare States* (1994), and author of *Social Capitalism* (1995).

❖ Introduction

Diane Sainsbury

The past decade has witnessed an exciting reorientation in welfare state research. The gender division of welfare, previously a neglected area of study in comparative scholarship, is currently a major focus of interest. Crucial to this reorientation have been feminist critiques of mainstream analyses of welfare states and the combining of feminist and comparative perspectives.

This reorientation has shed new light on the dynamics between gender and welfare state policies. First, earlier feminist theorizing and research on women and the welfare state were usually set in a specific national context. This limitation influenced theories and empirical understandings because they were based on invariance and a tendency to generalize on the basis of a single country's experiences. Comparative feminist studies have pointed to the diversity in welfare state policy outcomes (Leira 1992; Lewis 1993; Sainsbury 1994*b*, 1996; O'Connor *et al.* 1999) and multiple forms of women's politics (Katzenstein and Mueller 1987; Randall 1987; Chamberlayne 1993; Nelson and Chowdhury 1994; Ferree and Martin 1995).

Secondly, focusing on the quality of social rights, feminists have theorized that the principles of entitlement are decisive as to whether policies reinforce existing gender relations or transform them. The bases of entitlement differ in their emancipatory or regulatory potential for women. Again this contrasts with earlier feminist research, which stressed social control and the regulatory nature of welfare state policies. Feminist scholars have also expanded the sphere of rights by considering personhood and bodily integrity (Shaver 1993/4).

Perhaps the most important contribution has been to suggest how to bring gender into the comparative analysis of welfare states and social citizenship. As aptly put by Julia S. O'Connor (1996: 104), 'there has been a major shift in emphasis from making women in welfare states visible in the analysis to gender as a dimension of the analysis'. In gendering welfare states, feminist scholars have proceeded in various ways and produced different analytical frameworks (for overviews, see Gornick 1995, O'Connor 1996, and Orloff 1996).

At least two broad alternative approaches have emerged from these efforts. The first approach has been to build gender into mainstream theoretical frameworks. This has been done by reconstructing the core ideas and key analytical categories so that they include gender. A major rationale for this strategy has been that 'feminist research can thereby incorporate advances in the mainstream literature while transforming it to incorporate gender relations' (Orloff 1993: 305). The second approach holds that mainstream theories are fundamentally lacking, and new frameworks and models must be formulated. Proponents of this approach warn against a strategy that merely adds on women to frameworks where the male is the norm (Lewis and Ostner 1991, 1994; Lewis 1992; Sainsbury 1994a).

Each of these approaches has its strengths and weaknesses, but they largely complement each other. Although it may be useful, especially initially, to separate out gender because it focuses on facets omitted in mainstream analysis, such an approach is incomplete. It is necessary to examine the interplay between gender-relevant dimensions of variation with those identified as important by the mainstream literature. By contrast, building gender into mainstream frameworks retains their insights. A drawback is the potential difficulty of distinguishing between the influences of gender relations and other determinants of welfare state policies when feminist and mainstream perspectives are compounded in single ideal types or policy regimes. This strategy may also inadvertently incorporate the shortcomings of mainstream frameworks.

Feminist scholars have differed in their strategies of enquiry, but an underlying concern in feminist comparative research has been the conceptualization of gender-relevant dimensions of variation. One major thrust has been to incorporate gender in the welfare state regime concept, taking Gøsta Esping-Andersen's three dimensions of variation has a starting point (O'Connor 1993, 1996; Orloff 1993). The dimensions in his scheme are: the nexus of the state and market in the distribution system, the quality of social rights as reflected in decommodification, and the stratifying effects of welfare entitlements.

Ann Orloff's framework (1993) represents the most systematic effort to build gender into the welfare state regime concept. First, rather than taking the nexus between the market and the state, Orloff refashions this dimension of variation as *state, market, and family relations*. This modification recognizes the family and women's unpaid work as a variation in social provision. Her second dimension is the pattern of *gender stratification produced by entitlements.* She distinguishes between gender differentiation and gender inequality. Gender differentiation in entitlements occurs when claims to benefits are based on the traditional division of labour between the sexes. Men receive benefits as family providers and workers, while women claim benefits as wives and mothers. Gender inequality refers to differences in the benefit levels of women and men, which is often affected by gender differentiation. Benefits tied to participation in the workforce are usually more generous than benefits claimed on the basis of wifely or motherly labour.

Orloff adds two new dimensions of variation to decommodification— the key indicator of the quality of social rights in Esping-Andersen's analytical scheme. Decommodification, the ability to maintain a livelihood without reliance on the market (Esping-Andersen 1990: 22), presupposes social rights based on labour-market participation. This supposition is problematic, because many women work in the home. It is also problematic because employment provides a source of independent income for women and can alter their dependency within the family. To eliminate these difficulties Orloff proposes *access to paid work* as her third dimension. The fourth dimension of her framework is *the capacity to form and maintain an autonomous household.* This dimension parallels decommodification, which frees wage-earners from the dictates of the market. The ability to form and maintain an autonomous household frees women from the necessity to marry to gain access to a breadwinner's income in order to survive and support their children.

Other scholars have highlighted gender in isolation from mainstream theoretical frameworks. Jane Lewis, together with Ilona Ostner, have taken the breadwinner model as a point of departure (Lewis and Ostner 1991, 1994; Lewis 1992). They devise an alternative categorization of welfare state regimes based on the gender division of labour that prescribes breadwinning for men and homemaking/caring for women. In constructing their typology, Lewis and Ostner focus on how women are treated in the social-security system, the level of social-service provision, particularly childcare, and married women's position in the labour market. They distinguish between the strong, the moderate, and the weak male-breadwinner model or the dual-breadwinner model.

Drawing upon the feminist critique of mainstream welfare state research, Diane Sainsbury has outlined gender models of social policy (1994*a*, 1996). Her strategy has been to recast the generalizations of the feminist critique into dimensions of variation, constructing two contrasting ideal types: the male-breadwinner and the individual models. The dimensions of this scheme are largely a specification of the state–market–family relations and the stratification dimensions, but Sainsbury also emphasizes the importance of *gender and familial ideologies* as a key variation. Her framework additionally highlights whether *social rights are familialized or individualized*.

An advantage of this scheme is that it clearly specifies the dimensions of variation, whereas earlier discussions of the male-breadwinner model tended to conflate dimensions. A further asset of the framework is that it distinguishes between policy and behaviour, which are often confounded. Finally, it pays equal attention to the social rights of women and men, whereas other models have tended to make the rights of either women or men the focal point of analysis. The empirical application of Sainsbury's framework, however, pointed to the limitations of an analytical scheme based on two contrasting types. It suggested an additional ideal type that differentiates between women's entitlement as wives and as mothers, which is developed in Chapter 3.

Recently Lewis has revisited her earlier work, addressing criticisms and suggesting new lines of development (1997). She calls for the analysis of 'caring regimes', arguing that the crucial variations are how unpaid work is valued and how it is shared among women and men. Barbara Hobson (Hobson and Takahashi 1996) has developed the notion of care regimes, using them to analyse the social rights of solo mothers. She distinguishes between two alternative regimes that compensate care and represent coherent strategies towards the organization of paid and unpaid work. In the first regime all mothers are assumed to be carers and solo mothers are entitled to a social wage for their tasks as caregivers. The alternative regime assumes that all mothers are workers, care services are available to enable mothers to enter employment, and compensation for care is based on labour-market status.

❖ PURPOSE

Building on the insights produced by this reorientation, the major purpose of the book is to enlarge our understandings of how gender is constructed in welfare state policies and how these policies are a force in ordering gender relations through an examination of a wide range of national contexts. To accomplish this, we focus on three challenges in the literature.

First, as outlined above, feminists have proposed alternative frameworks and approaches. This book attempts to consolidate these approaches in two ways. The dimensions of variation from different analytical schemes can be brought together to provide a more rounded framework. In the chapters that follow, the dimensions of variation generated by the two approaches inform the authors' analyses. More importantly, we are interested in the patterning of variations as distinct gender policy regimes. A regime can be defined as a complex of rules and norms that create established expectations, and a gender regime consists of the rules and norms about gender relations, allocating tasks and rights to the two sexes. A gender policy regime entails a logic based on the rules and norms about gender relations that influences the construction of policies. We use gender regime and gender policy regime interchangeably in this volume.

Secondly, feminist criticisms of the welfare state and social policy regimes have questioned whether mainstream classifications—and in particular Esping-Andersen's welfare-regime typology—would hold up if gender were incorporated into the analysis. Initial probes, focusing on gender differentiation in entitlements, disclose a clustering of countries that differs from mainstream categorizations. However, most of these probes have dealt with a limited number of countries. Researchers have looked either at countries belonging to the same type or at contrasting countries. A point of departure for this book has been to evaluate these competing claims by examining gender and policies *both* within and across types of welfare states. This starting point leads to three questions. To what extent do gender regimes cut across welfare state regimes? What are the interlocking effects of gender regimes and welfare state regimes? How much regime variability exists and what accounts for the intra-regime variations?

The research design of this book offers us a strong handle to address these questions. As pointed out by Orloff (1996: 68), 'conclusions based on analyses that contrast countries purporting to represent different regime types are very likely influenced by which country is chosen to "stand in" for any given regime cluster, when we have not carefully assessed their differences and similarities across dimensions relevant for gender'. This observation necessitates a most-similar nations comparative strategy where countries representing the same welfare state regimes are analysed. Such a strategy, however, is prone to uncovering variations and fragmenting the regime cluster. Therefore, we also compare across welfare state regimes to determine whether the variations outweigh the commonalities and whether new clusters are formed.

Thirdly, feminist comparative analysis of welfare states has primarily dealt with how gender is coded in policies and mapped out variations across countries. So far less attention has been devoted to explaining gender variations in welfare state policies or cross-national differences in women's and men's social rights. When authors have engaged in explanation, the chief *explanans* has often been gender relations. Our third aim is to offer explanations that place women's politics and gender relations centre stage but also stress the importance of institutional arrangements and policy legacies.

❖ The Structure of the Book

The organizing concept in Part One is welfare state regimes, and each of the chapters deals with a specific type—the social-capitalist (or conservative), the liberal, and the social-democratic welfare state. The construction of gender in the policies of each type of welfare state regime is examined. A central issue is how the distinguishing characteristics of the welfare state regimes strengthen or counteract gender inequalities in social rights and policy outcomes. These chapters share three aims: to clarify the implications of each type of welfare state regime for the construction of gender in policies, to identify the major variations in women's and men's social rights across the countries representing each regime, and to explain the differences.

Chapter 1 discusses the contemporary predicament of social-capitalist welfare states, focusing on Germany, Italy, the Netherlands, and Belgium. Jet Bussemaker and Kees van Kersbergen argue that the institutional constraints and legacies of this welfare state regime distinctively structure gender relations in the labour market, systems of income maintenance, and the provision of social services. They initially present an overview of specific aspects of the social-capitalist or conservative welfare state and their influence on gender relations. The authors go on to discuss how changing gender and family relations are increasingly putting pressure on social-capitalist welfare states. They then map out the similarities and differences across the four countries in gender inequalities in the labour market, income maintenance programmes, and social services.

Chapter 2 turns to the liberal welfare states—Australia, Canada, the UK, and the USA. Julia O'Connor examines gender and strategies related to pay and employment equity. Her analysis reveals marked differences in policy implementation choices and success across the four countries. These differences are linked to policy legacies, the industrial-relations frameworks, the organizational strength of the labour movement, the level of party support for equality policies, and the strategies adopted by the women's movement.

Gender and the social-democratic welfare states are dealt with in Chapter 3. Diane Sainsbury develops an analytical framework identifying three gender policy regimes. The framework is then applied in analysing the inscription of gender relations in social provision in Denmark, Finland, Norway, and Sweden. In contrast to mainstream research that has emphasized the similarities between welfare state policies in Norway and

Sweden, and that these two countries are the closest approximation of the social-democratic welfare state regime, policy differences stand out when gender is considered. The next part of the analysis seeks to account for the differences between Norwegian and Swedish policies. The concluding sections discuss the features of the social-democratic welfare state regime that undercut gender inequalities and the emergence of a common gender policy regime.

In Part Two the focus shifts to policies and outcomes. We are interested in studying welfare state policies as a force in ordering gender relations. Policies are now the explanatory variable, and the chapters look at how policies affect women's and men's life chances and whether policies preserve or alter gender relations in a society. Through comparisons across types of welfare states, Part Two also explores whether gender regimes correspond to or cut across welfare state regimes.

More specifically, Chapters 4–7 provide 'global' comparisons of employment-support policies for mothers, policies affecting the income packages of solo mothers and their economic well-being, taxation as it privileges family types and affects employment incentives, and women's employment and earnings vis-à-vis men's. Each of the chapters takes a gender-relevant dimension of variation as its point of departure: state, market, and family relations, the ability to uphold a socially acceptable standard of living independently of family relationships, and access to paid work.

In theorizing about gender and welfare states, feminists have called attention to the nexus between the state, family, and market as a crucial welfare state variation. Welfare states vary in terms of public versus private responsibility for care of children, the elderly, and the disabled. Public policies, such as parental leave and childcare provision, or their absence shape the division of labour between the sexes in the home and society by structuring women's employment opportunities and access to paid work. In Chapter 4 Marcia Meyers, Janet Gornick, and Katherin Ross analyse the effects of parental leave and public childcare provision on mothers' employment in fourteen countries. Their results suggest that policy configurations influence the employment patterns of mothers primarily by providing an alternative to leaving the labour market for mothers who choose to combine employment and parenting. The analysis of national policy performance reveals a cluster of countries—France, Belgium, Finland, Denmark, Sweden, and Italy—that cuts across Esping-Andersen's welfare state typology.

Feminist scholars have grappled with the issue of the quality of social rights, arguing that decommodification by itself is inadequate when gender is central to the analysis. They have advocated supplementary gauges that underline the significance of independence in family relations. Apart from the ability to form and maintain an autonomous household (Orloff 1993), two other alternatives to appraise social rights and their emancipatory potential have been suggested: (1) personal autonomy 'insulation from dependence, both personal dependence on family members and/or public dependence on state agencies' (O'Connor 1993: 514), and (2) defamilialization—the capacity for individual adults to uphold a socially acceptable standard of living independently of family relationships (Lister 1994: 37).

In the current rethinking of social rights, solo mothers occupy a special place. As a group, they and their children have been extremely vulnerable to poverty; they provide a rigorous test in terms of justice and citizenship rights as well as the effectiveness of policies. Adopting the dimension of defamilialization, Majella Kilkey and Jonathan Bradshaw assess the impact of policies on the economic well-being of solo mothers in Chapter 5. The chapter commences by discussing the theoretical and policy relevance of solo mothers, and how they challenge both mainstream and feminist welfare typologies. The authors present trends in the growing prevalence of solo mothers across countries and the routes to solo motherhood. Using the most recent wave of data from the Luxembourg Income Study (LIS), they examine the economic well-being of single-parent families in relation to two-parent families, along with the poverty rates of solo mothers in paid work compared to those without paid employment. The chapter then analyses the influence of tax and benefit arrangements on mothers' employment. Kilkey and Bradshaw conclude by offering a classification of the countries based on the effectiveness of policies in enabling solo mothers to uphold a socially acceptable standard of living independently of men and the importance of employment and/or state benefits in contributing to their economic well-being.

Chapter 6 centres on taxation—a policy area frequently downplayed in typologies of welfare states—but emphasized by feminists. Taxation, for example, is a component of analytical frameworks based on the breadwinner model (Lewis and Ostner 1991; Sainsbury 1994a, 1996). This chapter argues that the tax system is a crucial nexus between the state, family, and the market. It looks at the preferential treatment of marriage and family obligations in taxation, along with taxes as disincentives or incentives for wives' employment, in fourteen OECD countries. Comparing tax systems in the mid-1980s and the mid-1990s, the chapter shows that diversity among the countries has actually widened with respect to tax relief for family responsibilities. A few countries have totally eliminated such tax relief, while others have substantially increased it during the past fifteen years. To understand the reasons behind the growing diversity, the author singles out four countries representing opposite cases for a more detailed examination of the politics of tax reform.

The topic of Chapter 7 is access to paid work and its impact on women's economic resources compared to men's in general and within the family. Janet Gornick examines cross-national variations in women's employment and earnings, relative to men's, across fifteen industrialized countries in the early 1990s, using the most recent wave of the LIS data. For nine of the countries, levels of gender equality in these labour markets are described and compared with respect to: (1) employment, (2) engagement in full-time work, and (3) earnings. She paints the cross-national earnings portrait from three angles: (1) 'net' earnings gaps, which capture levels of gender discrimination in pay; (2) 'gross' earnings gaps, which characterize the extent to which women workers' remuneration differs from men's; and (3) the share of the economy earned by women, a composite indicator of the degree to which women as a whole share the total labour-market returns. The chapter focuses initially on the labour-market attachment and earnings of working-aged women as a whole; subsequently it turns to married women and mothers of young children. The analysis explores the extent to which welfare state regimes are associated with unique labour-market outcomes.

Chapter 8 ties together the analyses of the earlier chapters by summarizing how gender-relevant variations cut across welfare state types and how they are specific to a particular regime. Together the chapters show the significance of the interrelationships between systems of income maintenance, taxation, public provision of services, and the labour market in structuring and transforming gender relations. The chapters underlined the welfare state as a central institution in the construction of different models of gender relations. In turn, differing strategies and demands of the women's movement, the organizational strength of the labour movement and industrial-relations frameworks, the level of party support for equality policies or conversely for policies reflecting a traditional division of labour between the sexes, and policy legacies have been crucial to how gender relations have been inscribed in welfare state policies across countries.

❖ REFERENCES

BALDWIN, S., AND FALKINGHAM, J. (1994) (eds.), *Social Security and Social Change: New Challenges to the Beveridge Model* (New York).

CHAMBERLAYNE, P. (1993), 'Women and the State: Changes in Roles and Rights in France, West Germany, Italy and Britain, 1970–1990', in Lewis (1993), 170–93.

ESPING-ANDERSEN, G. (1990), *The Three Worlds of Welfare Capitalism* (Cambridge).

FERREE, M. M., AND MARTIN, P. Y. (1995) (eds.), *Feminist Organizations: Harvest of the New Women's Movement* (Philadelphia).

GORNICK, J. (1995), 'Bringing Gender into Comparative Welfare State Research: An Assessment of the Typological Approach', paper presented at the Annual Meeting of the American Political Science Association, Chicago, 31 Aug.– 3 Sept.

HOBSON, B., AND TAKAHASHI, M. (1996), 'Care Regimes, Solo Mothers and the Recasting of Social Citizenship Rights', paper presented at Seminar 1 of the EC programme 'Gender and Citizenship: Social Integration and Social Exclusion in European Welfare States', Netherlands Institute for Advanced Studies, Wassenaar, the Netherlands, July.

KATZENSTEIN, M., AND MUELLER, C. M. (1987) (eds.), *The Women's Movements of the United States and Western Europe* (Philadelphia).

LEIRA, A. (1992), *Welfare States and Working Mothers: The Scandinavian Experience* (Cambridge).

LEWIS, J. (1992), 'Gender and the Development of Welfare Regimes', *Journal of European Social Policy*, 2/3: 159–73.

—— (1993) (ed.), *Women and Social Policies in Europe: Work, Family and the State* (Aldershot).

—— (1997), 'Gender and Welfare Regimes: Further Thoughts', *Social Politics: International Studies in Gender, State and Society*, 4/2: 160–77.

—— AND OSTNER, I. (1991), 'Gender and the Evolution of European Social Policies', paper presented at the CES Workshop 'Emergent Supranational Social Policy: The EC's Social Dimension in Comparative Perspective', Center for European Studies, Harvard University. 15–17 Nov.

—— —— (1994), 'Gender and the Evolution of European Social Policies', Working Paper No. 4/94, Centre for Social Policy Research, University of Bremen.

LISTER, R. (1994), '"She Has Other Duties"—Women, Citizenship and Social Security', in Baldwin and Falkingham (1994), 31–44.

NELSON, B., AND CHOWDHURY, N. (1994) (eds.), *Women and Politics Worldwide* (New Haven).

O'CONNOR, J. S. (1993), 'Gender, Class and Citizenship in the Comparative Analysis of Welfare State Regimes: Theoretical and Methodological Issues', *British Journal of Sociology*, 44/3: 501–18.

—— (1996), 'From Women in the Welfare State to Gendering Welfare State Regimes', *Current Sociology*, 44/2: 1–130.

—— ORLOFF, A. S., AND SHAVER, S. (1999), *States, Markets, Families: Gender, Liberalism and Social Policy in Australia, Great Britain, Canada and the United States* (Cambridge).

❖ DIANE SAINSBURY

ORLOFF, A. S. (1993), 'Gender and the Social Rights of Citizenship: The Comparative Analysis of State Policies and Gender Relations', *American Sociological Review*, 58/3: 303–28.

—— (1996), 'Gender in the Welfare State', *Annual Review of Sociology*, 22: 51–78.

RANDALL, V. (1987), *Women and Politics: An International Perspective* (London).

SAINSBURY, D. (1994*a*) 'Women's and Men's Social Rights: Gendering Dimensions of Welfare State', in Sainsbury (1994*b*), 150–69.

—— (1994b), (ed.), *Gendering Welfare States* (London).

—— (1996), *Gender, Equality and Welfare States* (Cambridge).

SHAVER, S. (1993/4), 'Body Rights, Social Rights and the Liberal Welfare State', *Critical Social Policy*, 39: 66–93.

❖ **Part One**

Gender Inequality and Welfare State Regimes

1 ❖ Contemporary Social-Capitalist Welfare States and Gender Inequality

Jet Bussemaker and Kees van Kersbergen

A leading hypothesis of comparative research is that the political institutions and mechanisms of a welfare state regime govern patterns of social inequality to a considerable extent. This effect of the welfare state was found to be relevant in many areas, ranging from patterns of urban poverty to changes in the general distribution of income, and from the structuring of post-industrial employment careers to the transformation of the class structure and the formation of new classes.

This chapter examines the relationship between gender inequality and social capitalism, a welfare state regime. Very briefly, this regime is defined as 'the distinctive arrangement between market, state, society and family by which resources produced in the private economy are channelled into social institutions that fail to secure their means of income themselves' (Van Kersbergen 1995: 190). What are the implications of this welfare state regime for gender relations? Does social capitalism correspond to a parallel gender regime? To what extent do gender relations contribute to the contemporary predicament of this welfare state regime? How do the existing yet changing institutions of the labour market, social security, social services, and taxation interrelate and structure gender relations? To what extent do empirical differences between social-capitalist nations call for a critical reformulation of regime theory?

We would like to thank Inge Bleijenbergh for research assistance and collecting data. Jet Bussemaker wants to thank the Foundation for Law and Government (REOB), which is part of the Netherlands Organization for Scientific Research (NWO), for financial support to work on this research.

As argued elsewhere (Bussemaker and van Kersbergen 1994), it is possible to distinguish analytically between two questions that can motivate the attempt to combine mainstream welfare state theory with the gender perspective. The first question is under which conditions and to what extent social policies affect gender relations. The second question deals with the reverse—namely, with the conditions under which and the extent to which gender relations affect social policies. In order to integrate the gender perspective into mainstream theories attention needs to be paid both to the manner in which gender dimensions are embedded in the formulation and implementation of social policies and to the effects of these policies on gender relations. In other words, assumptions about gender underlie the institutional characteristics of a welfare state regime, and the institutional constraints and historical legacies of a regime type are likely to have distinctive effects on gender relations.

In this chapter we try to generalize and substantiate these assumptions empirically by focusing specifically on the similarities and differences in patterns of gender inequality *among* social-capitalist welfare states. We therefore present an empirical analysis of within-group rather than between-group variation on the crucial features of social capitalism, concentrating on the core countries; Germany, Italy, the Netherlands, and Belgium. France does share some of the characteristics, but does not belong to the core countries of social capitalism,[1] and is therefore not systematically compared to the other cases. Occasionally we will pay attention to France, but mainly to highlight some striking contrasts with the other countries. In order to observe the extent to which the historical legacies of social capitalism still determine current developments and challenges as well as the extent to which new directions in policies have been developed recently, we concentrate on the period since 1980. This approach allows us to highlight changes over time and to examine whether empirically observed within-group variation is significant enough to justify a critical reformulation of the leading typology of welfare state regimes. Our central thesis is that social capitalism still has a strong gender bias. However, the manner in which social capitalism generates gender inequality and the kind of inequality have changed substantially over time as well as among countries. To explain the differences it is necessary, we argue, to take political factors into consideration.

The chapter is organized as follows. The first section deals with the manner in which assumptions about gender underlie the institutional characteristics of social capitalism. In addition, it concentrates on the manner in which assumptions about gender affect the contemporary challenges confronting social-capitalist nations. Subsequently our attention shifts to the distinctive effects of social policies on gender inequality.

In the second section we look briefly at patterns of social spending. The third section deals with gender and income maintenance (including care allowances) and concentrates on the changing breadwinner bias in social capitalism. The fourth section is devoted to gender and labour-market issues and focuses on the changing labour-market participation of women. The fifth section deals with the changing provision of services, particularly childcare facilities. The concluding section offers a discussion of the possible determinants of the observed empirical differences between the core social-capitalist countries.

❖ SOCIAL CAPITALISM AND GENDER: Features and Challenges

According to Gøsta Esping-Andersen (1990), a welfare state regime is the distinctive configuration of market, state, and family that a nation has adopted in the pursuit of work and welfare. Cross-national variation in welfare state development can be identified by looking at (1) the quality of social rights and the extent to which these rights liberate citizens from market forces (decommodification: 'the degree to which individuals, or families, can uphold a socially acceptable standard of living independently of market participation' (Esping-Andersen 1990: 37), (2) the resulting patterns of stratification, and (3) the way in which state, market, and family are interrelated. These three dimensions produced Esping-Andersen's renowned three types of welfare state regimes.

Approximately until 1980, the social-capitalist (conservative or corporatist) regime, composed of the welfare states of continental Europe, was characterized by its *passive or reactive type of social policy*. This type of social policy de-emphasized direct state intervention, but did stress the need to moderate the harmful outcomes of unfettered market forces by transferring considerable sums of money to support families. Social-capitalist welfare states have been transfer-oriented welfare states. Their focus has traditionally been on cash transfers to households rather than on the direct provision of services. An unconditional commitment to full employment never became a central element of social capitalism (see Therborn 1986), and active labour-market policies have never been an integral ingredient of this regime. Social policy did not aim at altering the logic of the market itself as it did in the social-democratic regime. It was to preserve the capitalist market, but—the crucial difference with liberal capitalism—at the same time tempers its harmful outcomes. This is why the term social capitalism is preferred over corporatism or conservatism. Social capitalism with its stress on moderating market outcomes is in this specific sense a middle way between social democracy and liberal capitalism: it is both social and capitalist. The regime is less state interventionist than the social-democratic model, but much more activist in the realm of social policy than the liberal regime.

Social-capitalist welfare states have been strongly characterized by the *principle of social insurance* and social-insurance schemes have been generally based on *labour-market participation and performance*. A historical legacy of corporatism concerns the status-differentiating nature of social insurance. Social rights have been linked generally to class and status, and the capacity to reduce income inequality has been small. The social-capitalist regime has aimed at retaining traditional status relations through 'a myriad of status-differentiated social-insurance schemes—each with its peculiar rules, finances, and benefit structure; each tailored to exhibit its clientele's relative status position' (Esping-Andersen 1990: 60). Historically, commodification was rejected on moral and religious grounds, and several strategies have been developed to combat it, notably corporatism and etatism, both leading to moderate levels of decommodification (Van Kersbergen 1995).

A further crucial element of this regime has been *the commitment to the defence and maintenance of the traditional family and its functions*. Social insurance has protected the family against the disruptive impact of the market. The family has been the unit of benefits, and benefits have been conferred upon the head of the household, the breadwinner. Social benefits for breadwinners, normally adult male wage-earners, were to replace the current level of family income. As a consequence, the continental welfare states have gradually developed rather generous benefit structures with regard to families. Family members have been covered but have typically lacked individual entitlements. A wife has been entitled to benefits only when she has become the head of the household through the death of her husband (widow pensions). Benefits for women in case of divorce have typically been absent. Social assistance and initially also charity have sometimes filled this gap in protection. The responsibility for the poor (among them many divorced or unmarried mothers), according to the principle of subsidiarity, has been decentralized to families, private initiatives, and charity organizations.

Subsidiarity refers to an organic totality in which all parts of the natural order have specific tasks in order to create the stability of the larger whole. Although the state should not interfere in the distribution of responsibilities, it is nevertheless the state's function to guarantee and facilitate that the lower social organs perform their duties and uphold the capacities of persons and social groups in their social environment (Van Kersbergen 1995: 181, 188). Accordingly, the state is assumed to guarantee that families can manage their responsibilities by helping them where necessary. Child allowances were typically granted to the breadwinner. Tax schemes have generally favoured a family unit consisting of a husband (breadwinner), a wife, children, and possibly members of the extended family. The assumptions were that men secured income, that women were only marginally present on the labour market, that the family unit was the prime provider of care, that this was a woman's responsibility, and that family allowances provided supplements, initially to large families.

Such images of the gender division of labour and the nature of the family have underlain social policies and have reinforced *typical male and female employment careers*. Generally speaking, the social-capitalist nations have been distinguished by their comparatively low levels of female labour-force participation. The discouragement of female labour-force participation through tax disincentives or even through explicit policies and the encouragement of women to leave the labour market— for instance, after marriage or first child—have been properties of social capitalism (Van Kersbergen 1995: 144).

The social-capitalist welfare states are confronted with pressures to adjust these social policies to changing demographic, social, and economic circumstances. The conditions under which post-war social capitalism emerged as well as the assumptions upon which the typical social policies were formulated and implemented no longer obtain. Ageing populations, changing family structures (for example, a growing number of divorced, single-person, and single-parent households), slackening economic growth and decreasing job security, unstable employment patterns, financial crises of social-security arrangements, changing social values, and the changing relations between men and women challenge the gendered assumptions of many welfare state arrangements (European Commission 1993; Esping-Andersen 1996*c*; George 1996).

One of the most striking features of developments in the social-capitalist welfare states in the 1980s and 1990s concerns the declining levels of employment, high (particularly long-term) unemployment, deteriorating dependency ratios, and severe financial crisis of social-security arrangements. Comparatively speaking, jobless growth and a crisis of inactivity are pivotal conditions of contemporary Europe. Both are hypothesized to be institutional effects of the working of the social-capitalist welfare-state regime and at the same time causes of the crisis of social protection.

In contrast to both the social-democratic and the liberal welfare state regimes, employment rates in the social-capitalist welfare states have actually fallen. From the 1970s to the mid-1980s social capitalism managed labour-market problems via supply reductions (Esping-Andersen 1996*b*). The policy was directed towards exit options rather than towards an increase of labour-market entrance. Such a policy has not only affected older male workers, who have been encouraged to retire early, but has also had substantial consequences for female workers, who have been discouraged from entering the labour market or have been encouraged to enter only in part-time jobs.

With regard to labour-market opportunities, the argument is that women, older men, and the young form a group of outsiders. This group depends on male breadwinners' pay or welfare state transfers and contrasts with a group of male insiders, which 'relies precisely on the guarantee of lifelong employment with high wages and heavy social contributions in order to ensure family welfare across the life cycle' (Esping-Andersen 1996b: 79). The insider–outsider problem and the labour-reduction route are partly endogenous to the social-capitalist welfare state, particularly to the manner in which social-security arrangements and social services either presuppose each other or conflict. It is worth quoting Esping-Andersen's view on the exit strategy:

> The roots of this strategy lie in the continental European welfare states' combination of highly (if not overly) developed social insurance (inordinately biased towards pensions) and underdeveloped social services. Social insurance means that entitlements are related to one's employment record, implying the necessity of a long unbroken career. The underlying assumption is that family members can depend on the full-time male breadwinner, and that wives are generally responsible for social care within the household. Hence, tax policies typically punish working wives, and the welfare state is extremely underdeveloped in terms of social services to families. . . . The continental European welfare state is thus essentially a familialistic transfer state.   (Esping-Andersen 1996a: 18)

The labour-reduction strategy, however, appears to be inherently self-destructive. In the absence of the capacity to promote job growth under the condition of a growing labour supply, particularly of women, the attempt to reduce the supply of labour reinforces the predicament of social protection, which, in turn, augments the incapacity to encourage employment. Labour-supply reduction implies higher claims on social-security schemes, particularly on pension systems, unemployment benefits, and early retirement schemes. Moreover, the inability to facilitate the labour-market entry of women aggravates the burden of social security through an increasingly unfavourable dependency ratio. As a result, labour costs remain prohibitively high, the growth of low-paid, stop–go jobs (for example, in the service sector) is frustrated, and an insider–outsider labour market is reinforced, as the insiders (predominantly adult male workers) are compelled to defend high wages, protected employment, and social-security entitlements at the expense of the labour-market opportunities and social rights of outsiders (women, the young, migrant workers).

The social-capitalist welfare states face a dilemma. Reducing labour costs in order to promote the growth of employment can occur only at the expense of the level of social protection. Welfare state retrenchment and the flexibilization of labour markets, however, do not automatically lead to an increase in the supply of labour. Active labour-market policies are required, for instance, to simplify the labour-market entry of women (for example, childcare facilities), to further the re-entry of the unemployed (for example, training), and to improve the opportunities of vulnerable segments on the labour market (for example, by activating the core passive schemes of social protection typical for the regime). But, of course, such measures are notoriously expensive. They contradict not only the logic of the transfer-oriented, passive welfare state regimes of continental Europe, but also the very project of retrenchment.

This brief sketch of the contemporary predicament of the social-capitalist welfare state may exemplify how labour-market institutions, social-security arrangements, and the development of social services are interrelated. It may also clarify that notions of gender inequality have been a fundamental condition for the foundation of social capitalism and that these are now endemic to the current dilemmas. So far we have concentrated on identifying the main features of social capitalism. We now elaborate empirically similarities and differences in patterns of gender inequality among the social-capitalist welfare states in the 1980s and early 1990s.

❖ THE TRANSFER ORIENTATION OF SOCIAL-CAPITALIST WELFARE STATES

The social-capitalist welfare states are transfer-oriented, passive regimes. Their focus has traditionally been on cash transfers to households rather than on the direct provision of services. In terms of aggregate (public) social spending, they belonged to the 'big spenders' (see Van Kersbergen 1995: ch. 5). In the period between 1980 and 1993 the social-capitalist welfare states spent either consistently close to the OECD average (Italy) or above it (Belgium, Germany, the Netherlands, and also France). Of the social-capitalist regimes, the Dutch welfare state appears to be the biggest spender in this period. With the exception of 1993, Dutch social expenditure has been significantly above the average (see Table 1.1).

Aggregate data as reported in Table 1.1 pose several problems of comparability and should be interpreted with care. In countries where local or other lower tiers of government rather than central government administer social spending, the reported figures are lower than actual spending. In some countries, private social schemes (particularly pensions) with public (mandatory) characteristics are sometimes included in the figures (France) and sometimes not (the Netherlands). Another difficulty is caused by mandatory continued wage payments by employers, which are usually not considered to be public.[2] A final problem concerns the fiscal treatment of benefits. The data in Table 1.1 are gross expenditures and are not corrected for taxes. The differences in total gross spending between welfare states may look larger than they are if one looks at net outlays—that is, taking account of taxes on social transfers.[3] Apart from these more technical difficulties, the spending variable is a poor indicator of welfare state development for theoretical reasons as well (see Van Kersbergen 1995: ch. 2). None the less, social expenditures reveal the transfer bias of this type of welfare state.

Old-age and disability cash benefits constitute the single biggest item of social expenditures. The percentage of these transfers in relation to total social expenditure (1993) was 33.3 in Belgium, 35.3 in Germany, 40.4 in the Netherlands, and 49.7 in Italy. Services for the elderly and disabled (for example, residential care, home-help services, rehabilitation) as a percentage of total expenditure for this group (1993) was 1.2 in Belgium, 2.5 in Germany, 1.6 in Italy, and 4.3 in the Netherlands. By contrast, these figures were 21.5 for Denmark, 27.2 for Norway, and 23.8 for Sweden. If one looks

Table 1.1. Total social expenditure as a percentage of GDP in Belgium, France, West Germany, Italy, and the Netherlands, 1980–1993

Country	1980	1985	1990	1993
Belgium	25.6	28.5	26.6	27.0[a]
France	23.5	27.0	26.0	28.7
West Germany	25.0	25.5	23.8	28.3[b]
Italy	18.2	21.6	23.0	25.0
Netherlands	28.7	29.0	28.8	30.2
Average[c]	20.2	21.9	22.4	25.0
Standard deviation	5.8	5.6	5.4	6.6

[a] 1992.
[b] Germany.
[c] This is an eighteen-country average based on data from Australia, Austria, Belgium, Canada, Denmark, Finland, France, Germany, Ireland, Italy, Japan, Netherlands, New Zealand, Norway, Sweden, Switzerland, the UK, and the USA.

Note: Figures in italics are more than 1 standard deviation above average.

Source: OECD (1996: 19, table 1.1).

❖ BUSSEMAKER AND VAN KERSBERGEN

at the relation between family services (for example, day care, household services) and family benefits, one would expect a comparable pattern (a high percentage of benefits to families and a low percentage of family services of the total expenditures to families). However, here there is considerable variation among the social-capitalist welfare states. Not all countries rank low on family services: while Belgium and Italy spend a relatively low portion (4.6 and 13.6 per cent), the Netherlands and Germany spend a relatively high ratio (35.5 and 36 per cent) on these services (calculated from OECD 1996: 34–5).

An important qualitative characteristic of social-capitalist welfare states has been the absence of an unconditional commitment to full employment. One way of illustrating this is by looking at active labour-market policies. Until recently these policies hardly found support in these welfare states, whereas, of course, extensive measures to compensate for loss of income have done so. Thus, the ratio of passive to active labour-market measures in 1985 was a high 3.2 in the Netherlands, 3.0 in Italy, 2.5 in Belgium, and 1.8 in Germany. However, the situation changed in the second half of the 1980s and the beginning of the 1990s. The social-capitalist welfare states seem to be activating their core labour-market policies. Nevertheless, the passive/active ratio in 1993 was still 2.4 in Belgium and 1.7 in Germany, but dropped to 2.1 in the Netherlands and 1.2 in Italy.

❖ INCOME MAINTENANCE AND THE CHANGING BREADWINNER BIAS

Not only were social-capitalist welfare states transfer-oriented, passive regimes, but they also focused primarily on the replacement of family income. They were essentially family income-maintenance states. We illustrate some of the characteristics in income maintenance, as well as recent changes, in three areas of social policy, respectively social security and pensions, the position of lone mothers, and maternal and parental leave.

Social-security arrangements were strongly influenced by the breadwinner model of provision, where benefits and other transfers were to replace the income of a family. This historically explains the relatively high replacement rates of core social-security schemes and the differentiation of benefits according to position in the household. There is a long-standing inequality between men and women and husbands and wives with regard to social security as well as a firm dividing line between public and private responsibilities. The dimensions of the model are represented in Table 1.2.

Table 1.2. Dimensions of the breadwinner model of social policy

Dimension	Characteristic
Familial ideology	Strict division of labour
	Husband = earner
	Wife = carer
Entitlement	Differentiated among spouses
Basis of entitlement	Breadwinner
Recipient of benefits	Head of household
Unit of benefit	Household or family
Unit of contributions	Household
Taxation	Joint taxation
	Deductions for dependants
Employment and wage policies	Priority to men
Spheres of care	Primarily private
Caring work	Unpaid

Source: Sainsbury (1996: 42).

The empirical question is to what extent the social-capitalist welfare states have fully implemented the logic of the breadwinner model. Family ideology was traditionally strong in all four countries. There was a sharp division of labour between men and women (where a husband earns a family wage), a marked differentiation among spouses, and a tax system that privileged families over single persons. Tax-benefit regimes positively reflected this family bias, although more so in Belgium and Italy than in Germany and the Netherlands.

Most countries have been compelled to adjust their social-security legislation as a result of the directives of the European Union (EU) and the binding decisions of the European Court of Justice with regard to equal treatment (Hantrais 1995; Ostner and Lewis 1995).[4] In addition, many countries have developed equal-opportunity policies and equality agencies. Although changes have occurred in the level and the basis of entitlements, the extent to which social policy arrangements favour the family over the individual, and traditional male careers over female working patterns, is still significant.

Many countries have changed their policies concerning old-age pensions and retirement. Inequalities that relate directly to gender have been removed. Since 1985 Belgian female employees who are breadwinners can receive a family pension. However, only a few women meet the requirements. Family pensions are almost exclusively granted to male breadwinners. The replacement rate for family pensions is higher than for singles

(75 per cent and 60 per cent). In the Netherlands the basis for entitlement changed in 1985 for married women, who can now claim the statutory pension in their own right. However, a means test was later introduced, which implies that the younger partner is not automatically included but that her part (most younger spouses are women) is dependent on a means test. But, if a pension for both has been accepted, the allocation since 1994 is 50–50. Although means-testing can have an equalizing effect for unmarried pensioners, the fact that usually the family or the household is taken as the unit of income-testing may—as Mary Daly (1996: 54) argues—reduce a married woman's chances of receiving a pension. In addition, it creates a disincentive for employment.

In most social-capitalist countries the strategy of labour exit by early retirement is changing. The period to be spent in employment in order to receive old-age pensions has been lengthened. Germany introduced a gradual increase of retirement age for women from 60 to 65 and for men from 63 to 65. In Italy, where women retire at 57 and men at 65, a flexible retirement age for both men and women any time between 57 and 65 is planned. Such policies are in line with notions of equality, but the lengthening of employment requirements may have unequal effects between men and women as a consequence of differences in their labour-market participation.

Much depends on the extent to which unpaid care responsibilities are incorporated into pensions policies, if labour-market status is the basis of entitlement. Both Germany and Italy have recognized unpaid care work in their pensions. In Italy a pension credit for carers was introduced in 1994 and for housewives a voluntary, but subsidized pension scheme was established, while in Germany child-rearing legislation, allocating pension rights for time devoted to caregiving work at home, was introduced in 1986. In 1992 the period of child-rearing credited for pension purposes was increased from one to three years per child for children born after 1991 (Daly 1996: 52).

Such policies certainly increase gender equality in pensions and may counterbalance some of the negative effects on the lengthening of time to be spent in employment. But the effect on the changing pension policies also depends on the flexibility of pension schemes (flexible retirement schemes are currently being developed in Belgium, the Netherlands, and Italy). Part-time workers in particular may be affected negatively by such policies, because part-time retirement may be restricted to a certain limit in working hours. In general, the development of pension and retirement policies in social capitalism shows that some gender biases are removed, although new gender inequalities may result from recent changes in these policies.

SOCIAL-CAPITALIST WELFARE STATES ❖

Another example concerns unemployment benefits. Social capitalism was confronted in the 1980s with high rates of unemployment and deficits. To cope with these problems, many countries have redirected their employment policies as well as the conditions and levels of benefits. Together with the EU directive on equal treatment, these policies affect gender inequality. Changes have been particularly numerous in the Netherlands. Apart from a reduction in benefits and tightened conditions for eligibility, unemployment benefits have been individualized. In 1985 married women were granted the right to claim the same unemployment benefit as men and unmarried women. Generally women's entitlements have increased as an effect of individualizing benefits (Bussemaker 1993; Sainsbury 1996). However, at the same time a contradictory policy of means testing has been introduced—although formally gender neutral—in minimum benefits. Moreover, unemployment benefits are required to correspond to contributions. This policy favours men with long contribution records (Sainsbury 1996: 213).

The other countries have experienced less radical changes, although small cuts in employment benefits also occurred in Germany. Already in 1981 Belgium had introduced a differentiation in unemployment benefits for singles, couples with a sole breadwinner, and dual earners. The replacement rate of unemployment benefits for dual earners is lower than for single persons, while the replacement rate for single persons is lower than for breadwinners. During the 1980s eligibility criteria for unemployment benefits were tightened and the duration of benefits was limited. Also the benefits for young unemployed persons were reduced. Now, Belgium is one of the few countries where above-minimum benefits for one-earner families are higher than for other households (Andries 1996).

In conclusion, the directives on equal treatment of men and women have certainly affected social legislation in social-capitalist welfare states, although this has not served as an improvement of social rights. Particularly in countries with strong breadwinner traditions, equal treatment may lead to a reduction of benefits for both men and women (Sjerps 1988: 101), as it has—indeed—in the Netherlands and, albeit to a lesser extent, in Germany and in some respects in Belgium. Further, formal gender equality does not always lead to equity—for example, if equality is related exclusively to paid work, without taking unpaid work into account.

Moreover, the specific way policies have been implemented depends upon power relations, particularly the influence of the women's movement. For example, the German women's movement did not focus extensively on legal rights, and to the extent that it did it sought a better accommodation of work and family responsibilities. Catherine Hoskyns concludes that 'Germany has the reputation of being the country which has done least to implement the European policy and where the situation of women shows least change . . . .The effects have been limited, mainly it would seem because it has not so far connected with any real mobilization by women' (Hoskyns 1988: 46). In contrast, in the Netherlands a strong women's lobby has contributed to the individualization of social entitlements, but has been less successful in combating increased means-testing. In France the EU directive has not been very influential at all, precisely because social legislation had already been directed towards gender equality for a long time.[5] In general, differences between countries in the balance of political power, the role of the feminist movement, as well as differences in attitudes towards welfare state retrenchment have resulted in striking differences among social-capitalist welfare states.

The breadwinner bias is also evident in income-maintenance programmes for lone parents. Social systems that are broadly similar in their emphasis on the breadwinner model and the privileging of the family nevertheless vary substantially in the treatment of single mothers—for example, in the balancing of paid work and care, and in the public–private mix of financial assistance. While traditionally lone-parent families were widows, usually well protected by social security, they are now mainly divorced or never-married women. Only in Italy are the majority of lone mothers still widows.

Lone-parent families constitute 10–15 per cent of all families in the OECD countries and are among the most vulnerable groups in these societies. As an OECD report (1990) accurately summarized, the causes of the problems for lone-parent (usually single mother) families are diverse:

> the lack of support from the absent parent, the inadequacy of earnings or the inability to work at all whether due to personal attributes, labour market characteristics or domestic responsibilities, and other limitations on work effort or the returns to working, or some combination of them. Public policies and income support systems, whether by acts of omission or commission, are at times inadequate to the task of assisting lone-mother families. (OECD 1990: 13)

Among the many problems these families face, the risk of poverty is generally high. However, the poverty rate of lone mothers within the group of social-capitalist welfare states varies significantly. Apart from widows who are entitled to insurance benefits, the problem of lone mothers is 'non-existent' in Italy—that is to say, lone mothers are not an official category in social-security arrangements and social policy. The invisibility of lone mothers can be explained by the fact that the percentage of lone mothers is lower than in other countries (8 per cent of all families with dependent children), while the poverty rates for lone mothers are much lower than in Germany and the Netherlands (Bimbi 1997). In addition to clientelism, the intergenerational family and kin play an important role in channelling income from different sources to lone mothers. In practice, however, single mothers often lack adequate family support and social security. Lone mothers in Italy are, therefore, highly dependent on the labour market, and this dependency explains the striking contrast between labour-market participation of single mothers (high) and married mothers (low) (Bimbi 1997; Lewis 1997: 12). Italy shares this feature with Germany, where there exists a comparably sharp contrast between high and more full-time labour-market participation rates of lone mothers and low participation rates of married women.

The pattern in the Netherlands is different. Labour-market participation of lone mothers is low, even lower than the participation rate of married women (Bussemaker *et al.* 1997). Poverty among lone mothers, however, was moderate in the Netherlands, although in the early 1990s it showed a sharp increase, from 9 to 20 per cent. Nevertheless, German single mothers are still more likely to be poor than their Dutch counterparts (Lewis 1997: 14; see also Hobson 1994: 177). Labour-market participation, therefore, is not a guarantee for being economically independent and escaping poverty. Of course, payment and working hours are important variables, but so is the impact of social assistance. The comparatively low poverty rate of Dutch single mothers until recently was a result of generous social transfers. Although single mothers until the mid-1990s were not defined as a separate category in social-assistance regulation, the system of transfers (social assistance, child allowances, housing benefits) worked as a protection against the risk of poverty. In Germany, lone mothers who earn their income on the labour market are traditionally better off than those who depend on transfers. This may explain the higher rate of labour-market participation among German lone mothers. In fact, almost 50 per cent of German single mothers who are dependent on transfers as their main income source are poor, compared to only 10 per cent of those who have a paid job (Hobson 1994: 180).

According to Barbara Hobson, the striking differences between Germany and the Netherlands should be explained by the different structures of assumptions about gender in the systems of transfers. In Germany, the breadwinner–carer model has been translated into a low level of benefits and a care benefit for children for all mothers as a supplement to husbands' earnings, not as a care wage (Hobson 1994: 182; see also Lewis 1997). In the Netherlands, breadwinner arrangements have been translated into a mother–carer model in social security for single mothers. Although this model was never officially recognized (in law), it was widely accepted in practice. Benefits allowed single mothers—at least until 1996—to remain at home as full-time carers. But both countries recently changed their policies towards lone mothers. In Germany, more attention is being paid to the role of fathers: the combination of a guaranteed maintenance scheme and deduction of maintenance payments by employers makes it difficult for fathers to avoid payment. This is another strategy to continue the notion of subsidiarity, which implies a minor role of the state, as well as to secure children's interest in welfare (Lewis 1997; Ostner 1997). In the Netherlands, the focus has changed, not so much towards the role of fathers, as towards treating mothers as workers who should participate in the labour market. Since a new law on social assistance was implemented in 1996, single mothers are required to seek employment actively and obliged to work if day care or other care is available. The responsibility for a child is no longer an argument for staying out of the labour market or for rejecting a job offer (Knijn 1994; Bussemaker *et al.* 1997; Lewis 1997).

Social-capitalist welfare states with their breadwinner bias support families by cash benefits rather than by benefits in kind. If we look at labour-market-related leave schemes, particularly maternity, paternity, and parental leave, we see that social-capitalist welfare states have developed maternity leave in both duration and income, while parental leave in most countries has been introduced more recently and differs in length, but is normally not very well paid. Thus, while breadwinner arrangements are usually paid as transfers and income-maintenance programmes, parental-leave arrangements are not generous and therefore cannot compensate the temporary loss of income.

We look first at the statutory leave for workers with children (see Table 1.3). All countries provide leave for women around the time of childbirth. The duration and income-replacement rates of maternity-leave schemes show some moderate variation across the countries. In Belgium statutory maternity leave is fourteen weeks and payment is earnings related: 80 per cent for the first four weeks, then 75 per cent up to a maximum. In Germany it is also fourteen weeks and payment is at full earnings. In the Netherlands maternity leave is longer, namely sixteen weeks, and also at full earnings. France's policies are in between Belgium and Italy (sixteen weeks with a replacement rate of 80 per cent), although France is exceptional because of its long leave of twenty-six weeks for the third and subsequent child (European Commission Network on Childcare 1992, 1996: 144–7; Gauthier 1996: 173–4). Italy has the most developed maternity leave in time, twenty weeks, at a high earnings-related rate (80 per cent). In most countries, maternity leave is a legacy of post-war policies. The duration of maternity leave has not been subject to any increase in Germany, Italy, and Belgium since 1980. Only the Netherlands shows a modest increase from twelve to sixteen weeks in the recent period. Payments have not changed.

And only Belgium has increased maternity payment—from 60 to 80 per cent in 1989 (Gauthier 1996: 173).[6]

Looking at parental leave, we see much more variation, as well as change in recent times. Parental leave has not been part of post-war welfare state policies. Only Italy already had such a policy. After 1953 Italy provided unpaid parental leave for twelve months. Since 1973 the replacement rate has been only 30 per cent for six months. It is a mother's entitlement, but it can be transferred to the father. The other countries were much later in implementing parental-leave schemes, but their policies are often more generous. In 1977 France introduced parental leave for two years; the leave was extended in 1987 to three years, while cash benefits were introduced in 1985, but only for families with three or more children. Germany established parental leave for six months in 1979. Since then, it has increased dramatically—from eighteen months in 1990 to thirty-six months in 1993. The benefit is flat-rate until the child is twenty-four months and

Table 1.3. Maternity and parental-leave schemes in Belgium, France, West Germany, Italy, and the Netherlands, 1990

Country	Maternity-leave schemes		Parental-leave schemes		
	duration (weeks)	benefit level (%)	duration (months)	paid/unpaid	benefit level
Belgium	14	80	6–12[a]	partly paid	flat-rate
France	16[b]	80	36[c]	paid	flat-rate
West Germany	14	100	36	paid	partly flat-rate, partly means-tested
Italy	20	80	12	partly paid	low earnings-related rate for the first 6 months
Netherlands	16	100	6	unpaid	

[a] This is not official parental leave, but part of the universal system of a 6–12 months 'career break' subject to employer agreement.
[b] 26 weeks for third or later birth.
[c] Parental leave is paid only for women with three or more children.
Source: European Commission Network on Childcare (1996).

means-tested; the last twelve months are unpaid (European Commission Network on Childcare 1996: 144–7). Belgium has no statutory parental leave, but since 1985 workers can take 6–12 months 'career breaks' (up to a maximum of five times) from employment, subject to employers' agreement. The interruption can be requested for various reasons, including childcare. Until 1991 benefits were flat-rate; since then the amount of cash benefit paid is reduced after the first year, or at the second and subsequent breaks (Gauthier 1996: 179). The Netherlands were very late in establishing a provision for parental leave. Only in 1990 did the Dutch introduce a provision of six months of reduced hours per parent (with a minimum of twenty hours a week). It cannot be transferred between parents.

The Netherlands is the only country where parental leave is unpaid (although in some sectors, especially the public sector, a certain percentage of earnings is paid). The level of payment in the other countries, however, is not very generous either. Benefits are at a very low earnings-related rate (Italy) or flat-rate (Belgium, France, and Germany). The duration of parental leave also varies considerably. While parental leave is short in the Netherlands, and to a lesser extent in Italy and Belgium, it is much longer in Germany, although the last year is unpaid. Paternity leave does not exist in Germany, Italy, and the Netherlands and is three days in Belgium. Finally, leave for family reasons exists in Belgium (ten days per parent in the public sector and four days in the private sector, unpaid), Germany (ten days per parent for one child; twenty-five days per parent for two or more children, at full earnings), and Italy (until the child reaches the age of 3, unpaid), but not in the Netherlands.

The patterns of maternity, paternity, and parental leave are difficult to explain. Family-oriented social-capitalist welfare states traditionally provide maternal leave and since recently also parental leave (with the exception of Italy where this leave scheme was introduced earlier), but maternity leave is better paid than parental leave, particularly in Germany and the Netherlands. Typically, social-capitalist welfare states are ambivalent in their arrangements of maternity and parental leave. They seem to be willing to support women in their capacity to give birth to a child, but in combination with labour-market participation they are hesitant to implement extensive and generous policies. On the one hand, the duration of maternity leave is not particularly generous, parental leave is not very well developed and shows a lot of variation, and paternity leave is non-existent (except for three days in Belgium). On the other hand, the payment for maternity leave is rather generous, especially in Germany and the Netherlands, although parental leave is unpaid (the Netherlands) or low-paid/only partly paid (the other countries). A possible loss of earnings as a consequence of parental leave easily extends the inequality between men and women on the labour market, because the earnings of men are not interrupted. When a father takes parental leave his loss of income is likely to be more extensive than a mother's, owing to the fact that generally men earn more than women. The sharing of leave (parental leave) may exist in countries with statutory leave schemes and there is the possibility to transfer entitlements, but in practice these are seldom used. Usually it is the mother who claims parental leave, which emphasizes the assumed relation of women and care and reinforces the difficulty of women to re-enter the labour market.

In sum, social-capitalist welfare states still have a gender bias in income-maintenance programmes. Although some gender inequalities have been removed—for example, in pension and retirement policies, as well as in unemployment benefits—the relation between benefits and contributions still favours men over women. In addition, policies to facilitate the combination of paid work and care for children are ill developed, which particularly affects lone mothers. The organization of maternal and parental leave is ambivalent and reflects the emphasis on family structures as well as the gendered structure of the family–labour-market nexus.

❖ THE CHANGING LABOUR-MARKET PARTICIPATION OF WOMEN

Welfare state regime theory argues that the social-capitalist welfare states are currently characterized by jobless economic growth, where a group of male insiders monopolizes the labour market and a group of predominantly female (but also young and migrant) outsiders depends on the income of a breadwinner or on welfare state transfers. As we have argued earlier, low female labour-market participation corresponds to one of the typical features of social-capitalist welfare states, particularly the social insurance model and the assumption of long unbroken employment careers.

Let us first look at aggregate trends. Although the female labour force in social capitalism has increased substantially since 1960, in 1990 it was, typically, still below the OECD average (see Table 1.4). The most recent data on the selected countries are found in the results for 1994 of Eurostat's *Labour Force Survey* (1996) and are represented in Table 1.5. Eurostat data, however, give the activity rate that is defined as the total labour force as a percentage of the population over 15, where the labour force is the sum of persons in employment and unemployed persons.[7] Table 1.5 shows that in Belgium and Italy total activity is considerably lower than in Germany and the Netherlands. The same holds true for the activity rates by sex. Female activity rates vary from about 34 per cent in Italy and 40 per cent in Belgium, to around 48 per cent in Germany and the Netherlands.

One hypothesis would be that the differences between Germany and the Netherlands (and France), on the one hand, and Italy and Belgium, on the other hand, can be accounted for by the variation in part-time work in these countries. The argument is that, to the extent that women in social-capitalist welfare states have entered the labour market in considerable numbers since the 1960s, they have done so predominantly via low-paid, part-time, and irregular jobs, and at the expense of fertility.

There is indeed a sharp gender difference with respect to part-time work. However, the variation among the social-capitalist welfare states with respect to the labour-market participation of women at face value does not seem to be related to the incidence of part-time employment (see Table 1.6). The Netherlands has an exceptionally high and Italy a compar-

Table 1.4. Female labour force as a percentage of the female population 15–64 in Belgium, France, West Germany, Italy, and the Netherlands, 1960–1990

Country	1960	1980	1990
Belgium	36.4	47.0	52.4
France	46.6	54.4	56.6
West Germany	49.2	52.8	56.6
Italy	39.6	39.6	44.5
Netherlands	26.2	35.5	53.0
OECD average	43.3	54.1	61.5
Standard deviation	10.0	10.9	10.7

Source: OECD (1992: 29, table 2.8).

Table 1.5. Activity rates by sex in Belgium, France, Germany, Italy, and the Netherlands, 1994 (%)

Country	Total	Male	Female
Belgium	50.3	61.2	40.2
France	55.5	63.7	47.9
Germany	58.2	69.4	47.8
Italy	47.4	62.4	33.7
Netherlands	58.9	70.4	47.7

Source: Eurostat (1996: 20–1, table 001).

Table 1.6. Part-time employment as a percentage of persons in employment by sex in Belgium, France, Germany, Italy, and the Netherlands, 1994

Country	Total	Male	Female
Belgium	12.8	2.5	28.3
France	14.9	4.6	27.8
Germany	15.8	3.2	33.1
Italy	6.2	2.8	12.4
Netherlands	36.4	16.1	65.9

Source: Eurostat (1996: 20–1, table 001).

atively low proportion of women working part-time. This does seem to correspond to the variation in female activity rates. The difference in part-time work between Germany and Belgium (as well as France) is much smaller and does not correspond to the variation in activity rates. Moreover, the gender differences are most pronounced in Belgium and Germany, where women work ten times more than men in part-time jobs, while in Italy and the Netherlands this is only four times. This is because in Italy the incidence of part-time work is very low, while in the Netherlands it is high, also among men. Therefore, the hypothesis that the variation in part-time work is a major cause of the variation in activity rates among the social-capitalist welfare states cannot be confirmed on the basis of these data.

Perhaps a better understanding can be arrived at if we look at employment careers over the life course of women. The Netherlands and Germany used to have an M-shaped pattern in female activity rates—that is, a sharp increase in labour-market participation at the age of 20, a drop in activity rates around the age of 30, and again a rise at the age of 40, corresponding to labour-market entry, labour-market exit at childbirth, and labour-market re-entry. By contrast, Belgium and Italy were characterized by a moderate left-hand peak in the pattern of activity—that is, a sharp and continuing rise in activity rates as of the age of 20 until 40, after which a gradual decline set in (Eurostat 1990).

The M-shaped curve can perhaps be explained by (1) the absence of developed childcare facilities, which impedes an employment career for women after childbirth, and (2) the presence of developed old-age care facilities that enable women to re-enter the labour market at an age at which they would otherwise have had to take care of elderly relatives and at which their own children have grown older. Such an approach might also explain the French plateau-pattern, indicating high female activity

Table 1.7. Female activity rates by age in Belgium, France, Germany, Italy, and the Netherlands, 1994 (%)

Age	Belgium	France	Germany	Italy	Netherlands
15–19[a]	6.3	8.6	29.9	16.6	39.0
20–24	56.2	57.0	71.4	50.1	75.3
25–29	81.4	80.1	74.2	60.1	77.3
30–34	78.0	77.0	73.7	59.3	67.0
35–39	73.7	77.6	74.5	58.8	66.7
40–44	66.1	79.1	76.5	55.3	66.1
45–49	56.2	76.1	73.5	46.3	60.3
50–54	36.7	66.3	67.1	36.4	45.7
55–59	21.9	41.8	44.4	19.1	29.0
60–64	4.9	11.6	9.0	8.3	7.4

[a] One possible explanation of the variation between countries in this age group, particularly between Germany and the Netherlands, may be found in the differences in financial support for students, which in the Netherlands stimulates labour-market participation of students.

Source: Eurostat, (1996: 24–5, table 003).

rates—that is, a relatively constant high participation rate until the age of 50, because childcare facilities in France are traditionally much better developed than in the other countries (see the next section). The left-peak curve indicates that having a child has less effect on labour-market partic- ipation. This poses the question whether the differences in these patterns are explained by greater access to childcare facilities or not. This does not seem to be the case, as labour-market participation in Belgium is relatively low, while childcare facilities are well developed. At the same time, the decline in activity in Italy and Belgium—which occurs at an earlier age and is sharper than in Germany and the Netherlands—would suggest that the absence of developed services for the elderly helps explain the labour- market exit of women at the age of 40 and older. As we saw earlier, services for the elderly indeed comprise only a small percentage of all expenditures to this group in Italy and Belgium.

Eurostat data, however, indicate that the typical career patterns of women have changed to the extent that the M-curve as found in Germany and the Netherlands is now disappearing (see Table 1.7). The decline in activity rates at the age of 30 is still noticeable, particularly in the Netherlands, and there is still a re-entry effect at the age of 40 in Germany, but in general the patterns seem to have become more alike. They all now indicate more or less a pattern in between a plateau or a moderate left peak. This seems to provide evidence that the social-capitalist welfare states are converging and that female employment patterns are becoming more similar.

In sum, it appears that, although labour-market participation has increased in all social-capitalist welfare states and seems to converge in terms of activity rates, there are still important differences in terms of full-time and part-time labour-market participation of both men and women.

❖ Changing Services: Childcare

Social-capitalist welfare states have traditionally been characterized by a low level of social-service provision. The literature, as well as an overview of services, seems to confirm the impression that childcare facilities are still not well developed. Anneli Anttonen and Jorma Sipilä (1996) distinguish a particular social-capitalist (continental) organization of services. They label the continental countries involved in their research (Germany, France, the Netherlands, and Belgium) as belonging to the subsidiarity model.[8] This means that the state plays a role only when lower organs in society (family, private religious initiatives) fail to take their responsibility. As we saw earlier, subsidiarity is a central feature of social-capitalist welfare states. Indeed, in most social-capitalist welfare states childcare is not a matter of the state, but a (semi-)private matter. In 1990, the Netherlands had the lowest number of places in publicly funded childcare services for young children, with places for only 2 per cent of children under 3 years of age. Germany with 3 per cent and Italy with 5 per cent hardly scored higher (European Commission Network on Childcare 1996). Italy had a lack of social services for childcare and here relatives normally take over the responsibility from working mothers. In 1985 the majority of children between 0 and 3 years (almost 55 per cent) were looked after by family members. In most cases these relatives were the grandparents (for 45.5 per cent of the children) (Istat 1985). In Germany and the Netherlands it was mostly mothers who took care of their own children. They did so by working part-time or by leaving the labour market.

France and Belgium did much better. The coverage of children under 3 years old in public childcare was 20 per cent in both countries. France has had extensive public childcare facilities, not so much to support women's labour-market participation, but rather as an effect of a strong pronatalist policy, together with a strong belief in the benefits of early education. In the 1980s France consolidated its childcare policies; it guaranteed child-care to all children aged 2–5. Also in Belgium the strong belief in pre-school education has contributed to publicly funded childcare, although more recently than in France, while statist and pronatalist notions have not been as strong as in France. The relatively high percentage of small

Belgian children in public childcare is also the result of the specific structure of childcare facilities. Publicly funded creches are supplemented by
childcare services at home by independent carers. About half of these
independent carers are supervised and subsidized by government and all
of them are subject to governmental regulations. So, the relatively high
degree of childcare services in Belgium can be explained by a combination
of governmental policy and private arrangements (Dumon 1992: 96–8).

The figures for children between 3 and 6 years of age are higher in all
countries. In 1990, the Netherlands still had the fewest places (50–55 per
cent), followed by Germany (65–70 per cent). In Italy publicly funded
childcare services provided for 85 per cent of the children of this age group
and in Belgium and France even a high 95 per cent (European
Commission Network on Childcare 1992). However, in most countries
this form of childcare is part of (pre-)education, often only part-time, and
sometimes even with an interruption in the middle of the day. In other
words, childcare does not always correspond to working hours. This is particularly a problem in Germany and the Netherlands.

However, since the beginnings of the 1990s there has been an increase in
the availability of public childcare facilities (see Table 1.8). The increase of
childcare facilities is primarily the result of national policies of growing
investments in childcare facilities. Belgium shows a substantial growth for
young children and has extended its commitment of universal coverage to
children 0–2 years of age, but not to older pre-school children (Gornick *et
al.* 1997: 18). The growth of public childcare provisions for children less
than 3 years old is spectacular in the Netherlands. In 1989 the government
initiated a 'Stimulation Programme for Childcare'. This legislation was
intended to expand services for young children between 1990 and 1994

Table 1.8. Percentage of children in publicly funded childcare services in
Belgium, France, West Germany, Italy, and the Netherlands, 1993

Country	For children under age of 3	For children aged 3 to compulsory school age
Belgium	30	95
France	23	99
West Germany[a]	2	78
Italy[b]	6	91
Netherlands	8	71

[a] 1990.
[b] 1991.

Source: European Commission Network on Childcare (1996).

(later extended to 1997). The policy focuses on services for working parents in particular. Employers were expected to supplement public funds by buying places for their employees. Childcare is recognized as an economically productive instrument to increase women's labour-market participation and thus to make the Dutch economy more competitive. New incentives were created for employers in 1996 through a tax deduction of 20 per cent for the costs of childcare made by their employees. Rather than a fairer redistribution of labour both within and outside the home (the feminist position), the rationale of economic efficiency has had the greatest influence on the policy to expand childcare facilities (Bussemaker 1998). Arguments of efficiency, combating wasted human (female) capital, and enhancement of productivity appear to have been highly persuasive for building broad-based support for investment in childcare. In fact, these are part of a larger and rapid restructuring of the Dutch welfare state (Hemerijck and van Kersbergen 1997).

A new German policy initiative, which cannot be detected from the data yet, occurred as an effect of unification. Germany passed a law in 1992 to guarantee every child 3–6 years old a place in a *Kindergarten*, to take effect from 1996 (Bussemaker 1997b), but in 1997 extended to 1999. However, most of the kindergartens are open only part-time and are not attuned to labour-market participation of parents. Therefore, their effect on gender equality is limited. Moreover, municipalities are confronted with problems for children between 0 and 2 years old. Because they have to guarantee childcare for children from 3 to 6 years old, less attention is being paid to childcare for younger children.

Although there are signs of an increase of public childcare in various countries, new policies may impede further expansion. In the Netherlands, Germany, and Italy national governments have delegated the implementation of childcare policies to local authorities. Since 1996 Dutch central government funds are distributed to local authorities as part of their block grant and without earmarking these funds for specific services. Germany has delegated the implementation of the new 1992 law to the *Länder* and municipalities. Only France and Belgium deal with this matter on a national level: in France this is done by one national institution; in Belgium by the establishment of a childcare institution in the Flemish community and one in the *Communauté Française*.

Another recent trend is that a growing number of companies are investing in private day-care facilities. Employers see such investments as a necessity to attract female employees or to encourage their current female workers to keep working after childbirth, especially in the Netherlands. Public–private arrangements to take care of children at home also increased. This kind of day care is already well developed in Belgium (so-called host parents). But there also appears to be an increasing number of such semi-private carers in the Netherlands (also called host parents) and in Germany ('day mothers') (Bussemaker 1997*b*). This kind of childcare is very difficult to identify in terms of state and market, or in terms of private and public. It seems best to describe these facilities as 'semi' (market and family, as well as public and private).

In sum, since the late 1980s the Dutch and German governments seem to have increased their efforts to provide or encourage childcare facilities. Childcare has become a political issue in some of the social-capitalist welfare states (Bussemaker 1997*b*). At the same time, public responsibility for childcare is moving from the central state to local or regional authorities, as well as to individual families, the market, and private business. This movement is to a certain extent dictated by the need to cut public budgets and leads to a loss of quality of publicly funded childcare (as in the case of facilities for young children in Germany) or to an expected decrease in the number of places in public childcare (as in the Netherlands).

Overall, there are still striking differences among social-capitalist welfare states. Concerning childcare, it is problematic to label the French and Belgian policy as a form of subsidiarity. The French and Belgian institutionalization of childcare provision seems to be midway between the traditional social-capitalist model of subsidiarity and the social-democratic model of universality. Despite the fact that public childcare has not been directed to create gender equality, it certainly has affected gender relations, particularly in France. Although there are signs of change in the other countries (more in the Netherlands than in Germany), they are still far away from the French situation, and illustrate the variety among conservative welfare states.

❖ Conclusion

On the basis of our analysis we conclude that a gender bias has not disappeared in the social-capitalist welfare states. There is still a strong gender bias in social-security legislation, an ambivalence in the treatment of lone mothers, gendered assumptions underlying parental leave and childcare provisions, and gendered patterns of labour-market participation. However, we also found considerable variation among countries and increasing divergence as a result of new departures in policies.

Traditionally, social-capitalist welfare states have had common features concerning gender. Among these were a passive social policy, low female labour-market participation, a strong emphasis on cash benefits (family transfers) rather than on services, a strong breadwinner bias in social security to support the traditional family, ambiguously defined policies towards lone mothers (apart from widows), statutory leave schemes that focus primarily on mothers, and notions of subsidiarity in childcare services. These are clear, gendered properties of the social-capitalist welfare states. All these policies reinforce gender inequality.

However, we also found considerable variation among social-capitalist welfare states. Female labour-market participation has been traditionally higher in France and Germany than in the Netherlands and Belgium. The patterns of female labour-market participation over the life course vary cross-nationally: a traditional M-shaped curve for both Germany and the Netherlands; a moderate left-peak curve in Belgium and Italy; and a plateau curve in France. The breadwinner bias in social-security arrangements is particularly strong in Belgium and, to a lesser extent, in Germany and the Netherlands. Maternity and parental-leave schemes show considerable variation among countries. Services also reveal important differences. Germany and the Netherlands spend more on social services (especially for the elderly and the disabled) than Belgium and Italy, but services for children are more developed in Belgium and France than in Germany and the Netherlands.

Variation in policies has increased since 1980. All social-capitalist welfare states have removed unequal definitions in social-security legislation, but they have done so in various ways: (1) by extending means-testing; (2) by expanding the basis of entitlement to new groups; or (3) by restricting the level of benefits for all. The vulnerable position of lone mothers has caught attention in most countries (Italy being the exception), although the policies implemented differ. These are sometimes directed towards the protection of lone mothers through social transfers, as was the case in the Netherlands until recently. In other cases the pressure to participate in the labour market is increased, as in Germany, Italy, and the Netherlands, or fathers are stimulated to pay (Germany). As a result, poverty among lone mothers varies cross-nationally. Most countries have not changed their maternity leave, but have extended parental-leave schemes. But 'leave' is defined in different ways. It may be related exclusively to children, as in Italy, France, and Germany. But it may also be part, as in Belgium, of a general interruption of career life. Duration varies: short, as in the Netherlands; and long, as in Germany. The level of payment diverges, too: unpaid as in the Netherlands; low and short as in Italy; flat-rate as in Belgium; and means-tested as in Germany. There does not seem to be a clear pattern, but rather a patchwork of several arrangements. Female labour-market participation has increased in all countries. The M-curve in Germany and the Netherlands seems to be disappearing. Current patterns of part-time work for both men and women vary considerably among countries, while the variation in the participation of women on the labour market is not related to the incidence of part-time employment. There is also considerable variation in childcare policies. Belgium and France still stand apart from the other countries, although childcare provision for small children has expanded in the Netherlands and is expected to increase for older children in Germany. Only in Italy does the notion of subsidiarity, particularly in relation to the extended family, still play a role, although the informal market is an obstacle to getting the picture right.

For several reasons it is difficult to evaluate policy variation, policy changes, and policy outcomes in terms of increasing or decreasing gender inequality. First of all, some of these policies were introduced only very recently, and the relation between intentions and outcomes is not yet clear. Furthermore, old gender definitions have been partly eliminated—for example, by removing inequality in entitlements for married women—but new gender inequalities may arise. These may result from policies that perhaps do not relate directly to men and women, but nevertheless affect them differently. An example is the greater emphasis on means-testing.

Difficulties also stem from the more normative question of how one defines equality. To measure equality—or inequality—things have to be measurable. An important issue is what the central point for measurability is. This can be labour-market participation, personal autonomy (O'Connor 1993; Bussemaker 1997a), the possibility to maintain an autonomous household (Orloff 1993), or a fair distribution of paid and unpaid work. If one focuses on labour-market participation, social-capitalist welfare states still have a long way to go. But if one emphasizes personal autonomy, the answer might be more positive for at least some social-capitalist welfare states. If one concentrates on a fair distribution of paid and unpaid work, there is still inequality. We should also be aware that the women's movements in social-capitalist welfare states did not always agree about the definition of gender inequality. For example, parts of the German and Dutch women's movement have been reluctant to accept a definition of gender equality in terms of economic independence. Instead, some have preferred to define equality in terms of time autonomy that allows the combination of paid work and care, or in terms of self-realization.

Social capitalism, precisely because of its traditional combination of preserving the capitalist market while simultaneously tempering its harmful outcomes, historically and theoretically may have good prospects to remedy the negative effects of contemporary inequality, inside and outside the labour market. The main question is whether the *new* inequalities are recognized. If so, is there a political willingness to combat these

42

inequalities and what are the institutional conditions for this? As argued, the differences between social-capitalist countries in dealing with these issues are considerable. At the same time, some countries are more dynamic than others. Specifically, there is considerable variation in how these welfare states adapt to new challenges. The differences between the Netherlands and Germany are striking: in the latter case changes in social policy and gender relations are small, in the former important. This is not to argue that gender inequality will disappear, but rather that policy logics are changing. For example, measures to facilitate part-time work for women as well as men may decrease gender inequality in terms of a fair distribution of paid and unpaid work. On the other hand, the tendency to view childcare provisions as a means to increase productivity may impede such a strategy of gender inequality, because it neglects the role of unpaid work. In addition, new inequalities among women may occur as a result of new policies. For example, individualization of social security has more positive effects on the incomes of middle-class women than on those of working-class women.

What does our analysis suggest for the interrelation between gender inequality and welfare state regimes? Policies are moving in new directions, although not in all countries and not in all policy areas. Consequently, social-capitalist welfare states show increasing divergence with respect to gender. Although we would maintain that policy legacies play an important role in the way all social-capitalist welfare states deal with gender issues, we believe that it is more important to focus on short-term political factors to explain variation in current welfare policies. In other words, we think that politics matter. Social-capitalist welfare states are at a crossroads of upholding some traditional gender-related policies and innovation through new policies. We expect more variation among social-capitalist welfare states in the near future, not so much as an effect of persistent historical legacies and long-lasting institutional arrangements, but rather because of short-term political factors such as change in governments and perceptions of economic crisis. In addition, the influence of state agencies, EU directives, the influence of the women's movement as well as different national perceptions of gender equality determine changes and new directions in policies.

Current variation in policies challenges the social-capitalist welfare state regime as an empirically useful concept. Developments since the late 1980s seen from a gender perspective cross-cut the standard classifications (see Meyers *et al.*, Chapter 4, this volume). Although it is too early to make a final judgement, we argue that it is important to concentrate on the differences rather than similarities between welfare states within specific clusters. This is particularly relevant for the cluster of social-capitalist welfare states, precisely because gender is such an important indicator of new directions in social policy.

❖ Notes

1 In contrast to social-capitalist nations, etatism has been one of the main characteristics of France. Social policies have been directed to support the glorification of the state, rather than to support social institutions that fail to secure their means of income themselves.

2 A recent example of the problem is the Dutch sickness compensation scheme. In the Netherlands sickness benefits were covered by social insurance (compulsory below a certain level of income) until 1996, after which a privatized system of continued wage payments by employers was introduced. Such payments are 'private' and now fall outside the scope of public social expenditures, despite a mandatory responsibility of employers. Comparable considerations are valid for benefits that are negotiated in collective agreements.

3 Again, the Netherlands may look the biggest spender within the social-capitalist cluster, but the Dutch welfare state has few fiscal benefits plus taxes on cash transfers. Unfortunately, there are no data available on net expenditures.

4 Other directives concern equal pay for equal work and equal treatment in the labour force—they are excluded here.

5 The EU directive on equal treatment originated because of differences in gender-equality policies in France, on the one hand, and other countries, particularly Germany, on the other hand, and their possible effects for international competition. See Hantrais (1995) and Ostner and Lewis (1995).

6 With these regulations all social-capitalist welfare states meet the requirements following from a directive on maternity leave by the European Community in 1992. According to this directive, countries have to provide a minimum of fourteen weeks maternity leave, with replacement rates that are at least equivalent to sick pay.

7 Unemployment is gendered to the extent that women are more often unemployed than men. This is a general European pattern. However, the unemployment rate of women in 1994 was in Italy 1.8 times and in Belgium 1.6 times the unemployment rate of men. The number for Germany is 1.4 and for the Netherlands 1.2. These data emphasize the position of women as outsiders in the labour market.

8 Anttonen and Sipilä (1996) focused on services for both children and the elderly. We exclude services for the elderly from our analysis.

❖ References

Andries, M. (1996), 'Omtrent het Bestsaansminimum: Enkele Doelmatigheidsproblemen in International Vergelijkend Perspectief', *CSB-Berichten*, June (Antwerp).

ANTTONEN, A., AND SIPILÄ, J. (1996), 'European Social Care Services: Is it Possible to Identify Models?', *Journal of European Social Policy*, 6/2: 87–100.

BIMBI, F. (1997), 'Lone Mothers in Italy: A Hidden and Embarrassing Issue in a Familist Welfare Regime', in Lewis (1997), 171–202.

BUCKLEY, M., AND ANDERSON, M. (1988) (eds.), *Women, Equality and Europe* (Houndsmill).

BUSSEMAKER, J. (1993), *Betwiste zelfstandigheid: Individualisering, sekse en verzorgingsstaat* (Amsterdam).

——(1997a), 'Citizenship, Welfare State Regimes and Breadwinner-Arrangements: Various Backgrounds of Equality Policy', in Gardiner (1997), 180–97.

——(1997b), *Recent changes in European Welfare State Services: A Comparison of Childcare Politics in the UK, Sweden, Germany and the Netherlands*. Minda de Gunzberg Center for European Studies, Working Paper Series, Cambridge, Mass: Harvard University.

——(1998), 'Rationales of Care in Contemporary Welfare States: The Case of Childcare in the Netherlands', *Social Politics*, 5/1: 70–96.

——AND VAN KERSBERGEN, K. (1994), 'Gender and Welfare States: Some Theoretical Reflections', in Sainsbury (1994), 8–25.

——VAN DRENTH, A., KNIJN, T., AND PLANTENGA, J. (1997), 'Lone Mothers in the Netherlands', in Lewis (1997), 96–120.

——AND VOET, R. (1998), *Gender, Participation, and Citizenship in the Netherlands* (Aldershot).

DALY, M. (1996), 'Modernising Gender Relations: The Nature and Effects of Recent Welfare State Policies and Reforms', paper presented at Seminar 1 of the EC programme 'Gender and Citizenship: Social Integration and Social Exclusion in European Welfare States', Netherlands Institute for Advanced Studies, Wassenaar, the Netherlands, July.

DUMON, W. (1992), *European Observatory on National Family Policies, National Family Policies in EC-Countries in 1991*, (i–ii) Brussels.

ESPING-ANDERSEN, G. (1990), *The Three Worlds of Welfare Capitalism* (Cambridge).

——(1993), (ed.), *Changing Classes: Stratification and Mobility in Post-Industrial Societies* (London).

——(1996a), 'After the Golden Age? Welfare State Dilemmas in a Global Economy', in Esping-Andersen (1996c), 1–31.

——(1996b), 'Welfare States without Work: The Impasse of Labour Shedding and Familialism in Continental European Social Policy', in Esping-Andersen (1996c), 66–87.

——(1996c), (ed.), *Welfare States in Transition: National Adaptations in Global Economies* (London).

——Assimakopoulou, Z., and van Kersbergen, K. (1993), 'Trends in Contemporary Class Structuration: A Six-Nation Comparison', in Esping-Andersen (1993), 32–57.

European Commission (1993), *Social Protection in Europe* (Brussels).

European Commission Network on Childcare (1992), *Childcare in the European Community 1985–1990* (Brussels).

Eurostat (1990), *Community Labour Force Survey: A User's Guide* (Luxembourg).

——(1996), *Labour Force Survey: Results 1994* (Luxembourg).

——(1996), *A Review of Services for Young Children in the European Union, 1990–1995* (Brussels).

Gardiner, F. (1997), (ed.), *Sex Equality Policies in Western Europe* (London).

Gauthier, A. H. (1996), *The State and the Family: A Comparative Analysis of Family Policies in Industrialized Countries* (Oxford).

George, V. (1996), 'The Future of the Welfare State', in George and Taylor-Gooby (1996), 1–30.

——and Taylor-Gooby, P. (1996), (eds.), *European Welfare Policy: Squaring the Welfare Circle* (Houndmills).

Gornick, J., Meyers, M., and Ross, K. (1997), 'Supporting the Employment of Mothers: Policy Variation across Fourteen Welfare States', *Journal of European Social Policy*, 7/1: 45–70.

Hantrais, L. (1995), *Social Policy in the European Union* (Houndmills).

Hemerijck, A., and van Kersbergen, K. (1997), 'A Miraculous Model? Explaining the New Politics of the Welfare State in the Netherlands', *Acta Politica*, 32/3: 258–80.

Hobson, B. (1994), 'Solo Mothers, Social Policy Regimes and the Logics of Gender', in Sainsbury (1994), 170–87.

Hoskyns, C. (1988), 'Give Us Equal Pay and We'll Open Our Own Doors: A Study of the Impact in the Federal Republic of Germany and the Republic of Ireland of the European Community's Policy on Women Rights', in Buckley and Anderson (1988), 33–55.

Istat (1985) Istituto Nazionale di Statistica: *Indagine sulle strutture ed i comportamenti familiari* (Rome).

Knijn, T. (1994), 'Fish without Bikes: Revision of the Dutch Welfare State and its Consequences for the Independence of Single Mothers', *Social Politics*, 1/1: 83–105.

Leibfried, S., and Pierson, P. (1995), (eds.), *European Social Policy: Between Fragmentation and Integration* (Washington).

Lewis, J. (1993), (ed.), *Women and Social Policies in Europe: Work, Family and the State* (Aldershot).

——(1997), (ed.), *Lone Mothers in European Welfare Regimes: Shifting Policy Logics* (London).

Lewis, J. (with B. Hobson) (1997), 'Introduction', in Lewis (1997), 1–20.

O'Connor, J. (1993), 'Gender, Class and Citizenship in the Comparative Analysis of Welfare State Regimes: Theoretical and Methodological Issues', *British Journal of Sociology*, 44/3: 501–18.

——(1996), 'From Women in the Welfare State to Gendering Welfare State Regimes', *Current Sociology*, 44/2: 1–125.

OECD (1990): Organization of Economic Cooperation and Development, *Lone-Parent Families: The Economic Challenge* (Paris).

——(1992), *Economic Outlook: Historical Statistics 1960–1990* (Paris).

——(1996), *Social Expenditure Statistics of OECD Member Countries: Provisional Version* (Labour Market and Social Policy Occasional Papers, 17; Paris).

Orloff, A. S. (1993), 'Gender and the Social Rights of Citizenship: The Comparative Analysis of Gender Relations and Welfare States', *American Sociological Review*, 58: 303–28.

Ostner, I. (1997), 'Lone Mothers in Germany Before and After Unification', in Lewis (1997), 21–49.

——and Lewis, J. (1995), 'Gender and the Evolution of European Social Policies', in Leibfried and Pierson (1995), 159–93.

Sainsbury, D. (1994), (ed.), *Gendering Welfare States* (London).

——(1996), *Gender, Equality and Welfare States* (Cambridge).

Sjerps, I. (1988), 'Indirect Discrimination in Social Security in the Netherlands: Demands of the Dutch Women's Movement', in Buckley and Anderson (1988), 95–106.

Therborn, G. (1986), *Why Some People Are More Unemployed than Others* (London).

Van Kersbergen, K. (1995), *Social Capitalism: A Study of Christian Democracy and the Welfare State* (London).

——(1996), 'The Politics of Inactivity and the Welfare State: A Preliminary Position Paper', paper presented at the workshop 'The Politics of Inactivity', ECPR Joint Sessions, Oslo 29 March.–3 Apr.

2 ❖ Employment Equality Strategies in Liberal Welfare States

Julia S. O'Connor

Australia, Canada, the UK, and the USA are widely designated as liberal welfare states in terms of their social policy frameworks. This chapter examines their strategies related to pay and employment equity. It reverses the concern of much work on welfare states with the level of decommodification, or protection from dependence on the labour market for survival (Esping-Andersen 1990: 21). This protection from forced participation, irrespective of age, health conditions, family status, or availability of suitable employment, is obviously of major importance to both men and women, although affecting them differently because of their different patterns of paid and unpaid work (Orloff 1993: 317). However, before decommodification becomes an issue for individuals, a crucial first step is access to the labour market—that is, the potential for commodification—or, alternatively, the existence of a full range of social rights that afford economic independence without links to the labour market. Since the latter is not the case in any welfare state, labour-force participation and the quality of that participation are crucial to the range and quality of social rights and to social stratification in contemporary welfare states.

As Carole Pateman has pointed out, independence has been 'theoretically and historically, the central criterion for citizenship'. What constitutes independence has changed over time; in 'the "democratic" welfare state . . . employment rather than military service is the key to citizenship' (Pateman 1988: 238). Employment affords the possibility of independence directly through monetary compensation but it may also condition access to, and the exercise of, formally gender-neutral citizenship rights. A tiered system of access to social services characterizes the typical liberal welfare state. The major distinction between the tiers is relationship to the labour market (O'Connor 1993: 504), but not all relationships to the labour market are equally facilitative of independence. Occupational segregation by gender, both horizontal and vertical, and gender-based pay differentials are evident in all capitalist economies (OECD 1988: 209; Maruani 1992). Public policies on pay and employment equity have the potential to enhance the quality of participation and consequently the potential for independence. Yet, despite employment-equity and/or affirmative-action policies dating from the 1970s in several countries, the OECD evidence indicates that gender-based occupational segregation is still pervasive, as are differences in hourly earnings between men and women. Furthermore, several of the countries with the best female/male earnings ratios have high aggregate levels of segregation—for example, Australia and Sweden.[1] In contrast, Canada and the USA, which have considerably lower aggregate indicators of occupational segregation by gender and which had marked decreases in these indicators over the 1970–86 period (OECD 1996), have relatively low female/male earning ratios.

In the next section I outline the employment equality strategies pursued in the liberal welfare states since the 1960s. This is followed by a discussion of the outcomes that result, including a discussion of the apparent contradictions in aggregate measures of occupational segregation and female/male wage ratios and how these apparent contradictions can be reconciled. In the concluding section political and institutional explanations for the cross-national differences across welfare states are discussed.

❖ EQUALITY STRATEGIES

The public policy employment equality strategies pursued in the liberal welfare states have some significant similarities but also differ cross-nationally in some significant respects (Tables 2.1 and 2.2). All the liberal welfare states except Australia have equal-pay legislation, but only some states in the USA and some provinces in Canada have strong legislation on equal pay for work of equal value or comparable worth (Weiner and Gunderson 1990: 110–14, 138–9) and in most of these jurisdictions it is confined to public-sector workers. Equal-pay measures are directed to the underpayment of women doing the same or broadly similar work to men in the same employment. Equal pay for work of equal value is directed to the effects of horizontal segregation and the undervaluation of work done primarily by women; equal value or comparable worth is generally based on a composite measure of skill, effort, responsibility, and working conditions and may be arrived at through a process of job evaluation (Kahn 1992: 3). Depending on the interpretation, it may allow for comparison of occupations in the same workplace or across workplaces.

All four countries have legislation relating to equal-employment opportunities and the prohibition of discrimination, but the approaches adopted vary from anti-discrimination through affirmative action to expanding opportunities (O'Donnell and Hall 1988; OECD 1988; Steinberg and Cook 1988). Legislation in these areas is directed to the effects of vertical segregation and seeks to remove barriers to the integration of women into all areas of the labour force; these barriers may be in hiring, training, and/or promotion procedures.

❖ Equal Pay and Pay Equity

The USA, Canada, and the UK have adopted a legislative approach to pay-equity (Table 2.1). The effectiveness of a legislative approach is dependent on several factors, the most important of which is whether the legislation is proactive or complaint based. Proactive approaches are more effective than complaint-based approaches. Under a complaint-based approach an individual, a group, or their representative is obliged to initiate a complaint and go through the process of demonstrating unfair pay. The national legislation in all three countries is complaint based.

The US legislation on equal pay dates from 1963 but the emphasis on comparable worth did not arise until the late 1970s. The pressure for change came from a variety of sources, especially from public-sector unionized employees at state and local level who were supported by the Women's Bureau and by the Equal Employment Opportunities Commission (EEOC), which is responsible for the enforcement of the federal legislation on equal pay. In 1981 the National Academy of Sciences produced a report for EEOC entitled *Women, Work and Wages: Equal Pay for Jobs of Equal Value* (Treiman and Hartmann 1981), which provided a scholarly analysis of the wage gap and a justification for comparable worth and the use of job-evaluation techniques (Blum 1991: 51–2). Several states have enacted pay-equity legislation covering state employees and in some cases local-government employees. Evans and Nelson (1991: 229) indicate that states that took early action on pay equity 'tended to meet three political criteria: collective bargaining for public employees, control by the Democratic party of state government, and a strong commission on the status of women'. Despite substantial gains at the micro-level, pay-equity legislation has had relatively little impact on pay differentials at the aggregate level. This may be associated with the fact that it is implemented at the level of individual plants, and such settlements cannot be used as a basis to generalize upwards because of the absence of effective collective-bargaining machinery at industry, sectoral, and national level (Rubery 1988: 261). Associated with this is the fact that the principle of comparable worth is still under legal challenge and plaintiffs are usually obliged to prove intentional discrimination (England 1992: 225–51; Kahn 1992). In

Table 2.1. Equal-pay provisions, coverage, and enforcement in Australia, Canada, UK, and USA

Provision	Country			
	Australia	Canada	UK	USA
Legislation/ agreement/ decision	Equal pay for equal work decision 1969 Equal pay for work of equal value decision 1972 Minimum wage extended to women 1974 Sex Discrimination Act 1984 (amended 1992)	Equal Pay Provisions of Canadian Labour Code 1971 Section 11 of Canadian Human Rights Act 1977	Equal Pay Act 1970 (in force 1975) amended by Sex Discrimination Act 1975 and Equal Pay Amendment Regulations 1983 (equal pay for work of equal value amendment)	Equal Pay Act 1963 Title VII of Civil Rights Act 1964
Legislative model	Conciliation and Arbitration Sex Discrimination Act is complaint based	Complaint based	Complaint based	Complaint based
Monitoring/ enforcement agency	Industrial Tribunals, Human Rights and Equal Opportunities Commissioner, Industrial tribunals on reference from Sex Discrimination Commissioner (1992 amendment)	Canadian Human Rights Commission Labour Standards Branch, Department of Labour	Industrial Tribunals	Equal Employment Opportunity Commission Courts

❖ Julia S. O'Connor

Coverage	Public and private employees covered by federal and state awards. Sex Discrimination Act applies to private-sector employees and Commonwealth public-sector employees. It also applies to commission agents, contract workers, and partnerships.	All federally regulated sectors including the federal public service, Crown corporations, banks, airlines and interprovincial transport.	Public and private sector (the principle of equal pay was put into practice for non-industrial civil servants over the period 1955–61).	Covers most private employees whose employers are covered by the Fair Labor Standards Act, including executive, administrative, professional and outside sales employees, who are exempt from the minimum wage and overtime provisions. Most federal, state, and local government workers are covered.
Implementation/ enforcement mechanism	Unions bring cases before industrial tribunals. Individuals or unions can make complaints to the Sex Discrimination Commissioner.	The Human Rights Commission can initiate complaints and respond to complaints brought by individuals, third parties such as labour inspectors, or groups. The Canadian Labour Code enables an inspector to notify or file a complaint with the Canadian Human Rights Commission where the inspector has reasonable grounds to believe that the equal-pay provisions of the Canadian Human Rights Act have been breached.	Claims are brought by individuals through their unions to industrial tribunals. Class actions are not possible. The Advisory Conciliation and Arbitration Service has a statutory duty to attempt conciliation. The Equal Opportunities Commission established in 1975 gives free advice and in some cases financial assistance for legal representation before an industrial tribunal.	Complaints can be filed under either Act or both. The Equal Pay Act provides for equal pay for jobs whose performance requires equal skill, effort and responsibility and are performed under similar working conditions. Title VII prohibits discrimination on the basis of sex. Cases can be closed by negotiation, conciliation, or court settlement. The Equal Employment Opportunity Commission has the power to sue employers.

Sources: Various country sources; see text.

LIBERAL WELFARE STATES ❖

addition, job evaluation is a highly political process and without worker's collective representation the scheme chosen may not positively evaluate the skills of most female-dominated jobs (Acker 1989).

In Canada, equal pay for equal work legislation has been in existence federally and provincially since the 1950s and was embodied in the Canada Labour Code in 1971. Up to 1985 only the federal and Quebec governments had enacted pay-equity legislation and this was part of their human-rights legislation and complaint based. Since then five of the ten provinces and one of the two territories have enacted such legislation and one other province has made non-legislative provision for pay equity. All of these cover the public service and all but one covers the broader public service (municipalities, school boards, universities), six of the eight cover Crown corporations, but only three cover the private sector: the federal legislation covers private organizations in federally regulated industries such as banking and transportation. Quebec is the only province where the total workforce is covered—90 per cent by the Quebec Charter and the remainder by the federal legislation. However, because of the vagueness of the guidelines regarding equal value, complaints are difficult to establish and few have been filed. The Ontario legislation is the most progressive: it is the only legislation that is both proactive and covers the private sector, although it excludes employers with less than ten employees; consequently, some of the most vulnerable workers are excluded from protection. The issue of proactivity is important, since it mandates employers to assess the extent of discriminatory pay practices and implement a wage-adjustment programme. As with the US legislation, there have been some substantial gains at the micro-level in Canada but little impact on the wage gap at the aggregate level.

The 1970 Equal Pay Act in the UK, which came into effect in 1975 and made it illegal to pay a woman less than a man working for the same employer and doing the same or broadly similar work, is acknowledged as the source of a significant improvement in the female/male wage ratio. Between 1970 and 1977 average hourly earnings of full-time women relative to men rose from 63 to 75 per cent; there were no further increases between 1977 and 1987—rather there was a slight widening in the differential (Gregory 1992). Rubery (1988) argues that the reason for the once-off improvement is that the trade unions did not pursue general policies of equalizing wage rates (p. 259); she acknowledges that unions did contribute to improving the wages of women through ensuring that the equal-pay settlements were based on the male minimum not the female minimum (p. 261). The Equal Pay Act was amended in 1983 following a European Court of Justice ruling that the original Act did not meet the requirements of European law as embodied in Article 119 of the Treaty of

Rome and subsequent Equality Directives.[2] The amendment meant a change to 'equal pay for work of equal value'; this allows for value comparisons across different occupations and, consequently, affords an opportunity to address some of the consequences of occupational gender segregation.

Jeanne Gregory (1992) argues that equal pay for work of equal value received only weak support and considerable opposition in the UK. The Conservative government was hostile and created a 'procedural minefield' for the processing of claims (ibid. 463). The industrial tribunal processing system has been severely criticized because of the complexity of the regulations, length of time involved in processing a claim, and the cost (Kahn 1992: 52). There are a minimum of fourteen different stages to complete an equal-value case and some take up to eight years to complete (*Labour Research*, Dec. 1993: 13). The problems with the legislation are reflected in the fact that the Equal Opportunities Commission (EOC), which has the statutory responsibility for monitoring the legislation, has put forward proposals to amend it (EOC 1990). Employers strongly opposed the legislation, as did male craft workers; initially the trade-union movement did not incorporate equal value into its negotiating strategy and there were no collective remedies for enforcing equal-pay legislation. Discriminatory collective bargaining is illegal under the Sex Discrimination Act as amended in 1986, but there is still no collective mechanism for enforcing this. Towards the end of the 1980s the situation improved: the EOC adopted a law-enforcement strategy and initiated several judicial review proceedings against the government (Lovenduski and Randall 1993: 190). Trade unions are now more active in supporting equal-value claims and highlighting the limitations of the legislation. The bias in most job-evaluation schemes towards higher-status jobs has been highlighted, as has the use being made by employers of job evaluation to avoid equal-pay claims. The latter is possible because the Equal Pay Act stipulates that a job-evaluation scheme that meets its standards is a bar to an equal pay claim (*Labour Research*, Oct. 1992: 14). In view of these problems unions are campaigning for job-evaluation schemes that take account of equal-pay principles and are fair to workers in all sectors of the occupational spectrum (ibid).

In contrast to the USA, Canadian, and UK systems the Australian system up to the early 1990s was highly centralized through federal and state Conciliation and Arbitration/Industrial Relations Commissions that ruled on pay issues. After 1969 they accepted the principle of equal pay for equal work and after 1972 the principle of equal pay for work of equal value—that is, that 'award rates for all workers should be considered without regard to the sex of the employee' (Equal Pay Decision Print B8506

LIBERAL WELFARE STATES ❖

1972: 7, quoted in Burton 1991: 130). When agreement could not be reached by unions and employers, work-value comparisons were to be conducted. Where possible these were to 'be made between female and male classifications within the award under consideration' (Principle 5b of Decision, quoted in DIR 1993: 7). Broader bases of comparison were deemed acceptable only in exceptional circumstances. Work-value enquiries were rare under the 1972 agreement, and, when they were undertaken, the emphasis was on job content rather than job value (Burton 1991: 132). Equal pay for work of equal value was implemented in three phases up to 1975. The acceptance of equal-pay and equal-value principles in Australia has been demonstrated to be associated with a significant reduction in the wage gap (Gregory and Duncan 1981; Burton 1991: 146–8). The principle of comparable worth was rejected in 1986, in a ruling relating to nurses' pay, on the grounds that it would result in too broad a range of work-value comparisons and hence would 'strike at the heart of accepted methods of wage fixation . . . and would be particularly destructive of the present Wage Fixing Principles' (Conciliation and Arbitration Commissioner's ruling, quoted in O'Donnell and Hall 1988: 58). The Commissioners pointed out that Canada, the USA, and the UK, where the principle is applied, although with different approaches in each country, have very different industrial-relations systems from the Australian one. The system in each of these countries is highly decentralized, and considerably lower percentages of their labour forces are covered by collective agreements. In May 1990, 80 per cent of Australian wage and salary earners (83.5 per cent of women and 77.3 per cent of men) were covered by awards made by the Commonwealth and state industrial tribunals or by collective agreements registered with them. It is estimated that in Canada only 50 per cent of the labour force are covered by collective agreements, in the UK about 70 per cent are covered, including almost all public-sector employees, and in the USA less than 20 per cent of the labour force are covered (Ries and Stone 1992: 369).

In summary, the equality strategies pursued in the four countries are based on similar principles and the sequence of adoption is similar. Equal pay for equal work gave way to equal pay for work of equal value in each of the countries. The major cross-national difference is the greater success of the Australian collective approach in reducing gender-based pay differentials.

❖ *Employment Equity*

Legislation on equal-employment opportunities ranges from anti-discrimination through affirmative action to expanding opportunity

❖ Julia S. O'Connor

approaches, and the sequence of adoptions tends to follow this pattern. Anti-discrimination policy concentrates on preventing individual employers and others from discriminating. The emphasis on policy is formulated in terms of what employers or others are prohibited from doing (Steinberg and Cook 1988: 319). The affirmative-action approach addresses the systemic behaviour of parties in the labour market. The essential difference between it and the anti-discrimination approach is that, while the former focuses on individual behaviour, the latter is concerned with the structure and functioning of the labour market and the implications of this for employment practices. The expanding-opportunities approach is based on a recognition of barriers to entry and/or progress in the labour market. The solution to discrimination is seen to lie to a significant extent in the expansion of training programmes for under-represented groups, childcare, and collective-bargaining agreements that incorporate anti-discrimination clauses relating especially to pay but also to employment conditions and benefits (Table 2.2).

The anti-discrimination approach in the USA dates from the 1964 Civil Rights Act. Title VII of that Act came into effect in 1965 and prohibited discrimination in employment practices and established the EEOC, 'to investigate and conciliate complaints and grant complainants the right to seek remedies in court' (Blum 1991: 22). Later the powers of the EEOC were expanded to include the ability to sue employers directly and its jurisdiction was expanded to include state and local-government employees. Executive order 11246, issued in 1965, required written affirmative action plans from all federal contractors with contracts over $50,000; those with contracts over $10,000 were required to practise affirmative action. Because of the extent of federal contracting—approximately one-half of all private-sector, non-agricultural employment is provided by such firms—the potential of the executive order is far reaching (Blum 1991: 22). The plans must specify goals and timetables, not quotas, for the achievement of an integrated labour force both in race and gender terms. The inclusion of women under Title VII came about by accident rather than design and few sex discrimination cases were brought in the early stages.[3] The institutional and legal frameworks developed in the USA are important resources and have proved effective when political commitment encouraged their use. The strength of this political commitment has varied—it was weak during the Nixon and Ford administrations, strong during the Carter administration, and weak during the Reagan and Bush eras. According to Linda Blum 'the lack of vigorous enforcement is the most frequently cited reason for the limited impact of affirmative action on women's economic status' (Blum 1991: 23). It is noteworthy that the gains made in the public sector have been considerably better than those in the private sector and have been consistent throughout this period.

The importance of the political complexion of the Supreme Court for achievements under the 1960s measures is reflected in the push for the Civil Rights Act 1991. This legislation was directed to countering 'the effects of nine Supreme Court decisions from 1986 to 1991 that made

Table 2.2. Employment equity provisions, principal implementing measures, in Australia, Canada, UK and USA

Country	Year	Title	Enforcement machinery
Australia			
Equal Employment Opportunity	1984	Sex Discrimination Act	Sex Discrimination Commission
	1992	Amendments	
	1984	Public Service Act	Public Service Commission
	1987	Amendments	
	1986	Affirmative Action (Equal Employment Opportunity for Women) Act	Affirmative Action Agency
	1992	Amendments	
	1993	Contract Compliance	
Canada			
Equal Employment Opportunity	1977	Canadian Human Rights Act	Canadian Human Rights Commission
	1986	Employment Equity Act	Canadian Employment and Immigration Commission
	1986	Federal Contractors Programme	
	1995	Employment Equity Act (amended)	Canadian Human Rights Commission
UK			
Equal Employment Opportunity	1975	Sex Discrimination Act	Equal Opportunities Commission (EOC); Industrial Tribunals
	1986	(amended)	
USA			
Equal Employment Opportunity	1964	Civil Rights Act, Title VII	Equal Employment Opportunity Commission
	1965	Executive Order 11246	Office of federal Contract Compliance Programs
	1968	Executive Order 11375	Office of Federal Contract Compliance Programs
	1972	Equal Employment Opportunities Act	Equal Employment Opportunity Commission
	1991	Civil Rights Act	

Source: OECD (1988: 167–8, table 5.11), and updates from country sources.

❖ JULIA S. O'CONNOR

it harder for workers to bring and win job discrimination lawsuits' (*Congressional Quarterly Almanac* 1991: 251).[4] The legislation provided guidelines for disparate impact lawsuits and expanded the scope of relevant civil-rights statutes to provide adequate protection to victims of discrimination (ibid. 258). In addition, it established a four-year Glass Ceiling Commission 'to study how business filled management and decision-making positions, the developmental and skill-enhancing practices used to foster qualifications for advancement, and the pay and reward structures used in the workplace' (*Congressional Quarterly Almanac* 1991: 259). The Commission chaired by the Secretary of Labour was mandated to make recommendations to help eliminate artificial barriers to the advancement of women and minorities on the job. The legislation also included a pay equity study by the Labor Department 'to study disparities in the wages of men and women and whites and minorities' (ibid). In its first report the Commission demonstrated that women have made gains at the middle-management level, where white women hold 40 per cent of jobs compared to 36 per cent of all jobs, and black women hold 5 per cent of these jobs compared to a similar percentage of all jobs. In contrast, the Commission concluded that, despite three decades of affirmative action, women and minority groups are to a significant extent blocked from top management, with women constituting less than 5 per cent of senior managers. They point to the difference between the rhetoric and the practice of inclusion (Glass Ceiling Commission 1995).

Canada's anti-discrimination approach dates from the Canadian Human Rights Act (1977). The right to equality in employment was constitutionally affirmed in the Canadian Charter of Rights and Freedoms, which forms part of the Constitution Act (1982). This explicitly permitted legislation such as employment equity. The federal Royal Commission on Equality of Employment, which reported in 1984, argued that, despite existing human-rights legislation and voluntary affirmative action, systemic barriers continued to exist for women, aboriginal peoples, visible minorities, and disabled people and that these barriers could be overcome only by systemic remedies. It referred to these measures as employment equity rather than affirmative action. It argued against the latter term because of its negative connotation and its association with quotas. The 1986 Employment Equity Act, which strongly reflects the Royal Commission recommendations, states that employment equity 'means more than treating persons in the same way but also requires special measures and the accommodation of differences' (Section 2). This Act excludes the federal public service, because it was already subject to an Affirmative Action Policy introduced in 1983. It applies only to a minority of employers and employees; these are federally regulated employers and

Crown corporations that have 100 or more employees, and operate primarily in banking, transportation, and communications industries. They employ about 5.5 per cent of the labour force. In addition to the Employment Equity Act, the federal government has a contract-compliance policy requiring employers of 100 or more workers bidding for federal contracts of $200,000 or more to commit themselves to employment equity. The programme applies to about 880 companies employing about 7.5 per cent of the labour force, primarily in manufacturing and such businesses as engineering services, printing, cleaning services, and university research.

The obligations of the Employment Equity Act are that companies must implement employment equity and design a plan, including goals and timetable, and must report annually on progress. These reports are sent to the Canadian Human Rights Commission and a consolidated report is presented to parliament. Public access to the reports is available on request. Failure to report can result in a fine of $50,000. Should there be an appearance of discrimination on the basis of the information provided, the Canadian Human Rights Commission can initiate a complaint under the Canadian Human Rights Act. The Canadian Human Rights Commissioner argued before a parliamentary review committee in 1992 that the Human Rights Commission lacked a clearly defined mandate to monitor implementation, and that the Act is too vague successfully to combat employment discrimination. A special parliamentary committee that reported on the operation of the Act in May 1992 made several recommendations for broadening its scope and increasing its effectiveness through such measures as training and childcare; this indicates that there is a recognition that some of the sources of women's labour-market inequality lie outside the labour market (Special Committee on the Review of the Employment Equity Act 1992). These recommendations imply the need for an expanding opportunities approach. A revised Employment Equity Act incorporating some of the recommended changes was passed in 1995. In particular, it extended coverage to all employees in the federal public sector—that is, the federal public service, agencies, and commissions; it empowered the Canadian Human Rights Commission to conduct audits of all public and private employers under the legislation to verify compliance and to empower the Canadian Human Rights Tribunal, acting as the Employment Equity Review Tribunal, to ensure final enforcement when needed in both the public and private sectors (Human Resources Development, Canada 1994). This answers one of the major criticisms of the original act—that is, non-enforceability of employers' obligations. The inclusion of the federal public sector brought an additional 10 per cent of the labour force under coverage of the Act and answered the criticism that the public-service affirmative-action policy was not being strongly enforced.

Ontario is the only other jurisdiction in Canada that has had employment equity legislation. It was passed in 1993 and came into effect in September 1994 under the New Democratic Party government. It covered the same four designated groups as the federal legislation but was broader in scope; it applied not only to the public service and the broader public service as does the federal legislation but also to private-sector employers with ten or more employees. It was the most comprehensive legislation in Canada and was the focus of concerted opposition by sections of the business community, by the Conservative and Liberal parties, and by the mainstream print media. In one of the first legislative acts of the newly elected Progressive Conservative government, it was abolished in October 1995.

The first sex-equality legislation in Australia was passed in 1975 in South Australia, and by 1985 three other states (Victoria and New South Wales in 1977 and Western Australia in 1985) had enacted sex-equality legislation. The federal Sex Discrimination Act, which was passed in 1984, is complaints based but does contain provisions against apparently neutral employment requirements that disadvantaged women. It was amended in 1992 to cover federal industrial awards and variation in industrial awards made after the date of the legislation. This was introduced to guard against discrimination in the changed climate of decentralized bargaining arrangements. The Affirmative Action (Equal Employment Opportunity for Women) Act was passed in 1986 and was fully operational by February 1989. It focuses on the removal of systemic discrimination. It covers all private-sector employers with 100 or more employees, as well as higher-education institutions; it requires employers to set goals and timetables for achieving a representative workforce (O'Donnell and Hall 1988: 78; OECD 1988). In 1992 it was extended to cover voluntary bodies with 100 or more paid employees, elected union officials, and trainees employed through group training schemes. With effect from January 1993, companies in breach of affirmative-action legislation for women workers are ineligible for Commonwealth government contracts, which are worth $A10 billion annually. The Australian Commonwealth legislation differs from the Canadian federal legislation in being focused exclusively on women, while the Canadian legislation covers four designated groups. It is broader in scope than the Canadian federal legislation in covering all firms with 100 or more employees. It covers 45 per cent of the labour force compared to 13 per cent in Canada. Until 1993, when the contract compliance provision was introduced, the only sanction for non-compliance was naming in parliament.

The Australian strategy incorporates measures to promote equality of opportunity in government employment. These have been taken at both the federal level and in Western Australia, South Australia, New South Wales, and Victoria. The New South Wales legislation covers colleges and universities and local government (O'Donnell and Hall 1988: 79). In addition to these measures there has been an increasing emphasis on training over the past decade. In 1992 women made up 62 per cent of the participants in the Australian Traineeship Scheme and women received about 42 per cent of Department of Education Employment and Training labour-market programme opportunities. In 1990 the Women's Employment, Education, and Training Advisory Group was formed to provide independent advice to government on employment, education, and training issues affecting women, and in 1991 the Commonwealth, State, and Territory Governments developed the National Plan of Action for Women in TAFE (technical and further education) to provide a coordinated approach to improving women's participation (Office of the Status of Women 1993: 31). The most significant difference between the Australian approach to equality in employment and that in the other three countries is that, in addition to these training elements, there is a commitment to meet all work-related childcare needs by the year 2000/1, and childcare expenses are now regarded as a legitimate expense for parents in the paid labour force (O'Connor 1994).[5] These measures in combination reflect a commitment to expanding opportunities.

The 1975 Sex Discrimination Act, as amended in 1986, provides the legal basis of employment equity in the UK. This act was introduced to meet EC equality requirements as reflected in Article 119 of the Treaty of Rome. Industrial Tribunals, which are quasi-judicial bodies explicitly established to deal with labour-relations disputes, are central to the UK system. The EOC is involved only when a dispute raises a question of principle or when a complainant cannot pursue a claim unaided. It monitors the Equal Pay and Sex Discrimination Acts and recommends amendments to the laws. The EOC has been active in using the European Court of Justice to clarify domestic law. Its 'Code of Practice for the Elimination of Discrimination', which received parliamentary approval in 1985, has been associated with an increase in the number of voluntary initiatives on employment equity and some of these have been aided by state subsidies. In addition, several local authorities have adopted contract-compliance practices (OECD 1988: 166). Thus, while the legislation in the UK reflects an anti-discrimination approach, there is encouragement of voluntary affirmative action. This action is for the most part confined to a relatively small number of companies and is often targeted at the upper levels of the occupational spectrum—for example, the Opportunity 2000 campaign, which has received high-profile support, including that of the former Prime

Minister, John Major.[6] In contrast, it is noteworthy that funding rules prevent Training and Enterprise Councils from helping employers run affirmative-action training targeted to women in low-paid jobs. An investigation by the EOC indicates that, because of underfunding, training is extremely limited in the UK and some programmes are being cut back (*Labour Research*, May 1993: 30).

In summary, there is anti-discrimination legislation in all four countries. The USA, Canada, and Australia have affirmative-action/ employment equity legislation and the UK has voluntary affirmative-action initiatives that operate for the most part at higher occupational levels. Australia has adopted the most extensive approach to expanding employment opportunities, as reflected in training and childcare initiatives, but there is some emphasis on training in all countries. Increasingly, there is a recognition in all four countries of the importance of childcare in facilitating labour-market participation, but the type and extent of public support varies significantly across countries (O'Connor *et al.* 1999: Ch. 3).

❖ Outcomes of Equality Strategies

Gender wage-differential measures give a clear ranking of the liberal welfare states, with Australia at the high end of the OECD spectrum, close to Norway and Sweden, while the USA and Canada are at the low end, with the UK midway between the two extremes. This pattern was evident in the 1980s and is still true in the mid-1990s (Tables 2.3(i) and (ii)). The figures presented in Table 2.3(i) are not directly comparable—those for Australia and the UK are for hourly earnings, the Canadian figure is for annual earnings, and the US figure is for weekly earnings. The latter two include overtime earnings, which men are more likely to have; consequently, the hourly male/female differential may be less than indicated. Notwithstanding this caveat, it is noteworthy that the rankings of countries in this table are similar to those evident in several sources for the mid-1980s to the mid-1990s (e.g. OECD 1988, 1991; table 2.16; Gornick 1992; Gregory 1992; O'Connor 1996). The mid-1990s figures also reflect a decrease in the male/female differentials over time. As with every other aspect of labour-market participation, it is important to recognize that these aggregate measures of gender differences conceal considerable variation in the experience of workers in the public and private sectors, in different occupations, in unionized and non-unionized employment, and in full and part-time work. For example, while the overall gender wage differential in the UK did not increase over the 1983–9 period, the pay differential amongst women in employment did: there was an overall pattern of

Table 2.3(i). Ratio of female to male earnings for full-time workers in
Australia, Canada, UK, and USA, mid-1990s

Country	Year	Female/male earnings ratio
Australia	1996	84.4 (hourly earnings)
Canada	1995	73.1 (annual earnings)
UK	1996	80.0 (hourly earnings)
US	1996	75.0 (weekly earnings)

Sources: Australia: ABS (1997); Canada: Statistics Canada (1995); UK: Office for National
Statistics (1996); USA: United States Bureau of the Census (1997).

Table 2.3(ii). Ratio of female to male earnings for full-time workers: public
and private sectors, in Australia, Canada, UK, and USA, early 1990s

Country	Year	Sector		Total full-time workforce
		Private	Public	
Australia	1992	79.1	89.6	84.5
Canada	1992	67.9	79.8	71.8
UK	1991	65.8	76.7	71.9
USA	1991	67.2	74.1	71.0

Sources: Australia: ABS (1994); Canada: Statistics Canada, Household Surveys Division,
Survey of Consumer Finances, unpublished data, UK and USA: Gornick and Jacobs (1997:
table 4).

increasing wages for highly paid women at the same time as wages at the
low end of the pay scale remained static or declined. In addition, the gap
between full and part-time hourly rates increased (Maruani 1992), and this
pattern has continued throughout the 1990s (Harkness 1998). The figures
in Tables 2.3(i) and (ii) do not differentiate between full and part-time
workers; as gender pay differentials are usually less for part-time workers
and the UK has higher rates of part-time work than the other countries, it
is probable that its gender pay differential for full-time workers may be relatively worse than the above figures indicate.

There are marked differences in gender pay differentials between
public-sector and private-sector full-time employees in the early 1990s
(Table 2.3 (ii)). The female/male pay relativity is higher for government-
sector workers in all four countries. This is not surprising, since unioniza-
tion is considerably higher in the public sector than in the private sector

❖ Julia S. O'Connor

and unionized workers are in a stronger position to exercise their rights, and there is generally greater visibility of procedures in the public sector than in the private sector. It is also noteworthy that employment in the public sector has been declining since 1968 in the USA and the UK and since 1983 in Canada and Australia (OECD 1993).

Data and measurement limitations are even greater in gender-based cross-national comparisons of occupational distributions than in pay comparisons. Despite this fact, there are some clear indications of over- and under-representation of women and men in particular categories of occupations in all OECD countries. Women are generally over-represented in clerical and service occupations and in the service sector and men are over-represented in the transport and communications and manufacturing sectors, and these patterns have changed little over the 1980s. In contrast, the representation of women in managerial and administrative occupations and to a lesser extent in professional occupations varies markedly across OECD countries in general and across the liberal welfare states in particular (Table 2.4). Despite these facts, women have made gains in all these countries—what is at issue is the location and extent of these gains.

A review of the country occupational distributions in the early 1990s indicates some marked differences in the female share of occupational groups across countries, and a comparison with the early 1980s

Table 2.4. Percentage of women in major occupational groups in Australia, Canada, UK, and USA, 1990

Occupational groups	Australia	Canada	UK	USA
Managers and administrators[a]	24	41	32	42
Professional	41 } 45	} 50	40 } 45	53 } 52
Para/semi-professional[b]	47		50	49
Clerical	77	81	75	79
Unskilled service		57	67	60
Sales	64	47	66	48

[a] Managers is categorization for Canada, UK, and USA; managers and administrators is categorization for Australia.
[b] Australia: para-professionals; UK: associated professional and technical occupations; USA: technical and related support.

Sources: Australia: ABS (1992); Canada: Statistics Canada (1993); UK: *Employment Gazette* (1993); USA: United States Bureau of the Census (1993: 405, table 644).

indicates some marked differences in the rates of change (Table 2.4). While in Canada and the USA in the early 1990s over 40 per cent of managerial/administrative jobs were held by women, 32 per cent were held by women in the UK and only 24 per cent were held by women in Australia. In professional and semi-professional occupations the differences are considerably less, but there is still a marked difference between the USA and Canada, on the one hand, where the percentages of professional and semi-professional jobs held by women were 52 and 50 per cent respectively, compared to Australia and the UK, on the other hand, where 45 per cent of these jobs were held by women. In all four countries unskilled service jobs are predominantly female occupations, but that predominance is stronger in the UK than in any of the other countries.

A comparison of country-specific major occupational distributions for the early 1990s and the early to mid-1980s indicates that segregation has declined in all the liberal welfare states but at a slow rate and then only at the upper end of the occupational distribution. With the exception of the USA, where it remained static, women's representation in clerical, sales, and service occupations increased slightly over the decade. The only occupational groups that showed substantial increases in the representation of women are the managerial/administrative and professional occupational groups. For the USA and Canada, the most marked increase in female representation was in the managerial/administrative occupational group, where the representation of women increased in both countries by 28 per cent over the decade from 1982 to 1992. Representation in the professional occupational group also increased but by far lower percentages—by 9 per cent in the USA and by 11 per cent in Canada—over the decade. While the percentage of women in professional and para-professional occupations is now 50 per cent in Canada and 52 per cent in the USA, it is important to recognize that women are concentrated in nursing, teaching, and social-science professions in these countries, as in the UK and Australia. In the UK there was a 45 per cent increase in the percentage representation of women in the managerial and administrative occupational group from 1981 to 1992, but at 32 per cent in 1992 the representation of women is still considerably lower than in the USA and Canada; it is midway between the high North American levels and the Australian level of 25 per cent in 1992. Similarly, the increase in the representation of women in professional occupations was exceptionally high, at 15 per cent, and brought the representation of women to the same level as in Australia in 1992. Because of changes in occupational classifications in Australia in the mid-1980s, the base year used is 1986. The representation of women in both the managerial/administrative and professional occupational groups increased in Australia between 1986 and 1992 by 10 per cent. But in the former group it

❖ JULIA S. O'CONNOR

started from a very low base (22.5 per cent) and reached only 25 per cent in 1992. In contrast, the increase of 10 per cent in the professional occupational group was higher than the increase in the USA for the whole decade, but, starting from a lower base, its 45 per cent representation of women in 1992 was still considerably lower than the USA and Canada.

As with pay differentials, it is important to bear in mind that different patterns are evident for full and part-time workers in relation to gender-based occupational segregation (Watts and Rich 1991, 1992; Hakim 1993). In analysing the British situation, Catherine Hakim demonstrates different patterns for full and part-time workers over the 1971–91 period. Specifically, she demonstrates that the percentage of women in female-dominated occupations—those with more than 55 per cent women—increased for the part-time workforce and declined for the full-time workforce. In contrast, the percentage of women in integrated occupations increased within the full-time workforce. She argues that these opposing trends explain the low decline in occupational segregation in Britain despite equal-opportunity legislation since the 1970s. In summary, there has been a decrease in gender-based occupational segregation across all four countries, but this is to a large extent confined to high-status full-time occupations and is most marked in the USA and Canada followed by the UK and is evident to a considerably lesser extent for managerial/administrative occupations in Australia.

These patterns are consistent with those identified through an index-of-dissimilarity analysis over the 1970–86 period (OECD 1988). However, the findings reported here specify that, even in those countries with sharp decreases in aggregate measures of segregation, increases in the representation of women are confined to a couple of occupational groups at the high end of the occupational spectrum. This is not an altogether surprising finding. Managerial/administrative and professional occupations tend to have well-defined career structures and training and promotion opportunities (Dobbin et al. 1993). The incumbents of these positions are also those who are in the best position to purchase support services necessary to maintain a full-time commitment to the labour market. This combination of factors is likely to contribute to a more equitable entry and promotion scenario than is the case for other occupational groups. However, it is important to bear in mind that numerical integration does not necessarily mean qualitative integration (Reskin and Roos 1990). The detailed analysis undertaken by Barbara Reskin and Patricia Roos in the USA of apparently integrated occupations identified a process of change in the occupations where integration was greatest that made them less desirable to men.[7] Specifically, these occupations were deskilled, autonomy and earnings declined, and working conditions deteriorated. They identified a pattern of vertical segregation within several of the numerically integrated occupations and conclude that the substantial segregation evident within desegregated occupations 'has bleak implications for women's prospects of achieving economic equity with men' (ibid. 307).

The lesser progress in gender integration in the managerial/administrative occupational groups in Australia is very marked relative to the other three countries. There are some indications that the progress for women in the public service in Australia may be considerably better than is reflected by the aggregate figures (Evaluation and Statistical Services Branch, Department of Finance, 1993). The effectiveness review of the Affirmative Action (Equal Employment Opportunity for Women) Act published in 1992 concludes that, generally speaking, the Act is working well, but points to concern about the quality of affirmative-action programmes, the lack of consultation with women and unions, and this 'the so-called glass ceiling inhibiting progress into senior management and board positions' (Affirmative Action Agency 1992: p. iii). The review concluded that the rate of affirmative-action progress was uneven and that some organizations were still largely untouched by equal-employment opportunity. Furthermore, it pointed out that, while high compliance with the Act's reporting requirement had been achieved, this does not necessarily mean high-quality programme development. Coupled with this pattern is the fact that contract compliance was not introduced until 1993 and prior to this the only sanction was naming in parliament. These facts are at least a partial explanation of the poor progress.

❖ PAY EQUITY VERSUS EMPLOYMENT EQUITY

The pattern identified in the previous section indicates an apparent incompatibility between success in pay-equity and employment-equity terms. In particular, while the USA and Canada have made most progress in relation to the lessening of gender-based occupational segregation, Australia has achieved greatest success in pay-equity terms. The UK is in an intermediate position on both measures.

Reasons for the poor success of the legislative approaches to pay equity in the USA, the UK, and Canada have been identified earlier—the complaint-based approach, the absence of a collective approach to implementation, weak government support, weak trade-union support in the early stages, and narrow coverage. Conversely, the individualistic legalistic approach to integration, pursued most strongly in the USA, works well at the upper end of the occupational spectrum, where internal labour markets and the merit principle can be demonstrated to make good business sense. Yet, it is important to remember that the 'upper end' of the occupational spectrum does not usually include the top management positions (Glass Ceiling Commission 1995) and there is evidence from the detailed case-study analysis that numerical integration may mask vertical segregation in some occupations (Reskin and Roos 1990). This is not to deny progress but to point to the importance of disaggregation and qualitative analysis.

It is noteworthy that the pay-equity–employment-equity pattern evident in Australia is similar to that evident in Sweden, an exemplar of the social-democratic welfare state. It has even lower female/male pay differentials than Australia, but relatively high gender-based occupational segregation. This raises the issue of a conflict between mass and élite equality strategies, or at least the possibility of different policy legacies and political configurations being favourable to one strategy rather than the other (O'Connor 1996: 78–100).

❖ CONCLUSIONS

This analysis of employment equality strategies does not support the characterization of Australia, Canada, the UK, and the USA as a coherent liberal welfare state cluster, at least as far as policy emphasis and implementation are concerned. While the broad principles on which employment equality policy is based may be similar across, Australia, Canada, the UK, and the USA, the mechanisms for implementation and the policy emphasis are very different. This conclusion is consistent with the body of work that questions the coherence of the liberal welfare state cluster as identified by Gøsta Esping-Andersen (1990) on the basis of the level of decommodification (Castles and Mitchell 1992; Castles 1994). The findings of this study lend some support to the ranking of these countries outlined by Ramesh Mishra (1990) in his analysis of the post-crisis period of the 1980s: he identifies two approaches to social policy, a neo-conservative (retrenchment) and a social-democratic–corporatist (maintenance). He identifies the USA and the UK as exemplars of the neo-conservative approach, with Canada also on this end of the continuum but considerably less extreme in its policies of retrenchment. It is noteworthy that Mishra is referring to the Canadian Conservative Party's mandate from 1984 to 1988; the neoconservative tenor of its administration became considerably more marked during their second mandate (Prince and Rice 1993; O'Connor 1998) and was strongly reflected in labour-market measures and policy relating to women's programmes. Mishra situates Australia on the social-democratic–corporatist end of the continuum, where Sweden and Austria are the exemplars. While the closeness of Australia to the traditional democratic–corporatist position, as outlined by Esping-Andersen, is clearly debatable in terms of its social policy framework, it is close to the collectivist end of a continuum when employment-equality strategies are considered. Yet, as Frances Castles and Deborah Mitchell (1992) and Castles (1994) have argued, the key characteristics of the Australian redistributive strategy are distinctly different from the Scandinavian one. While it cannot be denied that there is a liberal influence on policy, as evidenced by an emphasis on means-testing, the strategies adopted in Australia reflect a strongly collectivist approach relative to the other liberal countries. This is clearly evident in relation to pay, but is also evident in relation to expanding opportunities, especially childcare and the tripartite and consensual emphases adopted by the Affirmative Action Agency (Affirmative Action Agency 1992). This indicates that a collective approach is not confined to the social-democratic welfare state regime. This is not to suggest that the Australian collective approach is identical to the social-democratic one. Yet, it is important to recognize its existence.

What has differentiated Australia most strongly from the other three countries is its centralized wage-negotiation system and the organizational strength and structure of its labour movement, the dominance of the Labor Party during the 1983–95 period, and the relative success of the Australian women's and trade-union movements in effecting change in government policies from the early 1970s to the early 1990s (Sawer 1991). An example of this success is the recognition of childcare as an economic issue rather than a women's issue in the 1990s (Office of the Status of Women 1993: 53). In this regard the prominence accorded to International Labour Organization (ILO) and UN conventions by government, unions, and the women's movement also distinguishes Australia from the other liberal countries; I refer in particular to the United Nations (UN) Convention on the Elimination of All Forms of Discrimination against Women and ILO Convention 156 on Workers with Family Responsibilities; the latter was ratified by Australia in 1990 and has not been ratified by the other three countries. ILO Convention 156 (1981) and the associated Recommendation (No. 165) are intended 'to promote equality of opportunity and treatment in employment for men and women workers with family responsibilities as well as between workers with family responsibilities and those without such responsibilities' (ILO 1993: 9).

Unfortunately, the gender-equalizing impact of the centralized bargaining system that has been instrumental in narrowing the gender wage gap in Australia has been compromised owing to the introduction of enterprise bargaining. The evidence on the outcome of enterprise bargaining is not encouraging (Hall and Fruin 1993). Australian Bureau of Statistics (ABS) data for 1993 indicate that gender wage differentials widened shortly after the introduction of enterprise bargaining (ABS 1994). Tables 2.3(i) and (ii) indicate that gender wage differentials have not lessened between 1992 and 1996. The Industrial Relations Reform Act 1993, which came into effect in May 1994, created a floor of minimum entitlements that are progressive when considered relative to the other three countries; these relate to minimum wages, unpaid parental leave, termination of employment, including unfair dismissal, equal remuneration for work of equal value, which covers basic pay, over-award, and other work-related benefits. But the objective of this act is to facilitate enterprise bargaining, which has been demonstrated to militate against women and probably other weakly organized groups in the labour force. This is a good illustration of the contradictory forces at work in all countries in the movement towards gender equality in employment.

Several often contradictory factors impact on, and condition the outcome of, the equality strategies chosen in each of the countries. One that is common to all four is economic restructuring; this is likely to result in the exclusion of larger and larger proportions of the increasing female labour force from the benefits of the equality strategies pursued to date, which, despite their limitations, have contributed to the independence of those covered. Any lessening of their scope is likely to limit the possibilities for independence and autonomy potentially associated with labour-market participation.

❖ NOTES

1 Changes in occupational segregation are based on the index of dissimilarity. This measures the percentage of men and women that would have to change occupations in order to achieve gender equality in occupational distribution. It was the subject of considerable criticism in the early 1990s (Watts 1992, 1993; Hakim 1993). The principal criticism relates to the fact that, like all single-figure measures, it is 'uninformative when one goes beyond broad national trends' and is based on the unrealistic premiss that 'occupational segregation takes a value of zero only when there is an absolutely uniform sex-ratio in every occupational group in workforce' (Hakim 1993: 295). Alternatives to the dissimilarity index provide very useful insights into single-country analysis over time. They make possible an examination of trends for full-time and part-time employees and between broad categories of occupations (Watts and Rich 1992; Hakim 1993), both of which are essential to understanding the dynamics of segregation, but these measures do not solve significant problems associated with comparative analysis.

2 Article 119 of the Treaty of Rome mandates equal pay for equal work. Its scope has been broadened through subsequent Equality Directives and it is now interpreted as mandating equal pay for work of equal value.

3 The inclusion of sex discrimination came about through a coalition of two very different groups: southern politicians who wanted to make the legislation relating to race ineffective and saw the inclusion of women as the mechanism to achieve this, and women's groups advocating women as a legitimate category within anti-discrimination legislation. It is noteworthy that the inclusion of women in the 1991 Civil Rights Act, discussed below, also came about because of a political manœuvre to gain acceptance by President Bush and the Republican Party of civil-rights legislation (*Congressional Quarterly Almanac* 1991: 251–2).

4 The most problematic of these decisions was taken in 1989 (*Wards Cove Packing Co.* v. *Atonio*) and shifted the burden of proof to the employee: The employee had to disprove an employer's assertion that a practice that had a 'disparate impact' on women, black people, or other minorities served a legitimate business purpose. In order to forge the compromise necessary to pass the legislation, the 2,000 workers involved in this case were specifically excluded from the legislation. Wards Cove Packing Co. was described as a substantial employer in Alaska. The case had been in progress for twenty years.

5 A Childcare Cash Rebate Scheme came into effect in July 1994, which is designed to assist with the cost of work-, study-, or training-related childcare expenses for children under the age of 13 in informal as well as formal childcare arrangements. This was introduced as a non-income-tested scheme, since the cost of childcare was seen as 'a legitimate expense for parents earning an income' (Minister for Family Services, quoted in *Canberra Times* (1994: 13)). This approach by the former Labor government is consistent with the shift in emphasis relating to childcare in Australia from a welfare rationale to an economic rationale. However, the Coalition government, in power since 1996, has changed the scheme to an income-tested basis.

6 Some of the companies associated with the Opportunity 2000 campaign have been found to have distinctly poor industrial-relations practices. Unions are not always involved in setting the goals and some officials suspect that the campaign may be a business public relations exercise (*Labour Research*, Nov. 1993: 8–10).

7 Detailed case studies were carried out on pharmacy, public relations, typesetters and compositors, bank managers, insurance sales and insurance adjusters and examiners, residential real estate, systems analysts, bartenders, bakers; partial case studies were carried out on accountants and auditors, reporters, and bus drivers. They found that two occupations—insurance adjusting/examining and compositing/typesetting—had become re-segregated as predominantly female and a few occupational specialities had been relabelled as women's work.

❖ REFERENCES

ABS (1992): Australian Bureau of Statistics, *August Labour Force Australia* (Canberra).

——(1993), *1991 Labour Statistics Australia* (Canberra).

——(1994), *Distribution and Composition of Employee Earnings and Hours 1993 Survey* (Canberra).

❖ JULIA S. O'CONNOR

—— (1997), *Labour Force Australia 1996* (Canberra).

ACKER, J. (1989), *Doing Comparable Worth: Gender, Class, and Pay Equity* (Philadelphia).

Affirmative Action Agency (1992), *Quality and Commitment: The Next Steps. The Final Report of the Effectiveness Review of the Affirmative Action (Equal Employment Opportunity for Women) Act 1986* (Canberra).

BLUM, L. M. (1991), *Between Feminism and Labor: The Significance of the Comparable Worth Movement* (Berkeley and Los Angeles).

BURTON, C. (1991), *The Promise and the Price: The Struggle for Equal Opportunity in Women's Employment* (Sydney).

Canberra Times (1994), 3 May.

CASTLES, F. G. (1994), 'The Wage Earner's Welfare State Revisited: Refurbishing the Established Model of Australian Social Protection, 1983–1993', *Australian Journal of Social Issues*, 29/2: 120–45.

—— AND MITCHELL, D. (1992), 'Identifying Welfare State Regimes: The Links between Politics, Instruments and Outcomes', *Governance*, 5/1: 1–26.

Congressional Quarterly Almanac (1991) (Washington).

DIR (1993): Department of Industrial Relations, *Equal Pay Unit Newsletter*, Issue No. 5, Apr.

DOBBIN, F., SUTTON J. R., MEYER, J. W., AND SCOTT, W. R. (1993), 'Equal Opportunity Law and the Construction of Internal Labor Markets', *American Journal of Sociology*, 99/2: 396–427.

Employment Gazette (1993), 'Women in the Labour Market', Nov.

ENGLAND, P. (1992), *Comparable Worth: Theories and Evidence* (New York).

EOC (1990): Equal Opportunities Commission, *Equal Pay for Men and Women: Strengthening the Acts* (Manchester).

ESPING-ANDERSEN, G. (1990), *The Three Worlds of Welfare Capitalism* (Princeton).

Evaluation and Statistical Services Branch, Department of Finance (1993), *Promotional Opportunities for Women in the APS* (Canberra).

EVANS, S., AND NELSON, B. J. (1991), 'Translating Wage Gains into Social Change: International Lessons from Implementation of Pay Equity in Minnesota', in J. Fudge and P. McDermott (eds.), *Just Wages: A Feminist Assessment of Pay Equity* (Toronto), 229–46.

Glass Ceiling Commission (1995), *Good for Business: Making Full Use of the Nation's Human Capital* (Washington).

GORNICK, J. (1992), 'The Economic Position of Working Age Women, Relative to Men: A Cross-National Comparative Study', paper presented at ISA Research Committee 19 Workshop, University of Bremen, Sept.

—— AND JACOBS, J. (1997), 'Gender, the Welfare State, and Public Employment', Luxembourg Income Study Working Paper No. 168.

GRAHAM, K. A. (1989) (ed.), *How Ottawa Spends 1989–90* (Ottawa).

GREGORY, J. (1992), 'Notes and Issues, Equal Pay for Work of Equal Value: The Strengths and Weaknesses of Legislation', *Work, Employment and Society,* 6/3: 461–73.

GREGORY, R. G., AND DUNCAN, R. C. (1981), 'Segregated Labour Market Theories and the Australian Experience of Equal Pay for Women', *Journal of Post-Keynesian Economics,* 3/3: 403–28.

HAKIM, C. (1993), 'The Myth of Rising Female Employment', *Work, Employment and Society,* 7/1: 97–120.

HALL, P., AND FRUIN, D. (1993), 'Gender Aspects of Enterprise Bargaining: The Good, the Bad and the Ugly', in D. E. Morgan (ed.), *Dimensions of Enterprise Bargaining and Organisational Relations* (UNSW Studies in Australian Industrial Relations Monograph No. 36; Kensington).

HARKNESS, S. (1998), 'Why are Part-Time Women Workers Losing Out?', *Centre Piece,* 3/1:25–9.

Human Resources Development, Canada (1994), 'Lloyd Axworthy Tables New Employment Equity Act', News Release, 12 Dec.

ILO (1993), International Labour Organization, *Workers with Family Responsibilities* (Geneva).

KAHN, P. (1992), 'Introduction: Equal Pay for Work of Equal Value in Britain and the USA', in P. Kahn and E. Meehan (eds.), *Equal Value/Comparable Worth in the UK and the USA* (Basingstoke), 1–29.

Labour Canada (1990), *Women in the Labour Force 1990–91 Edition* (Ottawa).

Labour Research (various issues) (Labour Research Department Publications).

LOVENDUSKI, J., AND RANDALL, V. (1993), *Contemporary Feminist Politics: Women and Power in Britain* (Oxford).

MARUANI, M. (1992), 'The Position of Women in the Labour Market: Trends and Developments in the Twelve Member States of the European Community 1983–1990', *Women of Europe Supplement,* 36 (Brussels).

MISHRA, R. (1990), *The Welfare State in Capitalist Society* (Toronto).

O'CONNOR, J. S. (1993), 'Gender, Class and Citizenship in the Comparative Analysis of Welfare State Regimes: Theoretical and Methodological Issues', *British Journal of Sociology,* 44/3: 59–108.

—— (1994), 'Labour Market Participation in Liberal Welfare States: Dual Breadwinners without Dual Breadwinner Social Policy Frameworks', unpublished.

—— (1996), 'From Women and the Welfare State to Gendering Welfare State Regimes', *Current Sociology,* 44/2: 1–124.

—— (1998), 'Social Justice, Social Citizenship, and the Welfare State, 1965–1998: Canada in Comparative Context', in R. Holmes-Hayes and J. Curtis (eds.), *The Vertical Mosaic Revisited* (Toronto), 180–231.

❖ JULIA S. O'CONNOR

—— ORLOFF, A. S., AND SHAVER, S. (1999), *States, Markets, Families: Gender, Liberalism and Social Policy in Australia, Canada, Great Britain and the United States* (Cambridge).

O'DONNELL, C., AND HALL, P. (1988), *Getting Equal* (London).

OECD (1988), Organization of Economic Cooperation and Development, 'Women's Activity, Employment and Earnings: A Review of Recent Developments', *Employment Outlook*, Sept.: 129–72.

—— (1991), *Employment Outlook* (Paris).

—— (1993), *Employment Outlook* (Paris).

—— (1996), *Employment Outlook* (Paris).

Office for National Statistics (1996), *Labour Force Survey* (London).

Office of the Status of Women (1993), *Women—Shaping and Sharing the Future: The New National Agenda for Women 1993–2000*, (Canberra).

ORLOFF, A. S. (1993), 'Gender and the Social Rights of Citizenship: The Comparative Analysis of Gender Relations and Welfare States', *American Sociological Review*, 58/3: 303–28.

PATEMAN, C. (1988) 'The Patriarchal Welfare State', in A. Gutmann (ed.), *Democracy and the Welfare State* (Princeton), 231–60.

PRINCE, M. J., AND RICE, J. (1989), 'The Canadian Jobs Strategy: Supply Side Social Policy', in Graham (1989), 247–87.

RESKIN, B. F., AND ROOS, P. A. (1990) (eds.), *Job Queues, Gender Queues: Explaining Women's Inroads into Male Occupations* (Philadelphia).

RICE, J. J., AND PRINCE, M. J. (1993), 'Lowering the Safety Net and Weakening the Bonds of Nationhood: Social Policy in the Mulroney Years', in S. D. Philips (ed.), *How Ottawa Spends 1993–4: A More Democratic Canada?* (Ottawa), 381–416.

RIES, P., AND STONE, A. (1992), *The American Woman 1992–3* (New York).

RUBERY, J. (1988), 'Women and Recession: A Comparative Perspective', in J. Rubery (ed.), *Women and Recession* (London), 253–86.

SAWER, M. (1991), 'Why has the Women's Movement had More Influence in Australia than Elsewhere?', in F. G. Castles (ed.), *Australia Compared: People, Policies and Politics* (Sydney), 258–77.

Special Committee on the Review of the Employment Equity Act (1992), *Employment Equity* (Ottawa).

Statistics Canada (1993), *Labour Force Annual Averages 1991*, (Ottawa).

—— (1995), *Earnings of Men and Women* (Ottawa).

STEINBERG, R. J., AND COOK, A. (1988), 'Policies Affecting Women's Employment in Industrial Countries', in Stromberg and Harkness (1988), 307–28.

STROMBERG, A. H., AND HARKNESS, S. (1988) (eds.), *Women Working: Theories and Facts in Perspective* (Mountain View, Calif.).

TREIMAN, D. J., AND HARTMANN, H. I. (1981), *Women, Work, and Wages: Equal Pay for Jobs of Equal Value* (Washington).

United States Bureau of the Census (1993), *Statistical Abstract of the United States: 1993* (113th edn.; Washington).

—— (1997), *Employment and Earnings January* (Washington).

WATTS, M. J. (1992), 'How Should Occupational Sex Segregation Be Measured?', *Work, Employment and Society,* 6/3: 475–87.

—— (1993), 'Explaining Trends in Occupational Segregation: Some Comments', *European Sociological Review,* 9: 315–19.

—— AND RICH, J. (1991), 'Equal Opportunity in Australia? The Role of Part-Time Employment in Occupational Sex Segregation', *Australian Bulletin of Labour,* June: 155–74.

—— —— (1992) 'Labour Market Segmentation and the Persistence of Occupational Sex Segregation in Australia', *Australian Economics Papers,* 31: 58–76.

WEINER, N., AND GUNDERSON, M. (1990), *Pay Equity Issues, Options and Experiences* (Toronto).

3 ❖ Gender and Social-Democratic Welfare States

Diane Sainsbury

Concepts such as 'the Scandinavian model' and more recently 'the social-democratic welfare state regime' have often emphasized the shared traits of the Scandinavian welfare states,[1] and that these traits set Scandinavia apart from other countries in a number of ways. The hallmark of the Scandinavian model has been comprehensive social provision where entitlement to benefits and a wide variety of services has been based on citizenship or residence. Other characteristics have included generous benefit levels, the funding of benefits through taxation rather than contributions from insured persons, and egalitarian redistribution (e.g. Allardt 1986; Erikson *et al.* 1987; Sainsbury 1988; Stephens 1996).

The distinctive features of the Scandinavian welfare states have been further elaborated by Gøsta Esping-Andersen (1990). In constructing his welfare state typology, he specifies the nature of the social-democratic welfare state regime in contrast to the liberal and conservative/corporatist regimes. According to Esping-Andersen, the social-democratic regime type is characterized by universal schemes and programmes with high-income replacement rates, diminishing the importance of the market. The costs of familyhood are subsidized through the heavy involvement of the state in the care of children, the aged, and the helpless. A final feature is a major commitment to full employment, where 'the right to work has equal status to the right to income protection' (1990: 28). In his empirical analysis, Scandinavia and the Netherlands form the cluster of countries

This chapter has benefited from the comments of participants of the Comparative Gender Studies Workshop at the University of Stockholm and the workshop on comparative politics at the 1997 annual meeting of the Swedish Political Science Association. In particular, the author wishes to thank Barbara Hobson, Li Bennich-Björkman, and Christina Bergqvist.

whose policies approximate the social-democratic welfare state regime—especially with respect to decommodification, 'the degree to which individuals, or families, can uphold a socially acceptable standard of living independently of market participation' (1990: 37, 52, 74–6).

Feminist critiques of the welfare state and social policy regimes have questioned whether mainstream classifications—and in particular Esping-Andersen's typology—would hold up if gender were incorporated into the analysis. Feminists have criticized the concept of decommodification on the grounds that it centres on labour as a commodity and therefore applies exclusively to workers; it neglects individuals outside the labour force, especially women in the home. They have also noted that Esping-Andersen fails to distinguish between a socially acceptable standard of living of individuals and of families. Feminists have further argued that women's and men's entitlements are differentiated by the gender division of labour in the family and society, and that this has been totally overlooked by mainstream research. Exploratory studies, concentrating on gender differentiation in entitlements, have revealed a different clustering of countries from mainstream research (e.g. Lewis and Ostner 1991, 1994; Lewis 1992; Orloff 1994; Sainsbury 1994; Shaver and Bradshaw 1995).

The position of Scandinavian feminists has been more divided. Several of them have stressed a Scandinavian form of welfare state and its advantages for women (e.g. Hernes 1984, 1987; Siim 1990, 1993; Borchorst 1994), while others have argued that the gender dimension cuts across welfare states. Barbara Hobson documents that women's economic dependence within the family fails to conform to mainstream categorizations. Her analysis of dependency levels shows that Norway clustered together with the liberal countries—Australia, Canada, the UK, and the USA—rather than with Sweden in the early 1980s (Hobson 1990, 1994). In a similar vein, Arnlaug Leira details how Norwegian childcare, provision has differed from that in Denmark and Sweden. She concludes that the differences in services are at odds with the thesis of a common Scandinavian model. Norwegian childcare, because of its minimal provision for infants and toddlers, along with widespread reliance on informal care arrangements, resembled that in the UK and several continental countries (1992).

This chapter examines the competing claims of mainstream and feminist scholars concerning the Scandinavian welfare states by focusing on gender. How are gender relations reflected in the welfare state legislation of Denmark, Finland, Norway, and Sweden, and how much variation in women's and men's entitlements occurs across the Scandinavian countries? Do variations outweigh commonalities, undermining the clustering of the countries into a single welfare state regime?

❖ DIANE SAINSBURY

❖ GENDER POLICY REGIMES

A gender-relevant framework of analysis has been lacking in mainstream comparative research on welfare states. For the most part, when women have been included in the analysis, it has been as workers (e.g. Esping-Andersen 1990: ch. 8; Korpi 1994). While the inclusion of women workers is to be applauded as an advance over studies based on the typical production worker, this approach is inadequate for three reasons. First, the standard mainstream analytical framework centring on paid work is merely extended to women. This is problematic, because women's participation in the labour market cannot be equated with access to work-related benefits. Additional qualifying conditions bar women workers from benefits more frequently than their male counterparts (Sainsbury 1996: chs. 5, 6). Secondly, this framework pays no attention to unpaid labour and the interplay between the division of work in the home and the labour market. Thirdly, by concentrating on social rights conferred through labour-market status, the approach overlooks two eligibility criteria that are decisive to women's access to benefits: their entitlements as wives and as mothers.

To overcome these shortcomings we need to focus on how gender is constructed in policies—and regularities in the patterning of gender relations in legislation. The concept of a gender policy regime provides a handle to this problem. A regime embodies values, norms, and rules, thus providing a normative or regulatory framework that shapes behaviour. A policy regime shifts the analysis from behaviour to policies. Analogous to the notion of a social policy regime that emphasizes that a given state-economy organization provides a policy logic of its own, we conceive of a gender policy regime as a given organization of gender relations associated with a specific policy logic. Central to the organization of gender relations are principles and norms (gender ideologies and practices) that prescribe the tasks, obligations, and rights of the two sexes. Gender policy regimes can be distinguished on the basis of ideologies that describe actual or preferred relations between women and men, principles of entitlement, and policy constructions. Table 3.1 presents three gender policy regimes in a schematic form.

The male-breadwinner regime is characterized by a gender ideology of male privilege based on a strict division of labour among the sexes. It assigns different tasks and obligations to women and men, resulting in unequal entitlements in social provision. Being married and having a family carry advantages in relation to unmarried persons with a family and single persons without support obligations. As family providers, men have entitlements that stem from the principle of maintenance. They

Table 3.1. Three gender policy regimes

Regime attributes	Male breadwinner	Separate gender roles	Individual earner-carer
Ideology	Strict division of labour Husband = earner Wife = carer	Strict division of labour Husband = earner Wife = carer	Shared tasks Father = earner–carer Mother = earner–carer
Entitlement	Unequal among spouses	Differentiated by gender role	Equal
Basis of entitlement	The principle of maintenance	Family responsibilities	Citizenship or residence
Recipient of benefits	Head of household Supplements for dependants	Men as family providers Women as caregivers	Individual
Taxation	Joint taxation Deductions for dependants	Joint taxation Deductions for dependants for both spouses	Separate taxation Equal tax relief
Employment and wage policies	Priority to men	Priority to men	Aimed at both sexes
Sphere of care	Primarily private	Primarily private	Strong state involvement
Caring work	Unpaid	Paid component to caregivers in the home	Paid component to caregivers in and outside the home

receive social and tax benefits that correspond to their family responsibilities. Employment and wage policies are directed to men, who are assumed to have support obligations. Marriage, as the celebrated family form, particularly affects the social rights of women, whose entitlements derive from their status as dependants within the family. Married women's entitlements are primarily as wives. The married woman has a weak position on the labour market because of assumptions that she is supported by her husband and that her place is in the home. The prime obligations of married women are to care for her husband and children in the form of unpaid work. In this regime, unmarried mothers and divorced women are anomalous, and they fall outside regular policies.

The ideology of the separate gender roles regime emphasizes the significance of differences between the sexes, and social rights are allocated on the basis of these differences. It underlines a strict division of labour between the sexes and the importance of family responsibilities in social provision, but it attaches weight to both the principle of maintenance and the principle of care. Unlike the male-breadwinner regime, where social and tax benefits are solely the prerogative of the family provider, the separate gender roles regime confers these benefits upon both the male family provider and the female caregiver. The principle of care also erodes the importance of marriage for women's entitlements, so that social rights encompass unmarried mothers. Women may receive benefits for caring responsibilities irrespective of their marital status. However, the principle of maintenance privileges men on the labour market, and employment and wage policies are oriented to the male worker.

The ideology of the individual earner–carer regime differs fundamentally from the other two in that the preferred relations between women and men are shared roles and obligations, leading to equal rights. Both sexes have entitlements as earners and carers, and policies are structured to enable women to become workers and men to become caregivers. Social rights and tax obligations are attached to the individual rather than the family. Family responsibilities do not entitle the head of the household to supplements for dependants in income-maintenance programmes nor to tax relief. Instead the financial costs of children are shared through public provision of services and child allowances available to all families. There is strong state involvement in the care of children, the sick and disabled, and the frail elderly through provision of services and payments to carers. Entitlements based on citizenship or residence are important, because they eliminate the influence of marriage on social rights. When citizenship or residence is the basis of entitlement, unmarried and married persons have equal rights, and in marriage husband and wife enjoy the same rights. This basis of entitlement also neutralizes a gender differentiation in social rights, because paid and unpaid work provide equal benefits.

This scheme draws attention to four underlying dimensions of variations. The first is whether rights are attached to the individual or based on family relationships and marital status—that is, whether rights are individualized or familialized. When the family is the unit of benefit, rights are vested in the head of the family. The rights of family members are indirect and often not full rights. In other instances rights are contingent upon the absence of the male breadwinner. Such rights are tenuous, since changes in family or marital status can result in the loss of entitlement. By contrast, individualized rights are not affected by family relationships.

The second dimension is the degree to which a gendered differentiation in entitlements based on the traditional division of labour between women and men exists. Does legislation provide women with benefits as carers, while men receive benefits as earners? Or do policies promote gender equality in claiming benefits, so that both sexes are entitled to work-related benefits and care-related benefits?

The third dimension concerns the scope of state responsibility for caring tasks in a society, and it underscores the centrality of care in the welfare state project. At one extreme, care is a family obligation, and as such it is unpaid work. At the other, state responsibility can occur through provision of services and payments to carers in the home. Both forms of public involvement have the capacity to transform unpaid labour into paid work, but their implications for gender relations can be quite different. Provision of services enables women's employment and provides a potential to change the division of labour between the sexes, while payments to carers in home reinforce traditional roles.

The final dimension is women's and men's *equal* access to paid work. Employment provides not only an income but also eligibility for work-related benefits. In this way equal access to paid work undermines a gendered differentiation of social rights where men have predominantly claimed benefits as workers. Equal access to paid work can also put pressure on a familialized system of social provision. When work-related benefits and tax relief are based on family responsibilities, dual-income couples raise the issue of which earner is entitled to the benefits. Work-related benefits additionally have the potential to challenge familialized entitlements by lessening married women's dependency on benefits based on their husbands' rights.

Using this scheme, I initially analyse the inscription of gender relations in the welfare state legislation in order to establish the degree of similarities and variations between the four countries. To facilitate comparisons with Esping-Andersen's analysis, policies in the period around 1980 are taken as a benchmark. The gender differentiation in women's and men's utilization of benefits over time is then examined. Contrary to mainstream research, which has highlighted the similarities between Norway and Sweden, the analysis here points to differences between the policies of the two countries. The chapter then turns to an explanation of the variations. Subsequently I discuss the characteristics of the social-democratic welfare state regime and their impact on gender inequalities. The concluding section addresses the issue of a common gender policy regime.

❖ BETWEEN GENDER POLICY REGIMES

One of the most striking features of how gender relations are embedded in welfare state legislation in Scandinavia has been the strong entitlements of women as mothers, which have overshadowed their entitlements as wives.[2] Also distinctive of mothers' entitlements were that aid to needy mothers was delivered outside the poor-relief system, and that marital status did not affect claims to several of these benefits. These features run counter to the male-breadwinner regime, where policies reward marriage

❖ DIANE SAINSBURY

and privilege men so that they can support their families. For the most part, the earlier pattern of gendered entitlements in the Scandinavian countries has instead resembled a separate gender roles regime, conferring social rights upon men as family providers and earners and upon women as mothers and caregivers.

This pattern of entitlements, in varying degrees across the countries, has been challenged by policies moving toward the individual earner–carer regime, where women and men share the tasks of bread-winning and caregiving. An important set of cross-national variations is found in the extent to which policies have encouraged women and men to combine these roles. A second set of dissimilarities concerns the import-ance of family responsibilities in shaping entitlements and tax benefits.

The construction of gender in the social provision of each of the coun-tries around 1980 is examined below in an effort to categorize its policy regime. The analysis reveals that Norwegian policies corresponded most closely to the separate gender roles regime. Finnish policies combined elements of both regimes. Legislation recognizing family responsibil-ities coexisted with extensive public provision of childcare and parental benefits made available to both mothers and fathers. Of the four countries, Danish legislation conformed least to the separate gender roles regime. The major development in the direction of the individual earner–carer regime was the expansion of public services, which increased the paid component of care work outside the home and promoted women's entry into the labour market. Swedish social provision contained strong ele-ments of the separate gender roles regime in the 1960s (Sainsbury 1994, 1996), but since 1970 there has been a major shift towards the individual earner–carer regime.

❖ Norway: Privileging Men as Providers and Women as Caregivers

Family responsibilities, reflected in both the principle of maintenance and the principle of care, have shaped Norwegian legislation. Income-maintenance programmes and taxation have privileged the family pro-vider as well as the caregiver. At the same time, there was a reluctance to introduce policies to aid women in combining motherhood and employ-ment—which has helped to sustain the gendered differentiation in women's and men's social rights.

One policy area that has strongly advantaged the family provider is taxation. Of the four countries, only Norway has joint taxation of married couples, but couples have been able to choose individual taxation if it has been a more favourable option. The family provider has received tax exemptions for children, and marital tax relief has been achieved through different tax schedules for individuals and married couples rather than a tax allowance for a dependent wife. A wife with earnings has received a personal tax allowance, and working mothers an additional tax allowance. As wives have entered the labour market, married couples have increasingly opted for individual taxation. Rather modest earnings have made individual taxation more advantageous than joint taxation, and by 1980 around 40 per cent of married couples were taxed individually (Skrede 1984: 370–1). Nevertheless, slightly less than half of all dual-earner couples chose joint taxation in the early 1980s. The existence of joint taxation and the construction of tax relief appear to have made part-time work for a wife quite attractive. A part-time job with small earnings allowed a couple to utilize both partners' allowances to reduce taxes on their joint income but without pushing their income into the highest tax brackets.

Part-time employment among women was most prevalent in Norway in the early 1980s, and over half of the Norwegian women in the labour market were part-timers. As distinct from Danish and Swedish women who have also held part-time jobs, Norwegian women were more frequently employed in short part-time work (twenty hours or less a week). The gap in women's and men's employment has also been widest. Around 1980 Norwegian men had the highest employment rate (87.6 per cent) of the four countries, and Norwegian women had the lowest (59.3 per cent) (see Table 3.A1 at the end of the chapter). In short, proportionally fewer Norwegian women were in the labour market, and those in employment had a weaker attachment than other Scandinavian women. This pattern of labour-market participation has, as we shall see, posed difficulties for women in claiming work-related benefits, perpetuating a gendered differentiation in entitlements.

The principle of care has exerted a very strong influence on Norwegian policies, arguably the strongest of the four countries. Universal child allowances and maternity grants have been available to all mothers.[3] Moreover, child allowances were tailored to the size of the family, so that the amount increased with the number of children (up to the fifth child). Tax relief for working mothers also mirrored caring responsibilities. Allowances were larger for younger children (under 14) and if there were more than one younger child. Even more unusual, Norway provided benefits that resemble a mother's or carer's wage to single persons with caring responsibilities. In the mid-1960s mothers' pensions, previously provided by several municipalities (Seip and Ibsen 1991), were 'nationalized' when they became a part of the national-insurance scheme. These pensions were available to widows, unmarried mothers, and unmarried women who nursed a close relative. The pension furnished a minimum income to carers, but pension reductions for earnings and taxation rules discouraged combining employment with benefits.[4] Solo mothers also receive an extra child allowance and an extra maternity grant.

On the other hand, public responsibility for the organization of child-care lagged behind the other countries. Nor had the expansion of parental leave kept pace with Finland and Sweden. Maternity-leave benefits compensated working mothers 100 per cent of earnings, but the maximum duration of leave was eighteen weeks. The problem of a relatively short leave was worsened by the virtual lack of public provision of childcare for infants and toddlers in the early 1980s. Coverage for older pre-school children was also low, full-time care was at a premium, and family day care (care by public childminders) was not available. In the early 1980s state involvement in childcare was unimpressive (see Table 3.A2 at the end of the chapter), and working mothers often relied on private and informal care (Leira 1992). Policies sanctioning an earning role for mothers, especially mothers with small children, were underdeveloped. To sum up, Norwegian legislation, with the exception of entitlements based on citizenship conferring equal social rights upon women and men, hardly corresponded to the individual policy regime around 1980. Women's social rights *vis-à-vis* men's had largely been improved by strengthening their claims as caregivers, in accord with the separate gender roles regime.

❖ Finland: Mothers as Workers and Carers

Finnish policies represented a mixture of both gender policy regimes. Family responsibilities were a centrepiece of income-maintenance policies and taxation, strengthening both men's and women's claims—and a gendered differentiation in entitlements. In this respect, Finnish legislation resembled Norwegian policies. As distinct from Norway, however, Finland offered parental benefits and public childcare on a more ambitious scale in the early 1980s, and Finnish women have traditionally had a stronger foothold on the labour market, counteracting a key aspect of the gender differentiation in entitlements.[5] This contradictory pattern is perhaps best understood as inspired by a long-standing norm that mothers are workers and carers.

Family responsibilities have been reflected in supplements for dependants. In addition to pensions, sickness benefits and unemployment compensation (both insurance and assistance) provided supplements for dependants—spouses and children. Men were generally the recipients of these benefits. For example, supplements in the sickness insurance scheme were paid to married beneficiaries only if their earnings exceeded those of their spouse (Alestalo and Uusitalo 1987: 138). Family responsibilities also structured tax relief, although taxation was on an individual basis. The husband as family provider reaped the benefit of tax deductions for children and a spouse with modest earnings or no income. Although framed in gender-neutral terms, relief for a spouse was granted to the partner with the larger income. In the early 1980s the size of tax credits for children also increased with the number of children (OECD 1986).

Mothers' rights based on the principle of care provide benefits for mothers outside the labour market. As in Norway, child allowances have also taken family responsibilities into account, increasing the amount with the number of children, and (since 1973) additional allowances were paid for children under the age of 3. Other benefits to mothers without labour-market status have included flat-rate sickness benefits, maternity grants, advanced maintenance allowances, and since the early 1980s a childcare allowance.

The individual earner–carer regime has been reflected in policies that have enabled women to combine work and motherhood and later have encouraged men to engage in care. Working mothers both married and single have received tax advantages, strengthening the incentives to enter the labour market. The late 1970s and early 1980s witnessed the simultaneous expansion of childcare and parental benefits. The duration of leave with high compensation had been extended so that in the early 1980s Finland provided a period of leave that was twice as long as that allocated in Denmark and Norway. Finnish fathers were also entitled to a considerably longer leave measured in the number of days and as a proportion of the total leave per couple in the early 1980s (Hagen 1992: 144).

Women's labour-market participation counteracts the preponderance of men's social rights as earners based on labour-market status. In 1980 Finnish women's labour-market participation rates came closest to matching men's. Equally important, and in sharp contrast to the other Scandinavian countries, the vast majority of Finnish women have held full-time jobs, further increasing the parity in women's and men's attachment to the labour market (see Table 3.A1).

On the negative side, a stronger role of means-testing in unemployment compensation and the basic pension system adversely affected Finnish women's social rights. Contrary to the individual earner–carer regime, the unit of benefit is the family in income-testing programmes—and not the individual. Family earnings over a certain ceiling disqualify married persons from benefits or reduce their benefits. When partners in dual-earner couples work full-time, both are disadvantaged, but husbands' higher earnings have been more likely to disqualify married women. In the area of unemployment compensation, roughly equal amounts were spent on insurance benefits and means-tested assistance in the early 1980s (Alestalo and Uusitalo 1987: 140).

Even more detrimental to married women's social rights has been means-testing in the pension system. As a result of means-testing, the basic pension was not fully 'individualized' in 1980. The amount of the Finnish basic pension paid to *all* the elderly was extremely meagre (only around 7 per cent of average gross pay in the mid-1980s), and means-tested supplements topped up the basic pension so that it totalled slightly over 25 per cent of average gross pay (Kangas and Palme 1992: 210). However, the amount of the pension was reduced by a spouse's income (Alestalo and Uusitalo 1987: 128, 130). Women's better access to work-related benefits perhaps offset their more tenuous entitlements as citizens affected by means-testing.

❖ Denmark: The Decline of Men's Rights as Providers and the Rise of Women's Rights as Workers

Danish policies have least resembled the separate gender roles regime. Historically, means-tested programmes were central in the development of the Danish welfare state. The early extension of social rights occurred within a means-tested framework by expanding the categories of the deserving poor, and universal flat-rate benefits replaced means-tested benefits later than in Sweden and Norway (Johansen 1986: 298–301). Means-testing blocked the development of women's rights as wives and restricted their entitlements as mothers. Men's rights as family providers at their height included supplements for dependants in the major social-insurance schemes, tax credits for children, and a tax allowance for a dependent spouse. The relatively weak position of women's rights (until the major breakthrough of universal benefits based on citizenship in the 1950s and 1960s) and men's rights as family providers produced a gendered differentiation in entitlements that was closer to the male-breadwinner regime in the past. (Compared with other countries, however, women's rights as mothers still stand out, but they were limited to poor and vulnerable families.)

Reforms have altered this gendered pattern of entitlements by whittling away at men's claims as family providers and paving the way for women to join the labour force, strengthening their social rights as workers. Efforts to improve women's entitlements as caregivers have not been as strong as in the other Scandinavian countries, and less legislation was aimed at equal parenting or men's role as carers. In 1980 fathers had no statutory right to parental benefits, except in the case of adoption.

The social benefits and tax advantages of the family provider have dwindled, although the trend has been less pronounced in taxation. By the mid-1970s supplements for dependants were no longer a feature of sickness and unemployment insurance. In the early 1960s tax credits to ease the financial burden of families with children were abolished. Individual taxation was introduced in Denmark and Sweden around 1970.

The principle of care has been much weaker in Danish legislation, affecting the rights of women at home and working mothers. The introduction of universal benefits based on the principle of care lagged behind the other countries. Universal child allowances were not adopted until the early 1960s, and universal maternity benefits were delayed until the end of that decade. A decade after their introduction, child allowances became income tested and maternity grants were abolished within a few years. Maternity benefits have been awarded on the basis of labour-market status, but working mothers could hardly afford to take leave for a longer period than the legislated duration (payable for a maximum leave of fourteen weeks in 1980). On the other hand, day care for infants was more available than in the other countries in both the 1980s and the 1990s (see Table 3.A2).

The main policy thrust to improve women's social rights has been the expansion of public services, especially day care. This expansion has been crucial to women's entitlements in three ways. The public provision of day care has enhanced women's social rights as earners by enabling them to combine mothering and employment. The availability of services, as public goods, has strengthened women's entitlements based on citizenship; these entitlements assumed more importance because cash benefits based on the principle of care have periodically been means or income tested. Finally, services have provided job opportunities and enlarged the paid component of care work outside the home, while there have been fewer measures to increase the paid component for care work in the home.

❖ Sweden: Transforming Gender Differentiation in Social Rights

Swedish efforts to recast women's and men's social rights have proceeded on four fronts: (1) the tax system, (2) labour-market policy, (3) parental insurance, and (4) increased public responsibility for childcare. There has been a long-term trend towards 'individualization' of social-insurance benefits and tax relief. By 1980 family supplements had been eliminated from social-insurance schemes except for the basic pension. Tax exemptions for children had been removed as early as the mid-1940s with the introduction of universal child allowances, and separate taxation of married persons came into effect in 1971. The tax reform significantly increased deductions for a dual-earner couple in relation to a family with a single breadwinner, and it encouraged equal earnings of partners in dual-income couples. Minimum taxation occurred when each partner earned exactly half of the couple's combined income (Gustafsson 1990: 159).

During the 1960s active labour-market measures had been mainly directed to men who predominated in training schemes and job-creation programmes. Changes in the next decade removed barriers to women's participation and encouraged their recruitment. Most important was the elimination of income-testing to qualify for a training allowance, which had operated against married women. By the end of the decade women's enrolment in labour-market programmes was nearly on a par with men's. From 1970 to 1980 the female labour-market participation rate climbed from slightly less than 60 per cent to nearly 75 per cent. Jobs in an expanding public sector accounted for much of the increase, but active labour-market measures—especially training and placement services—aided women in joining the workforce.

Maternity insurance was transformed into parental insurance in 1974, bringing entitlements in line with a new familial ideology prescribing shared roles and equal parenting.[6] In 1980 Swedish fathers were entitled to paid leave, which could be taken during the child's infancy up until school age, to care for a sick child, and a two-week paternity leave at the time of the child's birth.[7] The legacy of the principle of care has influenced benefits so that *all* mothers have been entitled to paid leave, but mothers without earnings receive flat-rate benefits. As the duration of leave was extended, the number of infants in public day care dropped. Greater public responsibility for caring for children in Sweden, unlike Denmark, entailed a joint expansion of parental leave and provision of childcare.

The 1973 pre-school reform signalled a new commitment to day care by setting as its objective the availability of public childcare to all parents. The reform gave priority to full-time centre-based care. Responsibility for the provision of day care was assigned to local government, but state funding has subsidized both the construction and the operating costs of childcare centres. As part of their responsibility, the municipalities also licensed and employed childminders to run family day care. This 'socialization' of childminders converted them into public employees and their status as employees assured them work-related social benefits. Coverage grew from around 10–15 per cent of all Swedish pre-school children in the early 1970s to over one-third of pre-schoolers in 1980. Together with children cared for by a parent on paid leave, public measures supported the care of nearly half of all pre-school children that year (Sainsbury 1996: 99).

To sum up, this analysis reveals a different clustering of Scandinavian

SOCIAL-DEMOCRATIC WELFARE STATES ❖

policies from that presented in mainstream scholarship. Mainstream studies have often underlined the commonalities of Norwegian and Swedish policies, and Esping-Andersen describes the two countries as the purest cases of the social-democratic regime, while Denmark and Finland represent paler variants (Esping Andersen 1992: 52, 74; Kangas and Palme 1992).[8] By contrast, we find that on the dimension of family responsibilities shaping entitlements Norway and Finland were grouped together, while Denmark and Sweden came closer to the individual earner–carer regime. Danish and Swedish legislation provided no tax relief for children, and supplements for dependants were limited to pensions. There was a similar split between the four countries in how they socialized the costs of familyhood. The Danes and Swedes were the most enthusiastic in developing childcare services, while the Finns and especially the Norwegians put a larger share of their resources into cash transfers and tax exemptions (see Flora 1987: 20, 48–9, 87, 114, 142, 207, 239). Despite these similarities in Norwegian and Finnish policies, the two countries were polar opposites with respect to women's and men's equal access to work and encouraging mothers' employment. Furthermore, on the dimension of parental benefits Finland and Sweden were arrayed together against Norway and Denmark. In the early 1980s Finnish and Swedish legislation provided longer leave, a lengthier period of high compensation, a more generous policy towards fathers to take leave, rights to care for a sick child, and flexibility in taking leave (Hagen 1992: 143–8).

Looking at the policy profiles of the individual countries, Norway and Denmark exhibit the most interesting deviations from the other three countries. Norway stands out through its lack of policies to encourage mothers to become workers. Provision of day care for infants and toddlers was virtually non-existent. This, together with short maternity leave, created difficulties for working mothers with small children. Similarly, mothers' pensions, which penalized employment through reduced benefits because of earnings, discouraged solo mothers to combine caregiving and breadwinning.

Danish policies distinguished themselves from those of the other countries in two important ways. First Denmark had no policies to advance men's roles as carers and hardly any statutory rights based on fatherhood. This was not only a key variation *vis-à-vis* the other Scandinavian countries; it was the main way in which Danish policies deviated from the individual earner–carer regime. Secondly, benefits attached to the principle of care have been associated with the eligibility criterion of need in the past or more recently with labour-market status—and less with citizenship and residence. In 1980 there were no flat-rate benefits covering all mothers; child allowances were income tested, and maternity benefits were generally conferred by labour-market status. Public provision of day care has improved women's ability to combine motherhood and work, leading to a major increase of women in the labour force.

Danish policies seem to approximate what Nancy Fraser (1994) has described as a universal-breadwinner model—and not the caregiver-parity model. In the former, the breadwinner role is universalized through the promotion of women's employment, and in the latter the caregiver role is put on a par with the breadwinner role through public measures supporting informal care work. It also needs to be noted that mainstream analysis has singled out Denmark from the other Scandinavian countries, because its policies have prioritized unemployment compensation rather than measures to stimulate employment. This evaluation requires revision; it does not apply to women.

❖ Women's and Men's Utilization of Social Benefits: How Equal?

How have the differences in policy frameworks mapped out above affected women's and men's utilization of benefits? Has there been an erosion in the gender differentiation in the utilization of benefits—where men predominately claim benefits as workers and women as caregivers—since 1980? In other words, has the utilization of benefits moved in the direction of the individual earner–carer regime? In attempting to answer these questions, let us examine women's and men's utilization rates of work-related and care-related benefits over time to detect whether an equalization has occurred.

❖ Work-Related Benefits

Work-related benefits have become an increasingly important component of social provision in the Scandinavian countries during the past decades. Introduced to guarantee income security, occupational benefits form a second tier complementing benefits that provide basic security to all on the basis of citizenship or residence. Labour-market status constitutes an initial eligibility requirement, but additional qualifying conditions are usually attached to work-related benefits.

Among work-related benefits, retirement pensions are typically the most difficult to obtain because eligibility is based on lifetime employment. Occupational old-age pensions therefore constitute a litmus test. Since such a test may be too severe, I use two yardsticks: statutory occupational old-age and disability pensions (ATP in Denmark, Norway, and Sweden and the numerous Finnish schemes covering the total workforce).

Table 3.2. Women's and men's utilization of work-related benefits in the Scandinavian countries

Country	Old-age occupational pensions			Disability occupational pensions		
	Women as % of all female old age pensioners[a]	Men as % of all male old age pensioners[a]	Percentage difference between women and men	Women as % of all female disability pensioners[a]	Men as % of all male disability pensioners[a]	Percentage difference between women and men
Denmark						
1980	24.1	54.4	−30.3	n.a.	n.a.	n.a.
1994	38.8	71.7	−32.9	n.a.	n.a.	n.a.
Norway						
1981	12.4	48.9	−36.5	37.3	69.5	−32.2
1995	41.3[b]	84.4	−43.1	63.6	93.6	−30.0
Finland						
1981	43.5	79.0	−35.5	64.9	76.2	−11.3
1994	72.5	95.4	−22.9	79.8	84.0	−4.2
Sweden						
1980	20.8	67.7	−46.9	31.5	67.9	−36.4
1994	59.6	91.8	−32.2	68.3	80.5	−12.2

[a] These percentages are calculated using the number of beneficiaries of basic pensions which cover the entire population as the denominator. Figures for Norway and Sweden include only occupational pensions which exceed the minimum basic pension (basic pension + supplement for persons without or with a small occupational pension).
[b] Besides women whose pension is based on their own work record, this figure may include women with a survivor pension.

Note: n.a. = not applicable.

Sources: Denmark: Statistisk årbog (1981: 299, 300, 302) (1995: 143, 146); NOSOSKO (1984: 39); Finland: CPSI (1983: 28, 30, 33) (1995: 47, 51, 56–7); Norway: NOSOSKO (1995: 154, 163); Statistisk årbok (1996: 115–16); Sweden: RFV (1982: 269–70, 291) (1996: 212).

The qualifying conditions for occupational disability pensions have been less rigorous.

Table 3.2 presents women's and men's utilization rates of occupational pensions, and it reveals a split between the countries. Although women's utilization rates of occupational old-age pensions rose during the period in all four countries, the female/male differential increased slightly in Denmark and widened in Norway. By contrast, the gap in utilization rates has diminished in Finland and Sweden. Disability benefits show a similar pattern. The gap has narrowed in Sweden and Finland, but the Norwegian female/male differential remains sizeable. (The Danish occupational scheme differs from the other countries by not offering disability pensions.)

Norwegian women have faced stiff requirements for ATP old-age benefits at the same time as their attachment to the labour market has been weaker.[9] Forty years of employment with minimum earnings is required for a full pension, whereas the Swedish requirement was thirty years of employment.[10] Nor did care credits compensate for this difficult work test until the early 1990s. Simultaneously, the work histories of most Norwegian men have enabled them to meet the requirement and receive additional pension income.

In the Danish case we see that a smaller share of old-age pensioners receive ATP benefits compared to their Scandinavian counterparts, despite the fact that the scheme covers all employees. The lower utilization rate stems from qualifying conditions, which are based on working hours during a person's entire employment career.[11] This formula has proven vulnerable to erosion, and it excludes many part-time workers, the unemployed, persons experiencing long-term illness, employees on leave, and early retirees. Women are hit particularly hard, because they hold the bulk of part-time jobs, their unemployment rate has generally been higher than men's during the past fifteen years (*Statistisk årbog* 1995: 179), and they take leave more frequently than men.

In conclusion, at least 70 per cent of Scandinavian women in the working-age population were economically active in the mid-1990s (see Table 3.A1). Despite a major increase in women's employment rates, the change in the gender differentiation in work-related pensions has been less far-reaching in Denmark and Norway. Only around 40 per cent of female pensioners receive occupational old-age benefits compared to between 60 and 70 per cent of their Finnish and Swedish counterparts. In Finland and Sweden women's utilization rates of old-age benefits are closer to men's, and the gap in disability benefits has also diminished. The lower utilization rates of Norwegian and Danish women resemble US and UK women's access to work-related pensions.

❖ *Care-Related Benefits*

Of the benefits based on the principle of care available to both women and men, parental benefits are of central significance. They represent an initial effort to reshape the gender relations as reflected in social entitlements by extending care-related benefits to fathers. In comparison with other such benefits available to men,[12] parental benefits have a potentially large target group of claimants. All four countries have provided parental benefits since the mid-1980s, when Danish fathers gained the right to paid leave.

Women's and men's utilization of benefits as caregivers follows a more traditional pattern of gender differentiation than in the case of benefits as workers. It is overwhelmingly women who claim parental benefits, and roughly 75 per cent or more of all mothers giving birth in a particular year have received benefits in the four countries. Two notable differences can be observed for Denmark and Norway (Table 3.3). Both in 1980 and the mid-1990s Denmark had the least comprehensive coverage, because mothers had to be in the labour market to qualify for benefits. Secondly, a large share of Norwegian mothers did not collect earnings-related benefits in 1980, but by the mid-1990s most mothers did.

Growing numbers of fathers claim parental benefits but, as an inspection of Table 3.3 reveals, there are wide differences between the countries. On the whole, however, Scandinavian fathers take short-term leave, and in all four countries the proportion of parental leave days taken by fathers is infinitesimal compared to that taken by mothers.

That parental benefits have been superimposed on maternity benefits partly accounts for fathers' low utilization rates. The Swedish reform converted maternity benefits into parental benefits, and either parent can claim benefits at any time after the child's birth. In Norway, Finland, and Denmark parental benefits were grafted on to maternity benefits, and only the mother can take the first weeks of leave. After this initial period, leave can be shared by both parents. Fathers, in these countries, have faced more constraints in claiming benefits.

Most striking is the small number of Norwegian fathers who have utilized benefits since the introduction of parental benefits in 1978. The low figures seem all the more surprising since the replacement rate for parental benefits is 100 per cent, and in April 1993 a 'daddy quota' came into effect. Four weeks were reserved for the father, and benefits are forfeited if he does not make use of his right to parental leave. Before the introduction of the 'daddy quota' even fewer fathers took leave.[13]

More than in the other countries, Norwegian legislation has enshrined the conception of the mother as the natural caregiver whose rights are

❖ DIANE SAINSBURY

Table 3.3. Mothers' and fathers' utilization of parental benefits in the Scandinavian countries

Country	N of mothers receiving benefits	% of all mothers receiving benefits	% of mothers receiving earnings-related benefits	N of fathers receiving benefits	% of fathers taking paternity leave	% of fathers taking parental leave	% of parental leave days paid to fathers	% of fathers taking additional leave to care for a child of all parents
Denmark								
1981	46,000	••	••	n.a.	n.a.	n.a.	n.a.	n.a.
1994	88,712	72	72	38,604	54	3	0.6	8
Finland								
1980	95,900	97	81	8,000	••	••	••	••
1993	112,358	98	91	38,436	54	5	2	28[a]
Norway								
1980	46,735	92	46	57	n.a.	••	••	••
1994	59,617	••	73	14,273	n.a.	••	••	••
Sweden[b]								
1980	186,031	95	81	81,287	78	23	5	40
1994	372,004	98[c]	87[c]	146,766	78	40[c]	11	40

[a] Refers to special care allowances.

[b] Parents utilizing cash benefits for temporary care of a sick child are not included in the numbers of beneficiaries. On the basis of official statistics it is virtually impossible to determine the percentage of Swedish parents utilizing benefits, except for paternity leave. The most recent percentages of mothers' and fathers' utilization of parental leave are based on a special study of children born in 1989. The two percentages of fathers taking parental leave are for the first twelve months after the child's birth but the figures are not comparable. The 1980 figure refers only to married fathers who were eligible for benefits, while the most recent figure includes all fathers.

[c] 1990.

Notes: n.a. = not applicable; •• = not available.

Sources: Denmark: NOSOSKO (1984: 31); SD (1995a: 2; 1995b: 2, 7, 9); Finland: SII (1981: 75–6; 1994: 135–6, 138–9); SVF (1995: 99); Norway: *Statistisk årbok* (1982: 23; 1995: 105); Sweden: RFV (1982: 50, 52, 236, 239; 1986: 12; 1995: 33–4; 1996: 67).

transferred to the father. This has resulted in several conditions that have operated against fathers utilizing parental benefits—but three are of special importance. First, the mother has had to qualify for earnings-related benefits, and this requirement excluded half of all fathers in 1980 and one quarter in the 1990s. Nor did the 'daddy quota' apply to the father if the mother was employed less than half time. Secondly, as distinct from the other countries, the mother's employment record has determined the benefit levels of both parents. If a mother has had part-time employment, the father's benefit has been reduced. Thirdly, paid paternity leave in connection with the birth of the child is not part of the national-insurance scheme (Kaul 1991: 118). As can be observed in Table 3.3, paternity leave is the main programme that raises Finnish and Danish fathers' utilization rates.

In summary, not only have Norwegian women been the least likely to have benefits as workers, but Norwegian men have been the least likely to claim benefits as carers. The way the mother has been encoded in Norwegian parental-benefits legislation contains an ironic twist. More generally, Norwegian policies have enhanced women's social rights as mothers and carers, making it less necessary for them to enter the labour market. In the case of parental benefits, however, the mother's rights as a worker have determined the father's entitlement; yet, of the four countries, fewer policies have aided mothers to become earners and Norwegian women have had the weakest position in the labour market. The introduction of the 'daddy quota' and flexible leave allowing parents to combine leave and part-time work has prompted a major reconsideration of the rights of parents independent of each other—and may lead to an individualization of rights, which is one prerequisite for equal parenting.

In conclusion, the preceding analysis differs from mainstream discussions of the Scandinavian model in three significant ways. First, it shows how gender relations are inscribed in social provision, patterning women's and men's social rights and their utilization of benefits. Secondly, and also in contrast to important feminist contributions that have presented the experiences of one Scandinavian country as representative of the others without investigating whether this is truly the case (Hernes 1984, 1987; Siim 1990, 1993), the analysis reveals major variations between the countries. It cautions against generalizing about the Scandinavian model or the social-democratic regime on the basis of a single country. Danish policies, with fewer entitlements based on the principle of care, resembled a universal-breadwinner model. The Norwegian policy matrix corresponded to a separate gender roles regime or, in Nancy Fraser's, terminology the caregiver-parity model. The Swedish configuration of policies revealed stronger elements of an individual earner–carer regime.

❖ DIANE SAINSBURY

Thirdly, variations related to gender differentiation in entitlements cause us to question Esping-Andersen's emphasis on the similarities between Sweden and Norway and his conclusion that these two countries are the clearest cases of the same welfare state regime (Esping-Andersen 1992: 112). This is true only if gender is not included in the analysis. When gender is incorporated, Swedish and Norwegian policies have exhibited sharp contrasts.

❖ Explaining Variations

What accounts for the stronger influence of family obligations in Norwegian legislation and its closer approximation of the separate gender role policy regime? Both mainstream and feminist scholars have argued that variations in welfare state policies are related to the power resources of social agents. At first glance, this approach appears to offer little help in understanding this puzzle. Since the late 1960s the Social Democrats have dominated the executive as the party of government in Norway and Sweden for roughly the same number of years. During the same period women's representation in parliament has nearly tripled in the two countries (Sainsbury 1993; Skjeie 1993). None the less, the answer to the puzzle has to do with power resources, but we have to look more closely at the pattern of women's mobilization, the party system, and the policy legacy of the 1930s.

❖ *Women's Mobilization*

In assessing the impact of the 'new' women's movement, Drude Dahlerup (1986: 13–15) notes that the interaction between the challenging movement and those inside the system is decisive to influencing policies. Besides considering insiders and outsiders, I want to focus on pre-movement groupings and direct attention to a neglected aspect of the movement's impact. *The new women's movement often revitalized existing women's organizations*, and the dynamics between the movement and existing organizations represent a crucial cross-national variation configuring women's demands and strategies.

At least three differences between women's organizations in Norway and Sweden are of importance here. First, gender segregation in Norwegian organizational life was stronger than in Sweden in the late 1960s and early 1970s. To a greater extent, women had their organizations (humanitarian, religious, and temperance), and men theirs (unions, farmers' associations, and business) (Pestoff 1977: 172–3).[14] Secondly, the organizational strength of traditional women's associations had not yet waned in Norway, and these organizations were a part of the corporatist system of interest representation. The Norwegian National Council of Women, an umbrella organization with nearly half a million members, was able to speak for a larger number of women than any other Norwegian organization. By contrast, its Swedish counterpart—the National Association of Women—was dissolved in 1981, and the Association had never been able to claim to represent women.

Thirdly, several organizations with clout in Norway were associations that defined women's identities in terms of difference. Under the motto 'Different—but of equal value', organizations such as the Housewives' Association and the Women's Public Health Association advocated the upgrading of woman's traditional role (Dahlerup and Gulli 1985: 11–15). The key organizations in Sweden were the Fredrika Bremer Association and the women's federations of the political parties working for women's rights and gender equality. The dissimilar gender ideologies of these organizations underpinned the claims and strategies of Norwegian and Swedish women.

The Norwegian women's movement encompassed a wider range of claims than the Swedish movement. Norwegian feminists demanded not only political representation, better day care, and employment opportunities; they also wanted wages for housewives and a valuation of unpaid work in the social-security and tax systems. The Norwegian strategy for women's emancipation envisioned two roads to personal independence: (1) through wages and (2) through social-security and tax benefits that acknowledged the importance of unpaid work and care (Dahl *et al.* 1981; Dahl 1984, 1987).

The Swedish strategy of emancipation differed in that it did not emphasize a valuation of women's unpaid work. Instead it underlined women's access to paid work, and that unpaid work had to be shared by men and women. Already in the early 1960s, Eva Moberg (1961) had argued that paid work was insufficient to achieve women's emancipation; such a strategy would create a double burden for women as earners and carers. To ease the double burden of women who entered the labour market, men had to become involved in caring tasks. The most radical point of Moberg's argument was it required rethinking men's position in the family and society. Women's emancipation could not be secured unless policy measures were aimed at both women and men.

❖ Party Alliances and Policy Legacies

The women's movements deployed their strategies in national contexts where party alliances favouring policy changes also differed. In Norway the encoding of family obligations in legislation has reflected the strength of the constellation of parties espousing traditionalist values. First, and most obviously, a Christian People's Party has been a permanent fixture of the Norwegian political landscape since the inter-war years. A less obvious factor has been the sharper decline of the Liberal Party—formerly a major reformist force in Norwegian politics. The Liberals have been the principal victims of a distinctive feature of the Norwegian party system, the prominence of the centre-periphery cleavage. Internal strife over issues of urban liberalism and moral fundamentalism of the periphery resulted in two party splits. The weakening of the Liberal Party was accompanied by the rise of the Conservatives as the largest non-socialist party after 1945. The Conservatives, together with other parties that support the traditional family, have polled between 40 and 50 per cent of the vote since the late 1960s. The centre-periphery cleavage may also have made the Labour Party less amenable to radical family policies. The two strongholds of the party have been the capital and northern Norway, and the periphery has at times exerted substantial influence over the party.

Swedish parties celebrating the traditional family have been overshadowed by reform parties. Unlike the Norwegian Liberals, the Swedish party experienced an upswing in popularity after the Second World War and was the largest non-socialist party until the late 1960s. The Liberal Party was very active in putting equal rights and gender equality on the political agenda (Drangel 1984). During much of the post-war period the Liberals and Social Democrats have either vied or cooperated with each other to promote gender equality measures.

The Social Democrats have also pursued a more radical family policy compared to the Labour Party. A first wave of Swedish reforms in the 1930s had already incorporated reproductive areas, such as maternal health and benefits, easing abortion restrictions, and safeguarding the employment rights of working women who became engaged, pregnant, or married. These reforms signalled larger public responsibility *vis-à-vis* the family. The financial burden of children should be shared by the whole society rather than by individual families, and support for families should consist of public provision of services, not just cash transfers. The Norwegian legislation of the 1930s lacked the woman-friendly measures enacted in Sweden. Important in the long-term perspective was that in the Norwegian debate family allowances took precedence over the issue of services. Few Norwegians enthusiastically embraced the Swedish Social Democrats' notion that public responsibility for the upbringing of children could eliminate the shortcomings of parents, financial or otherwise (Seip 1987: 300).

The present-day significance of Norwegian party alliances becomes clearer through an inspection of their positions on family policies and equality legislation since 1970. The Conservative, Christian, and Centre parties have championed benefits based on the principle of care. From the late 1970s until their introduction in the early 1990s the parties consistently advocated care credits in the ATP pension system. They have also insisted that maternity benefits of mothers outside the workforce should not lag behind those of working mothers. On these grounds, the parties obstructed an extension of maternity leave in the early 1970s. When the leave was extended, benefits for mothers at home were raised. The three parties also opposed equality-status legislation during the 1970s. The Christian People's Party and the Centre Party were in principle against such legislation, while the Conservatives rejected quotas (Skjeie 1993: 244–58).

Gradually, however, the non-socialist parties have come to support the expansion of day care, and their opposition to equality legislation has weakened. The Labour Party also endorsed care credits in the pension system. Norwegian MPs attribute the changes in public policies to women's inclusion in party politics. The most commonly noted policy change for all parties was the expansion of childcare, while MPs of the three non-socialist parties also mentioned benefits based on the principle of care (Skjeie 1997: 305–6).

Women's representation and the strength of traditional parties in local politics have also been decisive to the introduction of the public provision of childcare. As noted by Arnlaug Leira, the difference between Norway and the other social-democratic countries was not the legislation but its slow implementation. The 1975 childcare reform assigned responsibility for the provision of childcare to the local governments, but it was not made a mandatory task (Leira 1992). Differences among the municipalities in the early implementation of the reform were related to women's representation in the municipal councils and the strength of the Centre and Christian parties (Reitan 1997).

In conclusion, Norwegian party alliances promoted policies typical of the social-democratic welfare state regime *and* the separate gender roles regime. In the area of social reforms, the Agrarians and Liberals supported Labour Party measures strengthening state intervention in the distributive system during the 1930s, while the Conservatives and the Christian People's Party joined the post-war welfare state consensus. On family policies, however, the party alignment against replacing family obligations with greater public responsibility was stronger than in Sweden. The women's movement and its strategy of seeking the valuation of unpaid work have also been crucial both in recent decades and in the past.[15] With the increase in their representation in parliament, women who were insiders could push for movement claims, including benefits based on care.

✦ Diane Sainsbury

❖ The Social-Democratic Welfare State Regime and Gender Inequality

Having examined how gender is constructed in welfare state legislation, a crucial question remains to be considered: the relationship between gender and mainstream theorizing on welfare states. What features identified by mainstream typologies of welfare states exacerbate or combat gender inequalities? Confining the discussion to the social-democratic welfare state regime and the Scandinavian model, five distinguishing features undermine gender differences in entitlements and promote equality between the sexes in social provision. It needs to be stressed that these characteristics are the defining properties of an ideal type, and the policies of the individual countries vary in deviating from these properties.

The first is entitlements based on citizenship or residence. Neither mainstream nor feminist scholars have fully appreciated the importance of this basis of entitlement. Admittedly, mainstream researchers have noted the equalizing effects of this principle (Esping-Andersen and Korpi 1987). Feminists have also pointed to the prevalence of entitlements based on citizenship as distinctive to the Scandinavian countries, and that this extends entitlements to groups outside the labour market and to disadvantaged groups in general (e.g. Siim 1990). These discussions have missed two crucial points. Entitlements based on citizenship or residence confer equal benefits within marriage, and they neutralize the effect of marital status on social rights. This basis of entitlement also places paid work and unpaid work on a par, transcending a gendered differentiation in social rights.

As we have seen, Norwegian policies most closely coincided with a separate gender roles regime. However, rights based on citizenship that have enabled women to claim benefits in their own right, most importantly old-age and disability pensions, counteract the gender differentiation in entitlements. Norwegian women have poorer access to work-related disability pensions, but they outnumber men as disability pensioners, largely because of 'citizen' pensions. In welfare states without disability benefits based on citizenship or residence, gender inequalities due to differentiated access to work-related benefits persist. If means-tested disability programmes are available, entitlement is normally familialized, and a married woman would not be eligible as long as her husband had a sufficient income.

The second feature is the marginal role played by public assistance in Scandinavian income-maintenance programmes. Comprehensive coverage and high employment rates have reduced the importance of means-tested benefits. Means-testing has a negative impact on women's entitlements because the unit of benefit is usually the family or household, and its pooled resources determine eligibility. Means-tested benefits are pitted against earnings, often creating employment disincentives and resulting in a poverty and unemployment trap.

Public assistance has been marginalized, but the importance of means- and income-testing varies in the income-maintenance programmes of the Scandinavian countries. Where means- or income-testing survives there is evidence that it is to the detriment of women's economic well-being, and that it generates gender inequalities in the risk of being poor. The Finnish basic pension was 'individualized' in the mid-1980s so that a spouse's income no longer affects benefits, but means-tested supplements continue to make up the bulk of the basic pension. While most of the Finnish aged have an occupational pension, those who do not are over-whelmingly women (see Table 3.2). Elderly women must rely on means-tested benefits much more than elderly men, and single elderly women experience much higher poverty rates than single elderly men. Although the overall gender poverty ratio is quite small in Finland, the difference between the poverty rates of Finnish single elderly men and women is sharper than the difference in the poverty rates of men and women in Scandinavia (see Table 3.4).

Another case in point is Norwegian solo mothers, whose poverty rate is higher than in the other countries, and contrasts markedly with Sweden and Finland (Table 3.4). During the 1980s the proportion of Norwegian solo mothers with the carer's pension—the transitional benefit—steadily climbed. The solo mothers who were most at risk of being poor were those without employment; and the pension, which is income tested, severely penalized earnings until changes in 1990. Furthermore, the pension, like means-tested benefits, is a familialized entitlement, where a change in family status disqualifies a carer from benefits.

The third characteristic is a commitment to full employment. Feminists have emphasized women's employment as a necessity for financial independence, and Ann Orloff (1993) has designated access to paid work a crucial welfare state variation. Besides an income, paid employment offers a path to individualized benefits. When the commitment to full employment encompasses the entire population, it has the potential to alter the previous imbalance between men's and women's labour-market status.

It needs to be stressed that a commitment to full employment and women's access to paid work do not always coincide. For example, main-stream scholars have classified Japan and Switzerland as full-employment

Table 3.4. Poverty rates by family type and sex in the Scandinavian countries, 1986/7 and 1991/2 (%)

Types of family and sex	Denmark		Finland		Norway		Sweden	
	1987	1992	1987	1991	1986	1991	1987	1992
Single elderly women	8.2	6.8	5.5	7.3	4.4	0.3	2.7	3.8
Single elderly men	10.9	8.3	0.0	3.3	2.2	1.5	0.9	2.2
Elderly couples	14.0	2.6	2.3	0.6	1.7	0.7	0.8	0.6
Single women, no children	14.1	16.3	10.9	11.1	13.2	10.9	16.5	18.7
Single men, no children	12.8	13.2	15.2	12.2	10.0	11.8	17.6	14.0
Couple, with children	5.2	4.8	3.7	3.4	2.6	3.1	4.5	3.7
Solo mothers	6.5	8.4	4.3	4.8	17.1	10.7	4.3	3.8
All women	6.9	5.9	4.0	4.4	4.5	2.8	5.7	5.3
All men	7.2	5.6	4.2	3.9	3.8	3.4	6.5	5.4

Note: Calculations based on individuals, not households. Poverty is defined as having an income that is less than half of the national median disposable income, adjusted for family size. The boxes indicate categories with unusually high poverty rates for the Scandinavian countries.

Source: LIS.

regimes, but the policies of these countries scarcely promote equal employment of women and men. In contrast, Denmark has been categorized as a soft compensatory welfare state because of high levels of unemployment and generous benefits (Pierson 1991: 186), yet the Danish record in advancing women's employment is impressive. In these days of high unemployment when the goal of full employment seems more elusive, it is increasingly relevant to maintain a distinction between *equal* access to paid work and full employment.

The fourth distinctive aspect is the provision of a wide variety of public services. State involvement in the care of children, the elderly, and the helpless allows women to choose between paid work and the household— or more aptly to combine work and the household. However, as the earlier analysis has shown, the policies of the countries have differed in the extent to which they have encouraged women to opt for work or stay at home. In some instances policies were not in place to make employment an easy choice, and in other instances policies are structured in favour of choosing care. On the other hand, the increased involvement of the public sector in reproduction and care work has been a major source of jobs for women, pulling them into the labour market in all four countries. State-provided services, as public goods removed from the market, are also a form of decommodification. This form of decommodification is beneficial to those having few financial resources and a weak position in the market; thus it often advantages women.

The fifth major welfare state variation, missing from Esping-Andersen's typology but often mentioned as a component of the Scandinavian model, that has major consequences for gender inequalities in social provision, is taxation.[16] Descriptions of the Scandinavian model usually note that benefits are funded through taxation rather than contributions and premiums. This feature is important, because contribution requirements frequently disqualify women from benefits or reduce their benefits. In the Scandinavian countries, the Danish ATP scheme serves as an illustration.

Also of major importance is the taxation of work-related benefits. The gendering of social rights across welfare states has usually been characterized by privileging paid work in relation to care and domestic tasks through more generous benefit levels. Consquently, men typically receive higher benefits than women. Taxation of work-related benefits—now a feature of all four countries—has an major equalizing impact.[17] Because these benefits are taxable income, the differences between women's and men's net benefits are much smaller than their gross benefits. The taxation of benefits reduces both gender and class inequalities.

❖ TOWARDS A COMMON GENDER POLICY REGIME?

To conclude this discussion let us examine the trends of convergence and the persistence of variations since 1980 to determine whether the contours of a common gender policy regime are discernible. This examination focuses on the four underlying dimensions of variation of our policy regimes: gender differentiation in entitlements, individualized versus familialized benefits, state responsibility in caring activities, and women's and men's equal access to paid work.

The gender differentiation in entitlements has eroded over time. The earlier analysis showed that women's claims to work-related benefits and men's claims to care-related benefits have increased since 1980. It also revealed, despite seemingly similar policies, such as parental benefits and public provision of childcare, significant cross-national variations in women's utilization rates of work-related benefits and men's utilization rates of care-related benefits in the 1990s. Claims to benefits based on citizenship or residence, however, reduce disparities in women's and men's entitlements. Nor is there a gendered utilization of public assistance, in contrast to the liberal welfare states, where women predominant as claimants of assistance.

Family-based benefits in taxation and social-insurance schemes have been replaced by individualized benefits. The erosion in family responsibilities structuring taxation has proceeded furthest in Finnish and Swedish legislation. In the mid-1990s Finland and Sweden had fully individualized tax systems with no tax relief for a dependent spouse and children.[18] The Danish and Norwegian tax systems continue to recognize family responsibilities. However, as larger numbers of married women are in the labour force and increase their working hours, individual taxation of spouses has become more widespread in Norway, and it is increasingly a shared feature.

In social-insurance schemes a common trend has been to eliminate supplements for dependants. By the mid-1990s supplements were limited to Finnish and Norwegian unemployment benefits and the basic pension schemes of the four countries. Wife supplements have been virtually phased out of the pension system. The Swedish tax system and social provision are distinguished from the other countries by the extent to which both are now individualized.

All four countries have adopted guarantees to provide day care for all pre-school children (SOU 1996: 37). The expansion of childcare provision in Norway has been very impressive, but coverage still trails behind Danish and Swedish enrolment. Moreover, a much larger component of care is provided on a part-time basis, and family day care as well as after-school programmes have hardly been developed. Childminders remain in the private sphere, and full-time centre care was available only to around 15 per cent of toddlers. Furthermore, the total coverage of children under 3 was only 20 per cent (see Table 3.A2), while the proportion of mothers of infants and toddlers in the workforce was nearly 70 per cent (Leira 1992: 109; Ellingsæter 1993). In other words, provision has not kept pace with mothers' entry into the labour market, and many mothers have continued to rely upon private and informal care arrangements.

Parental insurance reforms have generally strengthened mothers' and fathers' rights to leave, resulting in convergence. The Norwegians have lengthened the duration of leave from eighteen weeks in the early 1980s to 42/52 weeks in the mid-1990s.[19] Now Denmark stands out as the laggard in terms of the length of parental leave and benefit levels.[20] A policy innovation of the 1990s is that first the Norwegians introduced a 'daddy quota' and then the Swedes a 'daddy month', which have reserved a portion of the leave period exclusively for fathers. A chief variation among the four countries, however, is the degree to which fathers' rights are individualized or dependent upon the mother's entitlements. Fathers' rights are limited in Norway and Denmark, since a father is not entitled to parental leave if the mother lacks labour-market status, and the benefits of Norwegian fathers have been affected by mothers' earnings and part-time employment.

A convergence in access to paid work has occurred. During the 1980s the labour-market participation rate of women rose by roughly ten percentage points in Denmark, Norway, and Sweden. While Norwegian women's labour-market-participation rate was on a par with that of women in the other countries, the gender gap remained the largest in Norway. Part-time employment also continued to be most widespread among Norwegian women (see Table 3.AI), and their rate was one of the highest in the OECD countries in the mid-1990s (OECD 1997: 178).

Women's access to paid work has contributed to the economic independence of married women and mothers with young children as measured in terms of their share of family earnings (Gornick, Chapter 7, this volume). The earnings situation of married mothers with young children is very vulnerable, but income from social benefits also increases their share of family income.[21] Women's independence in marriage is further enhanced by the low poverty rates of solo mothers. Leaving an unhappy marriage or relationship need not entail an unacceptable deterioration in economic well-being. As a result of various cash benefits to bolster income and measures promoting employment, the poverty rates of Scandinavian solo mothers were relatively modest in the 1990s—ranging from 4 per cent in Sweden to 10 per cent in Norway (Table 3.4, and Kilkey and Bradshaw, Chapter 5, this volume). Despite Norway's lower performance, the four countries clustered together in terms of married women's economic independence and modest levels of poverty among solo mothers in the 1990s (Hobson and Takahashi 1997: 123).

In summation, several variations identified earlier, although diminished, persist. Denmark, in line with the universal-breadwinner model, has strengthened labour-market status as a basis of entitlement. Norwegian policies continue to reflect the separate gender roles regime. Reforms have often privileged women as caregivers, and policy constructions pose obstacles for both women and men to cross the gendered boundaries of market work and care. Swedish legislation has moved closer to the individual earner–carer regime.

On the other hand, the Scandinavian countries share the following policies and trends towards convergence: the weakening of familialized benefits in income-maintenance programmes and taxation, extensive childcare provision, ambitious parental-leave schemes with stronger enti-

✦ DIANE SAINSBURY

tlements for both mothers and fathers compared to most other indus-trialized countries, and labour-market policy measures aimed at both sexes. These policies have enhanced women's economic independence and their social rights. In these respects, Scandinavian policies appear to be moving towards the individual earner–carer regime. The distinctiveness of this policy configuration is further reinforced by the characteristic features of social-democratic welfare states that combat inequalities between the sexes.

None the less, the legacy of the separate gender roles regime creates major tensions in achieving the individual earner–carer regime. In all four countries legislation has strengthened the rights and entitlements of care-givers since 1980. These benefits have enabled women to combine caring and earning, and they ensure that caring responsibilities neither disqualify them for work-related benefits nor massively erode their benefits. Negatively, however, entitlements based on the principle of care can lock women into positions as caregivers, undercutting the goal of shared roles of caring and breadwinning for women and men.[22]

During the 1990s both Norway and Sweden introduced care credits in their ATP schemes. In the Norwegian system, 'persons' caring for pre-school children, the elderly, or the disabled are credited an amount that is slightly less than average male earnings but considerably higher than the average earnings of women workers (Hatland *et al.* 1994: 181). The reform reflects the Norwegian policy legacy of privileging women as carers and men as providers in three ways. First, pension credits elevate the remuner-ation of care above the market work of most women. Secondly, care cred-its are definitely targeted at women, since credits are granted to the parent who receives the child allowance. Thirdly, by pegging the credits at an amount less than average male earnings, the reform does not encourage men to share in caring tasks.

Equally damaging to mothers and fathers sharing the roles of earner and carer has been the introduction of care allowances for children under 3 in Finland and recently again in Norway (also for a brief interlude in Sweden). The Finnish care allowance, which has been in place since the mid-1980s, is an alternative to public childcare. It has provided better com-pensation to caregivers than child allowances but far lower benefits than work-related benefits (Anttonen *et al.* 1995), and the claimants are moth-ers—not fathers. A mother can also use the allowance to pay a childmin-der so she can hold a job.[23] Utilization of the allowance has risen steadily since its introduction, and the allowance became increasingly attractive as unemployment soared in the early 1990s. Increased utilization has been accompanied by three trends. First, socialization of the costs of familyhood through cash transfers has accelerated. Since 1980 the share of Finnish expenditures devoted to services for families has further declined in relation to cash benefits (*SYF* 1995: 421). Secondly, the availability of childcare in general and for toddlers in particular has stagnated, so that Finland had the poorest coverage in the early 1990s (see Table 3.A2). Thirdly, the growth in Finnish women's labour-market participation has slowed, and they had the lowest rate in the mid-1990s (see Table 3.AI). In short the legacy of the separate-gender-roles regime and the Finnish case alert us that policy developments are not unidirectional. Contradictory trends coexist, as the gendered boundaries of market work and care are continually contested. The development of a common gender policy regime is very much a matter of politics, shaped by the balance of political forces in the four countries.

❖ APPENDIX

Table 3.A1. Women's and men's employment patterns in the Scandinavian countries, 1979 and 1996 (%)

1979

Country	Labour-market participation rate			Employment rate		Part-time employment	
	Total	Men	Women	Men	Women	Men	Women
Denmark	79.8	89.6	69.9	85.4	61.6	5.3	46.3
Finland	75.5	82.2	68.9	76.0	63.4	3.2	10.6
Norway	75.6	89.2	61.7	87.6	59.3	10.6	51.6
Sweden	80.5	87.9	72.8	86.0	70.5	5.4	46.2

1996

Country	Labour-market participation rate			Employment rate		Part-time employment	
	Total	Men	Women	Men	Women	Men	Women
Denmark	80.1	86.2	74.0	81.4	67.8	10.2	24.2
Finland	74.1	77.6	70.6	65.4	58.9	5.5	11.2
Norway	80.8	86.1	72.3	81.9	68.9	12.3	46.3
Sweden	79.0	81.6	76.3	74.7	70.6	6.7	23.5

Notes: The employment rate is the labour-market participation rate minus the unemployment rate. Part-time employment refers to the percentage of the labour force in part-time jobs. For 1979 the figures are based on national definitions of part-time employment. For 1996 the definition is standardized and consists of working less than thirty hours per week.

Sources: OECD (1995*a*: 210, 214–15; 1995*b*: 475–7, 492–3, 498–9; 1997: 163–5, 178).

❖ DIANE SAINSBURY

Table 3.A2. Provision of public childcare in the Scandinavian countries, 1981 and 1993 (percentage of all children in age group)

1981

Form of childcare	Denmark		Finland		Norway		Sweden	
	Age of child		Age of child		Age of child		Age of child	
	0–2	3–6	0–2	3–6	0–2	3–6	0–2	3–6
Full-time centre care	15	31	6	15	4	12	13	26
Part-time centre care	—	8	—	10	1	23	—	24
Family day care	22	8	11	12	—	—	11	15
TOTAL	37	47	17	37	5	35	24	65

1993

Form of childcare	Denmark		Finland		Norway		Sweden	
	Age of child		Age of child		Age of child		Age of child	
	0–2	3–6	0–2	3–6	0–2	3–6	0–2	3–6
Full-time centre care	18	57	8	27	14	37	23	49
Part-time centre care	—	11	—	8	3	24	—	14
Family day care	29	6	8	16	3	2	9	14
TOTAL	47	74	16	51	20	63	32	76

Note: a dash = magnitude nil.

Source: *Yearbook of Nordic Statistics* (1995: 321–2).

❖ NOTES

1 Here I use the term 'Scandinavian' to refer to Denmark, Finland, Iceland, Norway, and Sweden, but I do not deal with Iceland.

2 Scandinavian women's entitlements as wives have been mainly confined to widow pensions, which were enacted relatively late—in Sweden 1946, Denmark 1959, Norway 1964, and Finland 1969 (Flora 1987: 78, 136, 200). In addition, occupational pension schemes providing widow benefits were introduced from roughly 1960 to 1970 in the four countries.

3 Prior to 1970, however, Norwegian child allowances did not cover the first child, whereas in both Finland and Sweden child-allowance reforms in the late 1940s initially provided allowances for all children.

SOCIAL-DEMOCRATIC WELFARE STATES ❖

4 Any income over half of the basic amount reduced the mothers' pension, and taxation could result in marginal effects of over 100% (NOU 1993: 17, p. 210).

5 The Finnish women's labour-market participation rate was already 65.6% in 1960—the highest rate in the OECD countries—whereas the rates in Sweden, Denmark, and Norway were 50.1%, 43.5%, and 36.6% respectively (O'Connor 1993: 11).

6 Finland and Norway soon followed suit, introducing parental benefits in 1978, but Denmark lagged behind until 1985.

7 Until the mid-1980s a Swedish father's right to paid leave, with the exception of paternity leave, was qualified: the mother had to be entitled to earnings-related benefits.

8 In Esping-Andersen's empirical analysis, Finland did not rank among the strongest decommodifying cluster of countries, and it had a lower score on socialism than the other Scandinavian countries and a higher score on conservatism.

9 Two other factors affecting the male/female gap in utilization rates of old-age occupational pensions need to be mentioned. The first is the different sequence of phasing in the ATP reforms in the two countries. Norway introduced the pension in the late 1960s and it is scheduled to be fully implemented in 2007 (Kjeldstad 1988: 79), whereas the Swedish reform was introduced earlier and implemented more swiftly, with full benefits first paid out in 1980. The second factor is that the amount of the minimum pension has steadily increased, creating a higher threshold before ATP benefits add to the pension income of the elderly (Hatland *et al.* 1994: 57–9). This situation exists in both countries, but men's lower utilization rates indicate that the threshold may be higher in Norway.

10 The Swedish pension reform of the mid-1990s stiffens the qualifying conditions by requiring forty years of employment (concurrently introducing care credits) and by calculating benefits on the basis of lifetime earnings. The new conditions are to be phased in, coming into full effect around 2020.

11 If a Danish employee meets the working hours requirement (in 1993 a minimum of twenty-seven hours per week or 117 hours per month), both the employer and employee pay an annual contribution, and the contribution record determines the size of the pension (NOSOSKO 1995: 142).

12 Other care-related benefits available to men are, for example, the Norwegian pensions for single carers and in Sweden cash benefits to care for a close relative and allowances to care for a disabled child.

13 In 1993 a mere 1,650 fathers utilized parental benefits, compared to 64,550 mothers (NOSOSKO 1995: 39).

14 For example, the members of Norwegian religious and temperance organizations were predominately women, while there was little difference between the sexes in the membership of these organizations in Sweden. Nor was the discrepancy between women and men's involvement in job-related organizations as large in Sweden as in Norway, and many more Swedish women were members of these organizations.

15 Maternalist politics during the earlier part of the twentieth century resulted in several municipalities adopting mothers' pensions, which were eventually incorporated into the national-insurance scheme. For a discussion of the early policy legacy, see Sainsbury (1998).

16 Apart from the discussion in Castles and Mitchell (1993), taxation as an instrument of redistribution has seldom been included as a major variation in welfare state typologies.

17 For empirical evidence of the distributional effects of taxes on work-related benefits in the Swedish and Finnish cases, see Sainsbury (1996) and Jäntti *et al.* (1996).

18 The Finns abolished the tax allowance for a dependent spouse in the late 1980s and tax exemptions for children in 1994.

19 Parents entitled to earnings-related benefits can choose between leave of forty-two weeks with a replacement rate of 100% or fifty-two weeks at 80%.

20 In the 1990s the right to paid leave to care for a child in Denmark was improved as a labour-market measure, and a condition was that a replacement be hired for the parent taking leave. This condition was later dropped, and since 1994 both parents have the *right* to six months of paid leave. The level of compensation, however, is lower than parental benefits—70% of unemployment benefits.

21 For example, a recent study shows that the share of family income of Swedish mothers with pre-school children rose from 30% to nearly 40% when social benefits were taken into account (Nyberg 1997: 51).

22 Not all entitlements based on the principle of care represent challenges to the individual earner–carer model. For example, all four countries improved child allowances, but these improvements have generally been neutral in their impact on women's employment, since the allowances are non-taxable benefits. Moreover, in the late 1980s the Danes eliminated income-testing of child allowances, which had tended to penalize dual-earner families.

23 Communication from Anne Maria Holli, Sept. 1996.

❖ REFERENCES

ALESTALO, M., AND UUSITALO, H. (1987), 'Finland', in Flora (1987), 123–90.

ALLARDT, E. (1986), 'The Civic Conception of the Welfare State in Scandinavia', in Rose and Shiratori (1986), 107–25.

ANTTONEN, A., FORSBERG, H., AND HUHTANEN, R. (1995), 'Family Obligations in Finland', in Millar and Warman (1995), 65–86.

BOCK, G., AND THANE, P. (1991) (eds.), *Maternity and Gender Policies: Women and the Rise of the European Welfare States 1880s–1950s* (London).

BORCHORST, A. (1994), 'Welfare State Regimes, Women's Interests and the EC', in Sainsbury (1994), 26–44.

CASTLES, F. (1993) (ed.), *Families of Nations: Patterns of Public Policy in Western Democracies* (Aldershot).

——and Mitchell, D. (1993), 'Worlds of Welfare and Families of Nations', in Castles (1993), 93–128.

CPSI (1983), Central Pension Security Institution, *Statistik över pensionstagarna i Finland 1981* (Helsinki).

—— (1995), *Tilasto Suomen eläkkeensaajista 1994* (Helsinki).

DAHL, T. S. (1984), 'Women's Right to Money', in Holter (1984), 46–66.

—— (1987), *Women's Law: An Introduction to Feminist Jurispurdence* (Oslo).

—— Fastvold, M., AND Sverdrup, T. (1981), *Husmorrett* (Oslo).

DAHLERUP, D. (1986) (ed.), *The New Women's Movement* (London).

—— and Gulli, B. (1985), 'Women's Organizations in the Nordic Countries: Lack of Force or Counterforce?', in Haavio-Mannila *et al.* (1985), 6–36.

DRANGEL, L. (1984), 'Folkpartiet och jämställdhetsfrågan', in *Liberal ideologi och politik 1934–1984* (Falköping), 342–425.

ELLINGSÆTER, A. L. (1993), 'Changing Roles: Trends in Women's Employment and Gender Equality', *International Journal of Sociology* 23/2–3: 153–71.

ERIKSON, R., HANSEN, E. J., RINGEN, S., AND UUSITALO, H. (1987) (eds.), *The Scandinavian Model: Welfare States and Welfare Research* (Armonk, NY).

ESPING-ANDERSEN, G. (1990), *Three Worlds of Welfare Capitalism* (Cambridge).

—— (1992), 'The Three Political Economies of Welfare Capitalism', in Kolberg (1992), 92–123.

—— (1996) (ed.), *Welfare States in Transition: National Adaptations in Global Economies* (London).

—— and Korpi, W. (1987), 'From Poor Relief to Institutional Welfare States', in Erikson *et al.* (1987), 39–74.

FLORA, P. (1986) (ed.), *Growth to Limits*, i (Berlin).

—— (1987) (ed.), *Growth to Limits*, iv (Berlin).

FRASER, N. (1994), 'After the Family Wage: Gender Equity and the Welfare State', *Political Theory*, 22/4: 591–618.

—— (1997), *Justice Interruptus: Critical Relfections on the 'Postsocialist' Condition* (New York).

GUSTAFSSON, S. (1990), 'Labor Force Participation and Earnings of Lone Parents: A Swedish Case Study Including Comparisons with Germany', in *Lone-Parent Families* (Paris), 151–72.

HAAVIO-MANNILA, E., DAHLERUP, D., EDUARDS, M., GUDMUNDSDÓTTIR, E., HALSAA, B., HERNES, H. M., HÄNNINEN-SALMELIN, E., SIGMUNDSDÓTTIR, B., SINKKONEN, S., AND SKARD, T. (1985) (eds.), *Unfinished Democracy: Women in Nordic Politics* (Oxford).

HAGEN, K. (1992), 'The Interaction of Welfare States and Labor Markets: The Institutional Level', in Kolberg (1992), 124–68.

HATLAND, A., KUHNLE, S., AND ROMØREN, T. I. (1994), *Den norske velferdsstaten* (Oslo).

HEDERBERG, H. (1961) (ed.), *Unga liberaler* (Stockholm).

❖ DIANE SAINSBURY

HERNES, H. (1984), 'Women and the Welfare State: The Transition from Private to Public Dependence', in Holter (1984), 26–45.

—— (1987), *Welfare State and Women Power* (Oslo).

HOBSON, B. (1990), 'No Exit, No Voice: Women's Economic Dependency and the Welfare State', *Acta Sociologica*, 33: 235–50.

—— (1994), 'Solo Mothers, Social Policy Regimes and the Logics of Gender', in Sainsbury (1994), 170–87.

—— and Takahashi, M. (1997), 'The Parent–Worker Model: Lone Mothers in Sweden', in Lewis (1997), 121–39.

HOLTER, H. (1984) (ed.), *Patriarchy in a Welfare Society* (Oslo).

JÄNTTI, M., KANGAS, O., AND RITAKALLIO, V.-M. (1996), 'From Marginalism to Institutionalism: Distributional Consequences of the Transformation of the Finnish Pension Regime', *Review of Income and Wealth*, 42: 473–91.

JOHANSEN, L. N. (1986), 'Denmark', in Flora (1986), 283–381.

KANGAS, O., AND PALME, J. (1992), 'The Private–Public Mix in Pension Policy', in Kolberg (1992), 199–238.

KAUL, H. (1991), 'Who Cares? Gender Inequality and Care Leave in the Nordic Countries', *Acta Sociologica*, 34: 115–25.

KJELDSTAD, R. (1988), *Inntekt over livsløpet: Pensjonsgivende inntekt og alderspensjon. Forskjeller mellom kvinner og menn i fire fødseskohorter*, INAS Rapport 1988: 2 (Oslo).

KOLBERG, J. E. (1992) (ed.), *The Study of Welfare State Regimes* (Armonk, NY).

KORPI, W. (1994), 'Class, Gender and Power in the Development of Social Citizenship', paper presented at the 13th World Congress of Sociology, Bielefeld, 18–23 July.

LEIRA, A. (1992), *Welfare States and Working Mothers: The Scandinavian Experience* (Cambridge).

LEWIS, J. (1992), 'Gender and the Development of Welfare Regimes', *Journal of European Social Policy*, 2/3: 159–73.

—— (1993) (ed.), *Women and Social Policies in Europe: Work, Family and the State* (Aldershot).

—— (1997), *Lone Mothers in European Welfare Regimes: Shifting Policy Logics* (London).

—— and Ostner, I. (1991), 'Gender and the Evolution of European Social Policies', paper presented at the CES Workshop 'Emergent Supranational Social Policy: The EC's Social Dimension in Comparative Perspective', Center for European Studies, Harvard University, 15–17 Nov.

—— —— (1994), 'Gender and the Evolution of European Social Policies', Working Paper No. 4/94, Centre for Social Policy Research, University of Bremen.

LOVENDUSKI, J., AND NORRIS, P. (1993) (eds.), *Gender and Party Politics* (London).

MILLAR, J., AND WARMAN, A. (1995), *Defining Family Obligations in Europe*, Bath Social Policy Papers No. 23 (Bath).

MOBERG, E. (1961), 'Kvinnans villkorliga frigivning', in Hederberg (1961), 68–86.

NOSOSKO (1984), Nordic Committee of Social Statistics, *Social trygghet i de nordiska länderna: Omfattning, utgifter och finansiering 1981* (Helsinki).

—— (1995), *Social tryghed i de nordiske lande. Omfang, udgifter og finansiering 1993* (Copenhagen).

NOU 1993: 17, *Levekår i Norge: Er graset grønt for alle?* (Oslo: Ministry of Finance).

NYBERG, A. (1997), 'Gender Equality and Economic Independence: Women's and Men's Incomes', SOU 1997: 87 (Stockholm).

O'CONNOR, J. (1993), 'Citizenship, Gender and Labour Market Participation in Canada and Australia', in Shaver (1993), 4–37.

OECD (1986), Organization of Economic Cooperation and Development, *The Tax/Benefit Position of Production Workers, 1979–1984* (Paris).

—— (1995a), *Employment Outlook 1995* (Paris).

—— (1995b), *Labour Force Statistics 1973–1993* (Paris).

—— (1995c), *The Tax/Benefit Position of Production Workers, 1991–1994* (Paris).

—— (1997), *Employment Outlook 1997* (Paris).

ORLOFF, A. S. (1993), 'Gender and the Social Rights of Citizenship: The Comparative Analysis of Gender Relations and Welfare States', *American Sociological Review* 58: 303–28.

—— (1994), 'Restructuring Welfare: Gender, Work and Inequality in Australia, Canada, the United Kingdom and the United States', paper presented at the Conference of Crossing Borders, Stockholm, 27–9 May.

PESTOFF, V. A. (1977), *Voluntary Associations and Nordic Party Systems* (Stockholm).

PIERSON, C. (1991), *Beyond the Welfare State?* (Cambridge).

REITAN, T. C. (1997), 'Getting a Head Start: Early Provision of Day Care among Municipalities in Norway', *Scandinavian Journal of Social Welfare*, 6: 268–78.

RFV (1982), National Social Insurance Board, *Allmän försäkring mm 1980* (Stockholm).

—— (1986), 'Föräldrapenning med anledning av barns födelse: Barn födda 1978–1983', *Statistikinformation Is-I 1986: 12* (Stockholm).

—— (1993), 'Vilka pappor kom hem? En rapport om uttaget av föräldrapenningen 1989 och 1990 för barn födda 1989', *Statistisk rapport Is-R 1993: 3* (Stockholm).

—— (1995), *Socialförsäkringsstatistik: Fakta 1995* (Stockholm).

—— (1996), *Socialförsäkring 1993 och 1994* (Stockholm).

ROSE, R., AND SHIRATORI, R. (1986) (eds.), *The Welfare State East and West* (New York).

❖ DIANE SAINSBURY

Sainsbury, D. (1988), 'The Scandinavian Model and Women's Interests: The Issues of Universalism and Corporatism', *Scandinavian Political Studies*, 11: 337–46.

——(1993), 'The Politics of Increased Women's Representation: The Swedish Case', in Lovenduski and Norris (1993), 263–90.

——(1994) (ed.) *Gendering Welfare States* (London).

——(1996), *Gender, Equality and Welfare States* (Cambridge).

——(1998), 'Gender and the Making of the Norwegian and Swedish Welfare States', paper presented at the MIRE conference 'Comparing Social Welfare Systems in the Nordic Countries and France', Gilleleje, Denmark, 4–6 Sept.

SD (1995*a*), Statistics Denmark, *Befolkning og valg*, Statistiske Efterretninger 1995: 4 (Copenhagen).

——(1995*b*), *Social sikring og retsvæsen*, Statistiske Efterretninger 1995: 17 (Copenhagen).

——(1996), *Arbejdmarked*, Statistiske Efterretninger 1996: 13 (Copenhagen).

Seip, A.-L. (1987), 'Who Cares? Child, Family and Social Policy in Twentieth-Century Norway', *The Scandinavian Journal of History*, 12: 331–43.

——and Ibsen, H. (1991), 'Family Welfare, Which Policy? Norway's Road to Child Allowances', in Bock and Thane (1991), 40–59.

Shaver, S. (1993) (ed.), *Gender, Citizenship and the Labour Market: The Australian and Canadian Welfare States*, Social Policy Research Centre Reports and Proceedings No. 109, University of New South Wales (Sydney).

——and Bradshaw, J. (1995), 'The Recognition of Wifely Labour by Welfare States', *Social Policy and Administration*, 29/1: 10–27.

SII (1981), Social Insurance Institution, *Kansaneläkelaitoksen tilastollinen vuosikirja 1980* (Helsinki).

——(1994), *Kansaneläkelaitoksen tilastollinen vuosikirja 1993* (Helsinki).

Siim, B. (1990), 'Women and the Welfare State: Between Private and Public Dependence: A Comparative Approach to Care Work in Denmark and Britain', in Ungerson (1990), 80–109.

——(1993), 'The Gendered Scandinavian Welfare States: The Interplay between Women's Roles as Mothers, Workers and Citizens in Denmark', in Lewis (1993), 25–48.

Skjeie, H. (1993), 'Ending the Male Political Hegemony: The Norwegian Experience', in Lovenduski and Norris (1993), 231–62.

——(1997), 'A Tale of Two Decades: The End of a Male Political Hegemony', in Strøm and Svåsand (1997), 289–319.

Skrede, Kari, (1984), 'Familieøkonomi og forsørgerlønn', *Tidsskrift for samfunnsforskning*, 24: 539–54.

SOU 1996: 37, Bilaga 2, *Building Family Welfare*, Supplement 2 of the Official Report from the Swedish Committee on the International Year of the Family (Stockholm).

Statistisk årbog (various years) (Copenhagen).

Statistisk årbok (various years) (Oslo).

Statistisk årsbok (various years) (Stockholm).

STEPHENS, J. D. (1996), 'The Scandinavian Welfare States: Achievements, Crisis and Prospects', in Esping-Andersen (1996), 32–65.

STRØM, K., AND SVÅSAND, L. (1997) (eds.), *Challenges to Political Parties: The Case of Norway* (Ann Arbor).

SYF: Statistical Yearbook of Finland (various years) (Helsinki).

UNGERSON, C. (1990) (ed.), *Gender and Caring* (New York).

Yearbook of Nordic Statistics (1995) (Copenhagen).

❖ **Part Two**

The Gendered Impact of Policies across Welfare State Regimes

4 ❖ Public Childcare, Parental Leave, and Employment

Marcia K. Meyers, Janet C. Gornick, and Katherin E. Ross

Welfare state scholars have paid considerable attention to the role of the state in protecting the interests of citizens, as workers, from the demands of private markets. The role of the state in mediating the demands of family and caregiving responsibilities has received less scrutiny. Family policies have typically been analysed as residual social-welfare functions, only tangentially related to the central tension between the individual and the market. A dramatic, four decade long increase in women's employment in industrialized economies challenges this treatment of the interdependencies among the family, the state, and the market. Government policies relating to the care and education of young children are emerging as a central concern not only for studies of child and family outcomes but for those addressing women's economic progress as well.

Between 1960 and 1990, women's participation in the labour force increased in every OECD country, more than doubling in some (OECD 1992). Employment has increased particularly rapidly among women with children. This increase has expanded opportunities for social, economic, and political participation for many women. It has also created new challenges, especially for mothers who balance the demands of employment with caregiving for young children. The tension between family and workplace responsibilities has elevated the importance of many government policies that provide for the care of dependent children. All of the industrialized countries provide a package of family policies that includes some form of parental leave, publicly subsidized childcare, and public education. Although adopted in response to a variety of social-welfare and demographic concerns, these family policies also have the effect of supporting maternal employment by reducing conflicts between market and family responsibilities.[1]

Because they reflect the interdependence of market and family work, patterns of maternal employment—and the family policies that influence them—are central issues in gendered welfare state analyses. Equality in access to employment is viewed by many as fundamental to women's achievement of full social citizenship because, as O'Connor (1996: 78) describes, 'independence is the key to citizenship and in the democratic welfare state employment is the key to that independence'. Orloff extends this idea by considering women's ability to form and maintain autonomous households—that is, 'to survive and support their children without having to marry to gain access to breadwinners' income' (1993: 319)—as an indicator of welfare state progress for women. Equal access to employment is essential to this autonomy.

While opportunity to participate in employment is not a sufficient condition, it is arguably a necessary condition for women's social citizenship. Government policies that promote these opportunities are correspondingly important indicators of the extent to which welfare states are 'woman friendly' in promoting equality in employment opportunities between those who do and those who do not assume caregiving work (Hernes 1987; Lister 1990; Fraser 1994; O'Connor 1996) and in supporting alternatives to the 'male-breadwinner–female-caregiver' model of social and economic relations (Orloff 1996).

❖ STUDYING THE ROLE OF GOVERNMENT IN SUPPORTING MATERNAL EMPLOYMENT

A large comparative literature has examined cross-national differences in welfare state structures, expenditures, and economic and labour-market outcomes. Comparative scholars have given relatively little attention, however, to cross-national variation in government policies that facilitate maternal employment.

This paucity of attention reflects, in part, the class-based analyses that have dominated recent welfare state scholarship. Prominent among these studies is Esping-Andersen's (1990) theory of welfare state regimes. His empirically based model identifies three variants of the capitalist welfare state: the *social democratic* (primarily the Nordic countries), the *conservative/corporatist* (dominated by the European continental countries), and the *liberal* (primarily the English-speaking countries). Each regime type has a characteristic configuration of social policies that differ in the extent to which they decommodify workers by providing alternatives to dependence on private markets. Each regime type is also seen to have a distinctive pattern of socio-economic and labour-market outcomes.

The class-based framework in the work of Esping-Andersen and other mainstream scholars overlooks potentially important differences in the implications of government policies for the employment decisions of men and women. In particular, the focus on decommodification as a central measure of welfare state development assumes a level of labour-market integration that has yet to be achieved by women in many highly industrialized countries. A small body of empirical work that has focused on government policies with particular relevance to women's employment has revealed substantial variation *within* country clusters proposed by Esping-Andersen (Gornick 1994; Leira 1992). These findings suggest that, if the focus is shifted from the decommodification of workers to the integration of women, the performance of advanced welfare states might be judged quite differently.

In the present study, we address the question of whether a subset of public family policies has influenced women's participation in paid employment in the Western industrialized nations, and how these policies and associated employment patterns have varied across countries. We do so by capitalizing on large variations observed in the late 1980s in government policy and in women's employment across fourteen countries at similar levels of economic development.

Although maternal employment has increased in all industrialized countries, both the rates and the patterns of employment continue to vary markedly across countries at similar levels of economic development. In the late 1980s, for example, only 25 per cent of mothers in the Netherlands were employed, while 89 per cent of Finnish mothers were working for pay (authors' calculations, the LIS micro-data). Cross-national variation was also dramatic in mothers' patterns of full-time and part-time employment and in their employment continuity (OECD 1994; Gustafsson and Stafford 1995; Rosenfeld and Birkelund 1995; Gornick and Jacobs 1996; Gornick *et al.* 1998).[2] Variations in the *pattern* of maternal employment are particularly important indicators of the interdependence of paid and unpaid work. Many women respond to the competing demands of employment and child-rearing by engaging in intermittent employment or reduced-hour and contingent work. Although these employment choices may help women accommodate multiple-role demands in the short term, they may also reduce their employment opportunities and wages in both the short and the long term (Callaghan and Hartmann 1991; Dex 1992; Rosenfeld 1993; Gornick and Jacobs 1996).

Government policies that provide alternative care for children are an important factor in women's capacity to manage the tension between workplace and caregiving responsibilities, and the characteristics and generosity of these policies also varied dramatically across industrialized countries during this same period (Kamerman 1991; Kamerman and Kahn

1991; Hofferth and Deich 1994; Gustafsson and Stafford 1995). While most industrialized countries (with the exception of the USA and Australia) provided paid maternity leave, for example, the weeks of coverage varied from as few as twelve to as many as fifty-two. In some Nordic countries, from one-third to nearly one-half of children under age 3 had access to public childcare; in the USA and Australia, fewer than 5 per cent of infants were in public childcare (Gornick *et al.* 1997).

These cross-national variations provide a 'natural experiment' for exploring interdependencies at the nexus of the state, family, and markets. A number of single-country studies have linked childcare and maternity leave to women's employment decisions. There is also a rich cross-national literature that describes variation in family policies and in women's labour-market outcomes. Comparative scholars have yet to use cross-national data, however, fully to specify and test the association between the two. A handful of recent studies have explored this terrain (Whitehouse 1992; Schmidt 1993; Gustafsson and Stafford 1995; Ruhm and Teague 1995; Bradshaw *et al.* 1996; Gornick *et al.* 1998). Progress has been limited, however, by the lack of a model that specifies the association between country-specific family-policy 'packages' and patterns of maternal employment. Even more importantly, researchers have been limited by the lack of comparable cross-national data.

This analysis begins to fill this gap by examining the effect of public childcare policy and public parental-leave provisions on the employment patterns of married mothers in fourteen industrialized countries during the late 1980s. We make use of cross-national variation in policy and in maternal employment patterns to answer three questions. First, how did the advanced industrialized democracies vary in the generosity of childcare and maternity-leave policies and in patterns of maternal employment? Secondly, to what extent were variations in policy associated with variations in women's employment patterns? Thirdly, how do the results of a gender-sensitive analysis of welfare state performance correspond to class-based analyses, particularly the three welfare state regimes proposed by Epsing-Andersen?

By developing comparable measures of policy effort and employment outcomes across several countries, this analysis moves beyond single-country studies to identify cross-national commonalities and dissimilarities in the ways countries 'package' support for women who engage in both market work and unpaid caregiving work. The policy indicators compare the extent to which states compensate mothers for their assumption of caregiving responsibilities; the employment indicators compare how mothers with young children fare, relative to other women, on employment outcomes. Using these indicators, we capitalize on naturally occur-

❖ MEYERS, GORNICK, AND ROSS

ring variations at the country level to analyse the association between policy inputs and economic outcomes. This design isolates the contribution of government policy by comparing employment outcomes *within* countries between otherwise similar women with and without young children, thereby controlling for individual and country-specific factors, and then analysing the association between policy and employment outcomes *across* countries at similar levels of industrial and economic development, to hold constant additional macroeconomic and political factors.

❖ THE LINK BETWEEN FAMILY POLICY AND MOTHERS' EMPLOYMENT

The underlying hypothesis that childcare and maternity-leave policies facilitate continuity in maternal employment, is supported by substantial economic theory and research.[3] The standard labour-supply model predicts that having children in the home will influence women's employment decisions by changing the value that they place on their time outside paid work. The cost of alternative childcare arrangements will also lower women's effective market wages. The empirical literature confirms that women who care for a greater number of children and those who care for more dependent (for example, younger, disabled) children have a lower probability of being employed than similar women with fewer caregiving responsibilities; for mothers who are employed, greater child-rearing responsibilities reduce hours in paid work (Connelly 1991; Joshi 1992; Leibowitz *et al.* 1992).

Economic theory also suggests two approaches to understanding the effects of *childcare* on women's employment. The first depicts childcare arrangements as affecting the value that a woman places on her time at home, with better childcare alternatives reducing the attractiveness of full-time caregiving work in the home (Blau and Ferber 1992). In the second approach, the cost of childcare is viewed as a 'tax' on mothers' wages. An increase in the cost of childcare would have the same effect as lowering wages—decreasing both the likelihood of employment and hours of paid work (Connelly 1992; Michalopoulos *et al.* 1992). Both approaches predict that improvements in women's childcare options will be associated with increases in employment, and this prediction is supported by a large body of empirical research (Blau and Robins 1991; Connelly 1991, 1992; Leibowitz *et al.* 1992; Michalopoulos *et al.* 1992).

The relationship between maternal-employment and *parental-leave* policies is understood differently by economists. Generous maternity-leave provisions are generally believed to increase women's attachment to paid work in the short term. In addition to offering income support, many maternity policies are explicitly designed to prevent women from leaving employment following childbirth (Trzcinski 1991). In the longer term, there is more ambiguity about whether extended absences from the workplace will advantage or disadvantage women in the accumulation of experience and human capital. A small empirical literature has examined the impact of maternity leave in the short term. Joesch (1995) and O'Connell (1990) report that the availability of leave increases mothers' attachment to paid work, in particular, the likelihood of an early return to work after first childbirth. In the USA, Klerman and Leibowitz (1995) find only weak evidence of a relationship between state maternity-leave statutes and employment, but Waldfogel (forthcoming) reports an increase in leave taking and a small positive effect on employment after the passage of the US Family and Medical Leave Act. Macran, Dex, and Joshi (1996) find evidence in the UK that family-leave coverage increases the likelihood that a woman will return to her employer after childbirth; Waldfogel, Higuchi, and Abe (1998) report similar evidence in a three-country study of Japan, the USA, and the UK. These studies suggest that short-term leaves are likely to increase the employment of women following childbirth; more research is needed to establish the impact of longer leaves on lifetime patterns of employment and earnings.

❖ DATA

Data for the analysis were obtained from the Luxembourg Income Study (LIS). LIS is an archive of datasets gathered from a large number of industrialized countries. Micro-datasets available for each country contain demographic, labour-market, and detailed income data at the household and individual level. Estimates of mothers' employment outcomes are derived using household-level data from the period of 1985 to 1987 from fourteen countries: Australia, Belgium, Canada, Denmark, Finland, France, Germany, Italy, Luxembourg, Netherlands, Norway, Sweden, the UK, and the USA.[4] LIS also provides a policy database that contains country-level information on major income tax and cash transfer programmes. Measures of childcare and parental-leave policy for the late 1980s were recently added by the authors to the country-level policy database.[5]

❖ APPROACH

The analysis proceeds in three steps. We begin by using the country-level policy indicators to develop composite indices of the generosity of government policies by country. First we disaggregate the larger complex of national policies in order to identify the subset of family policies that are expected to influence maternal employment. Separate policy indicators are then aggregated into two indices that measure country-specific 'packages' of employment-supporting policies. The first index combines eight indicators of policies affecting mothers with children under age 3 ('infants'): the coverage, length, and generosity of short-term parental leaves, tax relief for private childcare expenses, the existence of a legal entitlement to public childcare, and the availability of public childcare (enrolments in public or publicly subsidized care). The second index combines four indicators of government policies affecting mothers with children from age 3 until school enrolment ('pre-schoolers'): tax relief for private childcare expenses, a legal entitlement to public childcare, the supply of public childcare (enrolment of children between age 3 and 5) and the impact of the age of universal public school (enrolment of children aged 5 in public childcare, pre-primary, or primary school).[6] Rankings are provided to facilitate cross-national comparisons, but it is important to note that numeric scores are not directly comparable *across indices*.

The second component of the analysis uses a multiple-regression analysis to examine country-specific patterns of interruptions in women's employment associated with child caregiving, by using household-level data from LIS to compare employment among mothers with young children to the employment of otherwise similar mothers in the same country whose children are all older. A measure of this difference, termed the 'child penalty', captures the country-specific decrease in the employment rate of married mothers that is associated specifically with having children under age 6 in the home. (See the Appendix for details.) The use of this measure of employment continuity, in place of the more conventional maternal employment rate, strengthens our analysis by focusing on an outcome that is closely related to women's roles as primary caregivers for children. The use of the child penalty also helps to isolate the impact of government policy on women's employment outcomes. Because maternal employment varies cross-nationally for a number of demographic, economic, and cultural reasons, it is difficult to disaggregate the reasons for cross-national variation in employment *rates*. The cross-national differences in maternal employment *continuity* that are captured by the child penalty can be linked more directly to variation in national policy. The child penalty compares employment rates between mothers within the same country who differ only in terms of the presence of young children— that is, between mothers who have similar demographic characteristics, face similar labour-market conditions, experience similar social and cultural norms, and so on. The child penalty, therefore, controls for other, non-policy factors that influence cross-national employment variation.

PUBLIC CHILDCARE AND PARENTAL LEAVE ❖

To aid with the interpretation of the child penalties, we simulate the impact of having a young child in the home on the likelihood that a 'typical' or average mother in each country is employed. A hypothetical mother is created, with all characteristics set at or near the average for mothers in her country, and the regression results are used to calculate her likelihood of being employed. Our 'hypothetical mother' is a 35-year-old married mother with two children, both over age 12; she completed her country's 'medium' level of education and her other household income is set at the average for married mothers in her country. After predicting the likelihood of employment for this mother, two alternative scenarios are simulated. In the first, a child under age 3 is 'added' to her family, and, in the second, a child between the ages of 3 and 5 is 'added'. New employment probabilities are generated corresponding to the 'addition' of each child (with other characteristics, including family size, held constant).

Finally, we examine the association between government policies (using the employment-supporting policy indices) and maternal employment continuity (using the child-penalty measures). Our central hypothesis relates directly to the interdependence of family responsibilities, market opportunities, and state policies: we predict that cross-national variation in the package of public childcare and maternity leave policies will explain a large part of the inter-country variation in the child penalty—that is, the probability that women reduce their employment when family responsibilities are high. This provides an empirical assessment of the extent to which woman-friendly policies that compensate for caregiving burdens are associated with more equality in employment outcomes between women with and without young children.

❖ CROSS-NATIONAL POLICY VARIATION

As of the middle to late 1980s, the generosity of public maternity-leave provisions and public childcare varied dramatically across the fourteen countries in this analysis. Nearly all had near-universal provisions for job protection and wage replacement in the months following childbirth (Table 4.1). The USA and Australia were the most prominent exceptions. The USA had no national law providing job protection or wage replacement at the time of childbirth; in Australia, federal law guaranteed up to twelve months of job protection but provided no wage replacement.[7] The UK also lagged, primarily because eligibility restrictions (for example, on minimum earnings and job tenure) were such that only approximately 60 per cent of employed women had access to both job protection and wage replacement.

❖ MEYERS, GORNICK, AND ROSS

Table 4.1. Public parental-leave policies in fourteen countries

Country	Legislated job protection	Paid maternity leave (weeks)	Wage replacement rate (% wages)	Coverage (% employed women)	Extended leave (weeks)	Paternity benefits
Australia	yes	12	60	10	52	yes
Belgium	yes	14	77	100	0	no
Canada	yes	15	60	100	0	no
Denmark	yes	18	90	100	10	yes
Finland	yes	43	80	100	111	yes
France	yes	16	84	100	140	yes
Germany	yes	14	100	100	0	yes
Italy	yes	20	80	100	136	yes
Luxembourg	yes	16	100	100	0	no
Netherlands	yes	12	100	100	0	no
Norway	yes	18	100	100	26	yes
Sweden	yes	52	90	100	26	yes
UK	yes	18	46	60	22	no
USA	no	6	60	25	0	no

Source: Gornick et al. (1997: 57).

PUBLIC CHILDCARE AND PARENTAL LEAVE ❖

In the other countries, all or nearly all employed women were covered by national job-protection and wage-replacement benefits. The length of protection and adequacy of wage replacement varied substantially. On the high end, universal systems in three Nordic countries (Sweden, Finland, and Norway) provided full or nearly full wage replacement for six months to one year. In about half of the countries, paternal involvement in early childcare was facilitated by the extension of some form of paid or unpaid leave to fathers.

All fourteen countries made some public investments in childcare, but both the form and the intensity of support varied markedly (Table 4.2). Reasonably comparable data on direct childcare expenditures were available for only six countries. At the high end, Sweden spent $1,885, in 1987 US dollars, per year per child under 15 and Finland spent $1,212. At the low end, the USA and Canada each invested less than $50 per child. Data were available for all countries on indirect tax expenditures that are aimed at offsetting the cost of private household expenditures on childcare. Tax relief was provided in eight countries. The generosity of these provisions varied from a high of $1,118 in Belgium to a low of $198 annually for one child in Finland (in 1987 US dollars).

By the late 1980s, only Denmark, Finland, and Sweden had adopted legislation that established childcare as a right for all (or nearly all) children under the age of 6. France guaranteed childcare to all children aged 2–5; Belgium had extended the promise of universal coverage to younger children (birth to age 2) but not to older pre-school children.[8] National childcare guarantees signal intent; they do not guarantee availability. In the actual provision of childcare for infants, Denmark was the clear leader with 48 per cent of children under age 3 in publicly supported care. Four additional countries (Belgium, Finland, France, and Sweden) also had relatively high rates of public provision, with 20–32 per cent of children under age 3 in care. Provision for children under age 3 fell substantially in the remaining countries, with 12 per cent of children in Norway and fewer than 5 per cent of children in the remaining countries enrolled in public or publicly funded care.

Public childcare provisions were more highly developed for pre-school children in all fourteen countries. In four (Belgium, Denmark, France, and Italy), over 85 per cent of children were in public day care or pre-schools. At the other end of the spectrum, Australia, Canada, Norway, and the UK enrolled only 25–40 per cent of pre-school children; the USA lagged even further behind with only 14 per cent of pre-schoolers in publicly supported care. Levels of public childcare arrangements for children began to converge as compulsory school enrolment provided care for older children. When childcare and school enrolments are combined for 5-year-old

Table 4.2. Childcare policies: public support and public supply in fourteen countries

Country	Tax relief for childcare (1987 $US)	Guaranteed childcare coverage (0–2) (age) (years)	Guaranteed childcare coverage (3–5) (age) (years)	% children (0–2) in publicly funded childcare	% children (3–school age) in publicly funded childcare	% children (age 5) in pre-primary or school	% children in publicly funded after school care	Childcare expenditures (1987 $US)
Australia	0	none	none	2	26	90	••	••
Belgium	1,118	0–2	none	20	95	99	••	••
Canada	851	none	none	5	35	98	••	43
Denmark	0	0–2	3–5	48	85	80	29	••
Finland	198	0–2	3–5	32	59	59	••	1,212
France	699	2	3–5	20	95	100	••	630
Germany	0	none	none	2	78	85	4	••
Italy	0	none	3–5	5	88	88	••	••
Luxembourg	599	none	none	2	58	99	2	••
Netherlands	384	none	none	2	53	99	••	••
Norway	342	none	none	12	40	50	••	508
Sweden	0	>18 months	3–5	32	79	79	34	1,885
UK	0	none	none	2	38	100	<1	••
USA	685	none	none	1	14	87	<1	44

Note: •• = not available.
Source: Gornick *et al.* (1997: 56).

PUBLIC CHILDCARE AND PARENTAL LEAVE ❖

children, virtually all countries made public provisions for 80–100 per cent of children. Here, only Norway (50 per cent) and Finland (59 per cent) stand out for their lack of provisions.

❖ EMPLOYMENT-SUPPORTING POLICY INDICES

Multiple indicators of family policy paint a complex cross-national picture. It is difficult, however, to reach general conclusions about government support. The composite indices in Figure 4.1 compare relative country performance on the 'package' of policies available to women with young children. (Numeric scores for the indices are provided in Table 4.3). They serve as yardsticks for comparing the extent to which countries equalized employment opportunities between individuals with and without child-caregiving responsibilities, by providing mothers with alternatives to quitting their jobs (through maternity leaves), and to providing full-time childcare themselves (through public childcare).

Five countries form a cluster of high performers: three Nordic countries (Finland, Denmark, and Sweden) and two continental European countries (Belgium and France). These countries generally provided universal provisions for maternity leave with full, or nearly full, wage replacement, lasting for several months up to a year. In addition, space was available in publicly supported childcare for a third to a half of all infants and nearly all pre-school-aged children.

Three English-speaking countries (Australia, the UK, and the USA) form a cluster of low policy performers *vis-à-vis* families with children in either age group. These countries provided limited or no paid leave. None had adopted policies to guarantee access to childcare and levels of public care were correspondingly low. In the USA, only 25 per cent of women had access to any publicly supported leave (through state-mandated private disability insurance); only 1 per cent of infants and 14 per cent of pre-schoolers were in publicly supported childcare.

The contrast between the low and high performers is sharp. The remaining countries—a mixture of Nordic (Norway), continental European (Germany, Luxembourg, and the Netherlands), and English-speaking (Canada)—form a cluster of moderate performers. These countries were characterized by moderate to very generous maternity-leave provisions but limited childcare provisions for both infants and pre-school-aged children.[9]

For most countries, movement in ranking is modest between the indices corresponding to the two age groups. High-performing countries on policies aimed at families with infants were generally high performers with respect to policies aimed at pre-schoolers. There is, however, consid-

Fig. 4.1. Policies that support employment for mothers

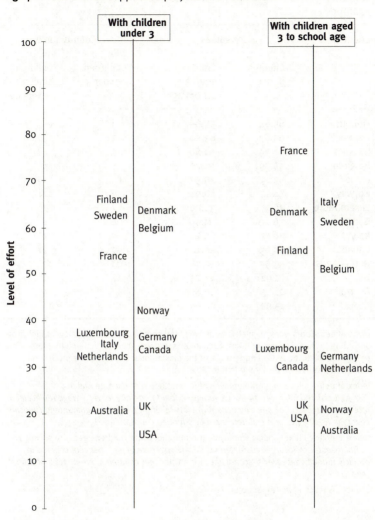

Source: Gornick *et al.* (1997: 60).

erable re-ranking *within* the clusters. France, for example, is among the high performers on both indices, but its relatively higher performance on policies for mothers with pre-schoolers reflects the strong French commitment to enrol children in *l'école maternelle* beginning at age 3. Finland represents nearly the opposite case, shifting from the most generous in

PUBLIC CHILDCARE AND PARENTAL LEAVE ❖

Table 4.3. Policy indices: index values and country ranks in fourteen countries

Country	Index values		Country ranks	
	Children under 3	Children aged 3 to school age	Children under 3	Children aged 3 to school age
Finland	65.84	55.85	1	5
Denmark	63.87	63.50	2	3
Sweden	62.29	61.60	3	4
Belgium	59.99	51.29	4	6
France	53.19	76.57	5	1
Norway	41.42	20.94	6	12
Luxembourg	36.27	34.06	7	7
Germany	36.20	31.90	8	8
Italy	36.04	65.20	9	2
Canada	34.69	30.12	10	9
Netherlands	33.97	30.08	11	10
UK	21.98	21.25	12	11
Australia	21.25	16.80	13	14
USA	13.59	20.65	14	13

Note: Index scores were calculated using weighted combinations of the relevant indicators according to the following formulas. Each index score was then converted into a final score of 0 to 100, with 100 representing 100% of the maximum achievable score for this index. These final values are presented in this table.

Index of policies that support employment for mothers with children under 3

0.50[*legislated job protection + (coverage) × (paid maternity leave) + wage replacement rate + coverage + 0.50(paternity benefits)] + tax relief for childcare + guaranteed childcare coverage (0–2) + per cent children in publicly funded childcare (0–2)*

Index of policies that support employment for mothers with children aged 3 to school age

Tax relief for childcare + guaranteed childcare coverage (3–5) + per cent children in publicly funded childcare (3–school age) + 0.33(per cent children in pre-primary or school (age 5))

Source: Gornick et al. (1998: 40).

support of mothers with infants to a position of relatively poorer performance in provisions for pre-schoolers. This reflects Finnish family policy during the period that emphasized both home care allowances and a childcare entitlement for families with infants. Although there was more public childcare for pre-schoolers, in absolute terms, it fell considerably short of demand.

Dramatic change differences in the relative performance of two countries—Norway and Italy—suggest more serious discontinuities in policy. Norway's relative performance declines markedly from the moderate tier on policies for infants to the lowest tier in provisions for pre-schoolers. During the late 1980s, Norway provided extensive and generous maternity leaves for employed women, but those leave benefits were coupled with low levels of public childcare for the under-3s and relatively modest investments in childcare for pre-schoolers. The problem was exacerbated for Norwegian mothers by the fact that compulsory school did not start until children were age 7—one to two years later than most other countries (Gornick *et al.* 1997). Although mothers had generous support in the months after childbirth, public support was limited once maternity leaves were exhausted. Italian family policy represented yet another combination. Italy provided generous maternity policies and widespread pre-school coverage for children over age 3; there were significant gaps, however, in public childcare for infants and toddlers. During the period between the end of maternity benefits and the beginning of public pre-school at age 3, Italian mothers faced significant barriers to employment.

❖ CROSS-NATIONAL VARIATION IN EMPLOYMENT PATTERNS

Variation was equally pronounced in employment outcomes across the fourteen countries (Table 4.4).[10] Employment rates of mothers varied from a low of 25 per cent in the Netherlands to a high of 89 per cent in Finland. Moderate rates are seen in most English-speaking countries.

The effects of caregiving for young children on employment continuity, measured as the country-specific child penalty, also varied markedly. Significant negative child penalties are seen in one-half of the countries: Australia, Canada, Germany, the Netherlands, Norway, the UK, and the USA. Penalties for women with infants were consistently larger than those for women with pre-school-aged children. In the remaining seven countries, mothers of young children were not significantly less likely to be employed than were similar mothers whose children are all 12 years old or older. Italy alone produced a surprising and inexplicable result: significantly positive coefficients on both young children variables.[11]

The largest child penalties are found in the UK, where the presence of an infant decreased the hypothetical mother's likelihood of employment from 82 to 37 per cent, a 45 percentage point decrease; the presence of a pre-schooler diminished her employment probability from 82 to 51 per cent. In the USA, the probability of employment also declined sharply for women

Table 4.4. Child penalties: logistic regression and simulation results in fourteen countries

Country	Employment rates (%)	Logistic regression coefficients[a]		Predicted employment rates[b] (%)		
		Age 0–2 (SE)[c]	Age 3–5 (SE)	(1) Base case	(2) Add 1 child age 0–2	(3) Add 1 child age 3–5
Australia (1985)	48	**-1.5401** 0.2091	**-0.7586** 0.2066	76	41	61
Belgium (1985)	50	0.4637 0.3572	0.4800 0.3447	41	—	—
Canada (1987)	62	**-0.6944** 0.1837	**-0.4920** 0.1759	72	57	62
Denmark (1987)	81	-0.2020 0.2640	-0.0434 0.2578	91	—	—
Finland (1987)	89	-0.3271 0.2306	-0.1497 0.2270	87	—	—
France (1984)	57	0.2959 0.1532	0.1796 0.1422	53	—	—
Germany (1984)	39	**-1.1102** 0.2360	**-0.7743** 0.2148	53	28	36
Italy (1986)	39	0.8574 0.1987	0.5366 0.1795	34	—	—

Luxembourg (1985)	29	−0.4454 0.4439	−0.4772 0.4307	33	—	—
Netherlands (1987)	25	**−1.1138** 0.3139	**−0.9182** 0.3065	60	35	39
Norway (1986)	60	**−1.3458** 0.2786	**−1.2524** 0.2859	81	52	54
Sweden (1987)	88	0.0359 0.2762	−0.3255 0.2559	96	—	—
UK (1986)	56	**−2.0584** 0.2454	**−1.4723** 0.2401	82	37	51
USA (1986)	57	**−0.9418** 0.1786	**−0.6752** 0.1748	72	50	57

[a] Control variables include marital status, number of children, mother's age and its square, education, other household income. Statistically significant negative coefficients ($p < 0.05$) are marked in bold.

[b] The 'base case' is a 35-year-old married woman with two children over age 12, with 'medium' education, and with other household income equal to the mean for this variable in her country. The three predicted employment rates should be interpreted as follows:
(1) the predicted employment rate for the base case (i.e. this hypothetical woman);
(2) the predicted employment rate for the base case if she is 'given' one child age 0–2, all else equal;
(3) the predicted employment rate for the base case if she is 'given' one child age 3–5, all else equal.

[c] SE = standard error.

Source: Gornick et al. (1998: 46).

with infants (22 percentage points) and pre-schoolers (15 percentage points).

There was surprisingly little relationship between overall maternal employment rates and the presence or magnitude of the child penalties. Child penalties are observed both in relatively low-employment countries and in moderately high-employment countries. While none of the three highest-employment countries had child penalties, some of the low-employment countries also had no child penalties.[12] This suggests that the *level* and the *continuity* of maternal employment are distinct and only weakly correlated phenomena.

❖ POLICY VARIATION AND ECONOMIC OUTCOMES

The final stage of analysis links the measure of breaks in employment with the subset of family policies that are predicted to facilitate continuous maternal employment. Figures 4.2 and 4.3 display the relationship between the magnitude of the child penalty and the generosity of employment-supporting policies in each country. Vertical lines represent the estimated range for the child-penalty measures; countries with a greater negative value indicate higher penalties or employment reductions among mothers with young children and those that cross zero indicate that no statistically significant child penalty is observed.[13] The sloping lines represent the regression estimates of the associations between the child penalties and the packages of employment-supporting policies; the upward slopes indicate positive relationships in which more generous policy packages are associated with *lower* child penalties (that is, smaller differences in the employment rates for mothers with young children and otherwise similar mothers whose children are all older.)[14]

Child penalties are seen to cluster along the sloping line in each figure. This demonstrates a strong positive association, across countries, between these public policies and mothers' attachment to employment. The statistical measure of association suggests that the first index of employment-supporting policy explains 36 per cent of the variation in the employment reductions associated with having an infant; the second policy index explains 52 per cent of the variation in penalties associated with having a pre-schooler in the home.[15]

❖ DISCUSSION

The consistency and strength of the association between employment-supporting policies and women's employment continuity suggest that these government policies may have influenced women's employment decisions. While this conclusion is consistent with the data, our use of

Fig. 4.2. Policy variation and child penalties for mothers with youngest child under 3

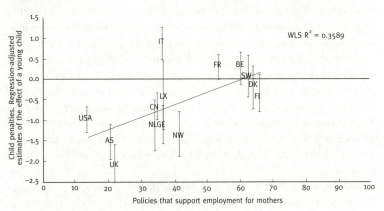

Note: The child penalties are indicated by the logistic regression coefficients. The vertical lines represent 95% confidence intervals for the child penalties based on the standard errors (SE) presented in Table 4.4.

Source: Gornick *et al.* (1998: 49).

Fig. 4.3. Policy variation and child penalties for mothers with youngest child age 3–5

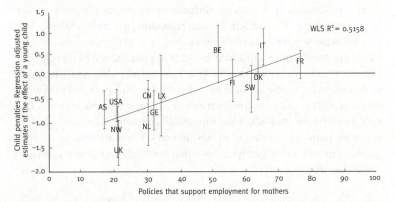

Note: The child penalties are indicated by the logistic regression coefficients. The vertical lines represent 95% confidence intervals for the child penalties based on the standard errors (SE) presented in Table 4.4.

Source: Gornick *et al.* (1998: 50).

cross-sectional data makes it difficult to interpret the results unambiguously. Several alternative explanations for the association are also possible. Most obviously, it is possible that the social, cultural, and economic factors that influenced women's decisions to go to work outside the home may have influenced the adoption of childcare and leave policies in their countries. In several Nordic countries, for example, cultural norms of gender equality may have contributed to both generous policy packages and continuous female employment. It is also possible that in countries where mothers of young children tend to choose employment, there may have been consumer demand and political pressure to increase the availability of such policies; in countries where most mothers choose to stay home when children are young, there may have been little demand for this form of assistance.

Although it is not possible fully to rule out these competing explanations, the case that policy influenced employment choices, especially in the short term, is strong. As noted earlier, economic theory and research have shown that women's short-term employment decisions are sensitive to public childcare and leave policies. Most of this research has been based on single-country studies that lack variation in both policy and employment outcomes. This analysis, by finding a strong association between cross-national variation in employment-supporting policies and the continuity of maternal employment, confirms and extends findings from these earlier single-country studies. It is particularly striking that this association is consistent even for the countries, such as Norway, that diverge from the 'cluster' of countries that welfare scholars characterize as having similar labour-market conditions, social norms, and welfare structures.

The conclusion that policy influences employment decisions is also strengthened by the design of the measures for this analysis. The employment-supporting policy indices improve on earlier studies by capturing the interactions and additive effects of policies, and by disaggregating the effects for mothers who face substantially different caregiving demands owing to the age of their children. The child penalty provides a measure of the effect on employment of caring for young children that controls, first, for individual and household characteristics and, secondly, for cross-national differences in labour-market and other factors—such as social norms about gender roles—that are likely to influence levels of maternal employment.

❖ Conclusions

Although the industrialized countries in this analysis had achieved similar levels of economic development by the late 1980s, their progress in adopting policies that supported women's employment opportunities was remarkably varied. A handful of countries—most of the Nordic countries along with France and Belgium—had developed extensive provisions that helped women with young children to manage their dual responsibilities to family and workplace. In these countries, women had access to job protections and generous wage replacements at the time of childbirth, and to public childcare as their children aged. In many, some form of leave was also available to fathers.

A second tier of countries, including the remaining continental countries along with Canada and Norway, provided more limited support for those with caregiving responsibilities. These countries were characterized by generous maternity leaves but much less extensive childcare for either infants or pre-schoolers. The laggards in the provision of employment-supporting family policy were the English-speaking countries of the USA, the UK, and Australia. These countries provided little or no maternity leave and only extremely limited public childcare assistance through either direct subsidies or tax credits.

The consequences of these policies for women is suggested by the cross-national variation in child penalties for mothers with children under age 6. In the countries with the most generous policies, mothers with young children were no less likely to be employed than were mothers with only older children. In the countries with middle and low levels of provision, women with young children had employment rates that were significantly lower than otherwise similar mothers without young children in the home. It is particularly noteworthy that moderate to high employment reductions were observed in a 'middle tier' of countries that combined generous maternity leaves with limited childcare. This suggests that these policies are not perfect substitutes in their impact on women's employment decisions. Maternity leave is consistent with both continued attachment to employment and a period of full-time caregiving in the home; childcare, on the other hand, is an essential support for women's participation in paid work. Those countries that have made generous commitments to both types of policy come closest to a universal-breadwinner model in which government policies equalize employment opportunities between adults who do and do not have child-caregiving responsibilities. Countries that have made a partial commitment, providing generous maternity leave but lacking extensive public childcare, represent a more ambiguous compromise between the universal-breadwinner and traditional male-breadwinner models.

The findings from this analysis challenge mainstream research on welfare state regime types. In particular, both policy and employment outcomes correspond only partially to Esping-Andersen's (1990) class-based regime model. In discussing women's employment, Esping-Andersen argues that each welfare state regime type is associated with a distinct trajectory. High levels of female employment are observed in the social-democratic countries, in which he suggests both supply and demand are driven by the large public sector with its extensive service provision. Moderate levels of female employment are observed in the liberal countries, driven largely by the demands of private markets and the weakness of social-insurance provisions. The lowest levels are observed in the conservative countries, which he attributes to the historic marginalization of female workers and the existence of policies that encourage mothers to remain in the home.

The configuration of government policies described in this analysis partially confirm and partially challenge the coherence of these regime types. In the provision of employment-supporting family policies, several countries are seen to diverge from the clusters predicted by the class-based welfare state models. The *social-democratic* regime type disaggregates as Norway diverges from the other Nordic countries in providing much less generous support for maternal employment, particularly in the areas of public childcare and early school enrolments. The *conservative* countries reveal little commonality: France is among the most generous countries in its provision of maternity leaves and childcare, whereas Germany is among the least generous. Among the *liberal* countries, Canada pulls away from the other English-speaking countries in providing more adequate maternity leave and somewhat better childcare coverage.

Standard welfare state typologies are also challenged by the pattern of child penalties. The lack of child penalties in most of the Nordic countries is consistent with predictions that social-democratic countries support full employment for women; substantial penalties observed in Norway, however, suggest that these countries are more heterogeneous than predicted. In the conservative cluster, Germany and the Netherlands have the significant child penalties that would be predicted by their support for traditional family structures, but France, Belgium, and Italy have none. And, while all of the countries in the liberal cluster have moderately high maternal employment rates, they also have significant child penalties—an outcome at odds with predictions that weak income supports necessarily propel women into the labour market.

The findings from this analysis vividly illustrate the consequences of welfare state policies for women's economic and social progress. The development of woman-friendly policies has been uneven across the rich, industrialized countries, with consequences for women's full economic integration. Progress has been mixed even within the cluster of Nordic countries, which, when characterized by class-based analyses of the role of

the state in decommodifying labour, have the most highly advanced welfare state policies.

Significant within-regime variations in policies and employment outcomes suggest that the traditional country clusters fail to cohere when
issues of particular consequence for women are considered. This argues
for new, more gender-sensitive measures of welfare state progress and generosity. It does not fully answer, however, the question of what combination of policies would be most woman friendly in supporting women's
multiple responsibilities for caregiving and labour-market work. This
analysis has identified policies that facilitate employment among mothers
with young children as one component of the woman-friendly welfare
state. Equal opportunities for women to participate in market work, and to
achieve parity with men, may be a critical first step towards full social citizenship for women. Employment also contributes to women's capacity to
form and maintain autonomous households, thereby lessening dependence on men. But, as Fraser (1994) has argued, policies that increase
labour-market opportunities for women, without affecting the gender
bias in responsibility for unpaid work in the home, will yield, at best, a partial form of gender equality. In the longer term, the contribution of
employment-supporting policies to the achievement of full economic and
social participation for women will depend on the extent to which they
influence the organization of both paid work in the market and unpaid
caregiving work in the home. A woman-friendly welfare state may well be
one that is 'parent-friendly' in supporting the efforts of both men and
women to combine caregiving and waged work without undue—and
gender-biased—sacrifices in either family or employment opportunities.

❖ Appendix

❖ Employment-Supporting Family Policy Index Construction

To compare government policies across countries, eleven indicators of childcare or
maternity-leave policy were combined into composite indices. Maternal employment is expected to respond to the form and intensity of several different policies
that, functioning as complements and/or substitutes, constitute a distinctive
employment-supporting policy package in each country. The implications of
these policies differ for families with children of varying ages. In order to capture
the interactions among multiple policies and disaggregate policy performance by
the age of the child, we develop two indices. (See Gornick *et al.* 1996*a* for a more
complete discussion of index construction.)

Four criteria were used to select individual indicators for the composite indices.
First, the indicator measured an aspect of policy reasonably assumed to be under
government control—that is, it constituted *public* policy. Secondly, it captured
a policy feature that labour-supply theory predicts has an effect on mothers'

decisions about entering or remaining in paid work. Thirdly, the indicator was exogenous or independent of individual mothers' short-term employment decisions. Fourthly, reliable and comparable data were available for the fourteen countries.

Eleven policy indicators were used in the construction of the indices. Data for the separate policy indicators were standardized as proportions of variable-specific maximum values. The two age-specific indices were constructed as weighted sums of the standardized measures. (The weights are presented in the notes to Table 4.3.) A second standardization converted index scores to a percentage of the theoretical maximum per index, so that scores range from zero to 100.

❖ EMPLOYMENT OUTCOMES

Our main measure of maternal employment outcomes is the child penalty. This is the regression-adjusted estimate of the effect of having young children on mothers' employment probability. Child penalties were estimated using a standard labour-supply model. (For more complete information on the estimation procedures, see Gornick *et al.* 1996*b*.)

In order to estimate country-specific child penalties, standard reduced-form logistic regression models were specified to predict a mother's employment probability. In these models, the explanatory variables of primary interest are two dummy variables that capture child-rearing responsibilities: one indicates that the youngest child in the household was under age 3 and another indicates that the youngest was between the ages of 3 and 5. Controls include: (1) the presence of a youngest child age 6–12 and the total number of children in the household under the age of 18; (2) human-capital variables (mother's age and education) as a proxy for the market wage; and (3) total other income in the household (primarily husband's earnings), as an indicator of economic need. Identically specified employment equations were estimated for mothers, separately by country.

The analysis for each country was limited to married women, aged 15–64, with at least one child under age 18 living at home. Mothers were coded as either 'employed' or 'not employed'. Mothers who were employed but on maternity leave were coded as employed; those who were unemployed as well as those not in the labour force were coded as 'not employed'.

There are several benefits associated with using the child-penalty measure. First, by focusing on the difference in employment between mothers with and without young children, it isolates an employment outcome that may be *specifically* tied to child-rearing responsibilities. Secondly, by using regression techniques to control for individual human-capital and household characteristics, it allows cross-national comparisons of employment outcomes that are net of inter-country variation in demographic variables; the penalty captures within-country employment differences among women who differ only (or primarily) in the age of their youngest child. Finally, by first estimating the impact of having young children on employment outcomes for mothers *within* the same country and then comparing these estimates *across* countries, the child penalty captures cross-national variation in employment outcomes that is largely independent of inter-country differences in labour-market conditions. In regression terms, both overall maternal employment rates and factors that affect those overall employment rates (such as demand-side factors) are captured in the constant term, while the impact of child-rearing responsibilities is captured in the regression coefficients.

❖ LINKING POLICY WITH EMPLOYMENT BEHAVIOUR

The final step in the analysis assesses the central hypothesis that cross-national variation in policy will explain a substantial portion of the inter-country variation in the child penalties. Country-specific child penalties are regressed on the corresponding index of employment-supporting government policies, using weighted least squares (WLS) regression techniques. In these estimations, the child-penalty coefficients are weighted by the inverse of their standard errors to take into account varying levels of precision in the child-penalty estimates.

❖ NOTES

1 Still other issues arise in the case of private provision of employment supports—e.g. the extensive use of family and market childcare arrangements in many countries and the provision of maternity leave through employer-sponsored benefits in some. These private arrangements raise important issues about interdependencies among government, family, and private markets, but are beyond the scope of this analysis.

2 Women's accommodations to home and workplace responsibilities are visible in their age-based employment profiles. While continuous labour-force participation is the norm among men in all of the developed countries, limited and intermittent participation is more often the norm for women. These patterns vary, however, cross-nationally (OECD 1994). As of the late 1980s, for example, women's labour-force participation in some developed countries—including Finland, France, and Sweden—resembled men's, rising and falling smoothly with age in an 'inverted U-shaped' pattern. In other countries, women's labour-force participation was characterized by the withdrawal by many women from waged work during their twenties, a pattern sharply different from that of their male counterparts. In the Netherlands and Germany, for example, women's participation rates were highest among those in their mid-twenties and fell steadily with age in a 'left-peak' pattern. In Australia and the UK, their rates rose then fell (among women in their late twenties), and then rose again, in an 'M-shaped' pattern (OECD 1994).

3 Extending the basic microeconomic consumption model, mothers' labour supply is viewed as a consumption choice between market income (hours of paid work) and time spent outside paid work (non-market time). A large body of empirical literature demonstrates the influence of personal, market, and policy factors on labour supply, both on participation and on hours worked (Killingsworth and Heckman 1986; Berndt 1991).

4 The years for which LIS micro-data are available for each country dictated the selection of the analysis period. See de Tombeur (1997) for information about LIS and for details on the individual datasets.

5 For more detailed information about data sources used for this study, see Gornick *et al.* (1996*a*).

6 This analysis uses enrolments as a proxy for childcare supply. Although this utilization measure is arguably responsive to female employment and demand for care, spaces in public programmes at a specific time will depend on past government decisions rather than current demand and can therefore be considered exogenous to individual employment decisions. OECD (1990) also notes that enrolments are a reliable proxy for available spaces because utilization rates are approximately 100 per cent.

7 Although the USA did not have national maternity-leave provisions, some women had access to paid leave, typically for six weeks, through employer-provided disability insurance. After the passage of the Pregnancy Disability Act of 1978, companies that provided disability insurance were mandated by federal law to include pregnancy as a covered disability. Five states had passed additional laws mandating provision of Temporary Disability Insurance by most employers; these laws covered an estimated 25 per cent of female workers. In Australia, women employed by the federal government had access to twelve weeks of maternity leave; this is estimated to have benefited 10 per cent of female workers.

8 Two other countries had developed policy in this area, but with such weak provisions that no entitlement to employment-supporting childcare can be inferred. Italy had extended its guarantee of childcare down to children under 3, but with a service target so low (5 per cent) and so poorly funded as to be meaningless. Germany had an entitlement for pre-school children, but the programmes to which it applied—part-day, part-week pre-school—were poorly attuned to the working schedules of employed parents.

9 In several of the countries, the supply of public childcare is further limited by providing part-day care. Notable examples include playgroups in the Netherlands and pre-schools in Germany. With schedules poorly matched to parents' working hours, these childcare arrangements provided little support for women's participation in paid employment.

10 The names of the individual surveys, country-specific sample sizes, complete regression results, and sample means for all independent variables are available in Gornick *et al.* (1996*b*).

11 In Table 4.4 changes in employment probabilities are simulated only for countries in which the coefficients on the presence of young children are negative and statistically significant at the 0.05 level (i.e. there is at least a 95 per cent probability that the penalty observed in the data is not due to chance). Only one country, Italy, was observed to have a statistically significant positive coefficient on the presence of young children. This would suggest that Italian mothers experience a 'child bonus'—i.e. that there is a higher probability of employment among moth-

❖ MEYERS, GORNICK, AND ROSS

ers with children under age 6 in the home. This may reflect an interaction of fertility, employment, and policy factors in this country. Alternately, it may reflect data problems associated with the reporting of informal work and childcare arrangements, which are particularly common in Italy. Other countries have small positive or negative coefficients, but, because they are not statistically significant, the impact of having a child under age 6 on maternal employment is assumed to be zero.

12 The weak association is confirmed by small correlation coefficients between maternal employment rates and child-penalty magnitudes (0.28 and 0.27, for infants and pre-schoolers, respectively).

13 Child penalties are presented with confidence intervals. The vertical line for each country represents the range of possible values for the child-penalty coefficient at the 95% confidence level. Negative values represent a penalty; a positive value would imply a child bonus. If the vertical line for any country crosses zero—i.e. if the range of possible values for the child penalty includes zero—this implies that there is neither a child penalty nor a child bonus in that country.

14 The fitted regression line is displayed in Figures 4.2 and 4.3, based on a weighted least squares (WLS) estimate (see the Appendix).

15 The measure of association is the R^2 for the WLS regression.

❖ REFERENCES

ASHENFELTER, O. C., AND LAYARD, R. (1986) (eds.), *Handbook of Labor Economics, i* (New York).

BERNDT, E. (1991), *The Practice of Econometrics: Classic and Contemporary* (Reading, Mass.).

BLAU, D. (1991) (ed.), *The Economics of Child Care* (New York).

——AND ROBINS, P. (1991), 'Child Care Demand and Labor Supply of Young Mothers Over Time', *Demography*, 28/3: 333–51.

BLAU, F., AND FERBER, M. (1992), *The Economics of Women, Men, and Work* (Englewood Cliffs, NJ).

BRADSHAW, J., KENNEDY, S., KILKEY, M., HUTLON, S., CORCLEN, A., EARDLEY, T., HOLMES, H., AND NEALEY, J. (1996), *Policy and the Employment of Lone Parents in 20 Countries* (York).

CALLAGHAN, P., AND HARTMANN, H. (1991), *Contingent Work: A Chart Book on Part-Time and Temporary Employment* (Washington).

CASTLES, F. G. (1993) (ed.), *Families of Nations: Patterns of Public Policy in Western Democracies* (Aldershot).

CONNELLY, R. (1991), 'The Importance of Child Care Costs to Women's Decision Making', in Blau (1991), 87–117.

——(1992), 'The Effect of Child Care Costs on Married Women's Labor Force Participation', *Review of Economics and Statistics* 74/1: 83–90.

De Tombeur, C. (1997), *LIS/LES Information Guide, Revised Edition*, Luxembourg Income Study Working Paper No. 7 (Luxembourg).

Dex, S. (1992), 'Women's Part-Time Work in Britain and the United States', in Warme *et al.* (1992), 161–73.

Esping-Andersen, G. (1990), *The Three Worlds of Welfare Capitalism* (Princeton).

Fraser, N. (1994), 'After the Family Wage: Gender Equity and the Welfare State', *Political Theory* 22/4: 591–618.

Glendinning, C., and Millar, J. (1992) (eds.), *Women and Poverty in Britain in the 1990s* (New York).

Gornick, J. C. (1994), 'Women, Employment, and Part-Time Work: A Comparative Study of the United States, the United Kingdom, Canada, and Australia', unpublished Ph.D. dissertation, Harvard University.

—— and Jacobs, J. (1996), 'A Cross-National Analysis of the Wages of Part-Time Workers: Evidence from the United States, the United Kingdom, Canada and Australia', *Work, Employment and Society*, 10/1: 1–27.

—— Meyers, M., and Ross, K. (1996a), 'Supporting the Employment of Mothers: Policy Variation Across Fourteen Welfare States', Luxembourg Income Study Working Paper No. 139 (Luxembourg).

—— —— —— (1996b), 'Public Policies and the Employment of Mothers: A Cross-National Study', Luxembourg Income Study Working Paper No. 140, (Luxembourg).

—— —— —— (1997), 'Supporting the Employment of Mothers: Policy Variation Across Fourteen Welfare States', *Journal of European Social Policy*, 7/1: 45–70.

—— —— —— (1998), 'Public Policies and the Employment of Mothers: A Cross-National Study', *Social Science Quarterly* 79/1: 35–54.

Gustafsson, S., and Stafford, F. (1995), 'Links between Early Childhood Programs and Maternal Employment in Three Countries', *The Future of Children: Long-Term Outcomes of Early Childhood Programs*, 5/3: 161–74.

Gutmann, A. (1988) (ed.), *Democracy and the Welfare State* (Princeton).

Hernes, H. (1987), *Welfare State and Woman Power: Essays in State Feminism* (Oslo).

Hofferth, S., and Deich, S. (1994), 'Recent US Child Care and Family Legislation in Comparative Perspective', *Journal of Family Issues*, 15/3: 424–48.

Hyde, J., and Essex, M. (1991) (eds.), *Parental Leave and Child Care: Setting a Research and Policy Agenda* (Philadelphia).

Joesch, J. (1995), 'Paid Leave and the Timing of Women's Employment Surrounding Birth', paper presented at the Annual Meeting of the Population Association of America, San Francisco, Calif., Apr.

Joshi, H. (1992), 'The Cost of Caring', in Glendinning and Millar (1992), 110–25.

Kamerman, S. (1991), 'Parental Leave and Infant Care', in Hyde and Essex (1991), 11–23.

❖ Meyers, Gornick, and Ross

——and KAHN, A. (1991), *Child Care, Parental Leave, and the Under 3s: Policy Innovation in Europe* (New York).

KILLINGSWORTH, M. R., AND HECKMAN, J. J. (1986), 'Female Labor Supply: A Survey', in Ashenfelter and Layard (1986), 103–204.

KLERMAN, J., AND LEIBOWITZ, A. (1995), 'Labor Supply Effects of State Maternity Leave Legislation', paper presented at the ILR–Cornell Institute for Labor Market Policies Conference, 'Gender and Family Issues in the Workplace', Ithaca, NY, Feb.

KORENMAN, S., AND NEUMARK, D. (1992), 'Marriage, Motherhood, and Wages', *Journal of Human Resources*, 27/2: 233–55.

LEIRA, ARNLAUG (1992), *Welfare States and Working Mothers: The Scandinavian Experience* (Cambridge).

LEIBOWITZ, A., KLERMAN, J., AND WAITE, L. (1992), 'Employment of New Mothers and Child Care Choice: Difference by Children's Age', *Journal of Human Resources*, 22/1: 112–33.

LISTER, R. (1990), 'Women, Economic Dependency, and Citizenship', *Journal of Social Policy*, 19/4: 445–67.

MACRAE, S., DEX, S., AND JOSHI, H. (1996), 'Employment after Childbearing: A Survival Analysis', *Work, Employment and Society*, 10/2: 273–96.

MICHALOPOULUS, C., ROBINS, P., AND GARFINKEL, I. (1992), 'A Structural Model of Labor Supply and Child Care Demand', *Journal of Human Resources*, 27/1: 166–203.

O'CONNELL, M. (1990), 'Maternity Leave Arrangements: 1961–85', *Work and Family Patterns of American Women* (Current Population Reports, Special Studies Series P-23), 165: 11–27.

O'CONNOR, J. (1996), 'From Women in the Welfare State to Gendering Welfare State Regimes', *Current Sociology*, 44/2: 1–130.

OECD (1990), Organization of Economic Cooperation and Development, *Economic Outlook* (Paris).

——(1992), *Economic Outlook* (Paris).

——(1994), *Women and Structural Change: New Perspectives* (Paris).

ORLOFF, A. S. (1993), 'Gender and the Social Rights of Citizenship: The Comparative Analysis of Gender Relations and Welfare States', *American Sociological Review*, 58: 303–28.

——(1996), 'Gender in the Welfare State', *Annual Review of Sociology*, 22: 51–78.

PATEMAN, C. (1988), 'The Patriarchal Welfare State', in Gutmann (1988), 231–60.

ROSENFELD, R. (1993), 'Women's Part-Time Employment: Individual and Country-Level Variation', paper presented at the Meeting of Research Committee No. 28 of the International Sociological Association, Durham, NC, 11 Aug.

——and Birkelund, G. E. (1995), 'Women's Part-Time Work: A Cross-National Comparison', *European Sociological Review*, 11/2: 111–34.

Ruhm, C., and Teague, J. (1995), 'Parental Leave Policies in Europe and North America', paper presented at the ILR–Cornell Institute for Labor Market Policies Conference, 'Gender and Family Issues in the Workplace', Ithaca, NY, Feb.

Schmidt, M. (1993), 'Gendered Labour Force Participation', in Castles (1993), 179–237.

Trzcinski, E. (1991), 'Employers' Parental Leave Policies: Does the Labor Market Provide Parental Leave?', in Hyde and Essex (1991), 209–28.

Waldfogel, J. (forthcoming), 'The Impact of the Family and Medical Leave Act on Coverage, Leave-Taking, Employment and Earnings', *Journal of Policy Analysis and Management*.

——Higuchi, Y., and Abe, M. (forthcoming), 'Family Leave Policies and Women's Employment and Earnings after Childbirth in the United States, Britain, and Japan', *Journal of Population Economics*.

Warme, B., Lundy K., and Lundy L. (1992), (eds.), *Working Part-Time: Risks and Opportunities* (New York).

Whitehouse, G. (1992), 'Legislation and Labour Market Gender Inequality: An Analysis of OECD Countries', *Work, Employment, and Society*, 6/1: 65–86.

5 ❖ Lone Mothers, Economic Well-Being, and Policies

Majella Kilkey and Jonathan Bradshaw

The concept of gender, both as *explanandum* and as *explanans* (Busse-maker and van Kersbergen 1994: 9), has emerged in the 1990s as a significant focus of research in comparative welfare state scholarship. The initial catalyst for this development was indubitably the work of Gøsta Esping-Andersen, and in particular his *Three Worlds of Welfare Capitalism* (1990). Methodologically, that study makes a major contribution to the field of comparative macro social-policy research. It moves us beyond the dominant 'welfare-effort' approach (exemplified, for example, by Wilensky 1975, 1981), which compares welfare states along the single dimension of expenditure on social programmes, and directs us towards a multidimensional and more qualitative approach, that of 'welfare state typologies'. Furthermore, Esping-Andersen attempted to develop a typology that is both historical and dynamic, and in which the dimensions of variation are explicit, and sufficiently narrow to be operationalized in an examination of more than three or four cases—precisely the qualities that are generally lacking in previous typologies of welfare state variation (see e.g. those of Titmuss 1974; Furniss and Tilton 1977; Mishra 1977, 1990; Korpi 1980).

While making a considerable methodological contribution, Esping-Andersen's theoretical and conceptual advance is limited, however, by one crucial factor; the absence of attention to gender. Analyses by feminist[1] scholars have revealed not only that Esping-Andersen's study, like its predecessors, is 'gender blind', but that the theoretical perspective underlying his analysis, and the dimensions of variation he employs, are deeply gendered. The result is that, when applied empirically, the typology has been found incapable of predicting variations across states in elements of welfare provision that might be considered important from the perspective of gender. Such observations have prompted feminist researchers to undertake the task of constructing a gender-sensitive typology of welfare state variation. The aim of this chapter is to contribute to that effort.

We begin by outlining the most salient elements of the feminist critique of Esping-Andersen's study. In the second section, we examine the frameworks that have been developed by those attempting to place gender centre stage in comparative welfare state research. Drawing on our assessment of these, we adopt Ruth Lister's (1994a,b) dimension of 'defamilialization',[2] and, in an empirical attempt to operationalize this, we follow Barbara Hobson (1994) and Bettina Cass (1992) in utilizing lone mothers as an analytical category. We then employ the 'model-families' method to compare the policy environment for lone-mother families in the fifteen EU member states. We conclude by reflecting on both the empirical and methodological significance of our findings.

❖ The Three Worlds of Welfare Capitalism: It's a Man's World

The central theoretical plank of Esping-Andersen's study is T. H. Marshall's (1950) citizenship paradigm. Following Marshall, Esping-Andersen (1990: 21) identifies social citizenship as constituting 'the core idea of a welfare state', and he seeks to compare welfare states according to the quality and nature of the social rights of citizenship. Incorporated in Marshall's thesis (1950: 87) is the notion of 'an image of an ideal citizenship against which achievements can be measured and towards which aspirations can be directed'. Marshall, however, was concerned with the amelioration of class-based inequalities, and his ideal is formulated in juxtaposition with the differentiation and inequality associated with social class. Thus, the ideal status of the citizen should be undifferentiated and equal.

Feminist scholars (Stacey and Price 1981; Vogel 1991; Fraser and Gordon 1994; Walby 1994), however, have problematized Marshall's concept of citizenship. In the first place, it negates consideration of gender-based inequalities. More crucially, in asking the question of in whose image is the 'ideal citizen' cast, Marshall's concept of citizenship is revealed to be a gendered construct. As Julia O'Connor (1993) notes, the paid worker in the public sphere is the model, and the appropriate citizenship rights are those associated with paid employment. Women, however (to a greater degree than men), have roles and responsibilities other than, or in addition to, that of a paid worker—for example, a carer in the private sphere. Moreover, precisely often because of these other responsibilities, women

❖ Majella Kilkey and Jonathan Bradshaw

have a differentiated and unequal material condition that undifferentiated citizenship rights fail to address: formal equality in their status as citizens, thus, may not translate into equality in practice (O'Connor 1993).

It is in applying Marshall's theory of citizenship without regard to its feminist critique that Esping-Andersen's examination of the quality and nature of social rights across welfare states assumes its gender bias. This is apparent in his dimension of the public–private nexus in welfare provision where private is analysed solely in relation to the market, and the family is ignored (Langan and Ostner 1991; Sainsbury 1994b). Yet, the family is one of the most important contexts for the structuring of women's lives. In particular, feminists identify the family as a key site of male power over women (see e.g. for reviews Walby 1990 and Pascall 1997). The family is also the main source of welfare provision in all welfare states (Taylor-Gooby 1991). Largely as a result of gendered-power relations, familial welfare in all countries remains overwhelmingly the responsibility of women (Bryson *et al.* 1994; van der Lippe and Roelofs 1995; Eurostat 1997). It has well-documented implications for women's lives in relation to their employment patterns, pay levels, economic well-being, capacity for independence, and ultimately their power *vis-à-vis* men.

While the relationship between the welfare state and the family is, therefore, of central importance to women, Esping-Andersen's key dimension for assessing the quality of welfare states for citizens, decommodification, fails to analyse this. As Mary Daly (1994a) argues, decommodification— the degree to which social rights free individuals from reliance on the market—is constructed in relation to male lifestyles, and has only limited relevance to women.[3] While independence from the market is likely to be a significant criterion for men's emancipation, 'female independence is of a different calibre' (Daly 1994a: 108). Since men's control over women is a central feature of womens lives, independence from this is an important prerequisite for women's emancipation. One source of autonomy is access to an independent income. It gives women 'voice' to negotiate power relations within families, and 'exit' to opt out of an unsatisfactory relationship (Hobson 1990: 236).

Welfare states are deeply implicated in shaping women's access to an independent income. Social policy may, for example, support women's waged labour. It may provide services or cash transfers that reduce both the burden of women's domestic labour and the costs entailed in undertaking paid work (Orloff 1993; Sainsbury 1994a). It may seek to strengthen women's attachment to and position in the labour market via provisions for maternity leave and equality policies (O'Connor 1993). Finally, welfare states may present an important source of employment for women (Orloff

LONE MOTHERS AND ECONOMIC WELL-BEING ❖

1993; Daly 1994*a*; Meyer 1994). Alternatively, social policy may award those not engaged in the labour market with an independent income. Depending on the amount, method, and conditions of payment, child benefits, extended parental-leave programmes, social assistance when child-rearing responsibilities preclude the obligation to seek work, and carers' allowances can represent an important economic resource to women.

Conversely, welfare states may also reinforce women's dependency on men by not facilitating their access to an independent income. Thus, if welfare states fail to intervene along the lines outlined above, they are likely to contribute to women's subjugation in the family. Feminist research also demonstrates, however, the manner in which welfare states actively compound women's dependence via, for example: the status of 'dependant', which may be accorded to women in the social-security and taxation systems; the designation of the 'couple' as the unit of assessment for the purposes of taxation and social-assistance benefits; the non-recognition of women's caring responsibilities during the life course in the social-security system, especially contributory schemes; and the rolling-back of care services, particularly for the elderly, sick, and disabled (Land 1993; Lewis 1993; Orloff 1993; Daly 1994*b*; Sainsbury 1994*a*, 1996).

In structuring women's access to an independent income along the above lines, the welfare state is an active force in the ordering of gender relations. Esping-Andersen's study, however, fails to capture the implications of the quality of social rights for gender relations, since his third and final dimension—stratification—is concerned solely with the manner in which social rights structure class hierarchies.

The feminist critique of each of Esping-Andersen's dimensions suggests that his typology is limited in its ability to understand both how gender relations have influenced the substance of welfare states and how the substance of welfare states affects gender relations. Early feminist engagement with Esping-Andersen's typology applied it to elements of the welfare state that might be considered important from the perspective of women and gender relations—for example, childcare provision (Leira 1993; Gustafsson 1994); the treatment of women's unpaid work within the tax/benefit system (Shaver and Bradshaw 1995); women's bodily and reproductive rights (Shaver 1992*a*); and the role that the welfare state plays in the direct employment of women (Meyer 1994). In general, the results of those applications confounded Esping-Andersen's observed variations in welfare states. The focus of feminist scholarship has, thus, shifted to one of constructing typologies more sensitive to gender.

❖ Majella Kilkey and Jonathan Bradshaw

❖ Wollstonecraft's Dilemma and Welfare Typologies

Research on the construction of gender-friendly models of welfare state variation remains, however, very much in its infancy. A key impediment to progress is the difficulty in identifying appropriate dimensions for analysis. While Esping-Andersen employed the dimension of decommodification to reflect what he believed to be the interests of paid workers, the task of identifying women's interests appears to be more contentious. In part, the difficulty is due to the centuries-old dilemma that has permeated feminist theory (and action): how to conceptualize women's (social) citizenship. Termed by Carole Pateman (1989) as 'Wollstonecraft's dilemma', it is characterized by somewhat more nuance among those currently engaging with the construction of welfare state typologies. Thus, with a view to feminist criticisms of Marshall's 'ideal citizenship', a consensus appears to have developed: it advances that a recognition of women's difference on the part of welfare states is necessary if women are to achieve equality with men in respect of social rights. It is, as Helga Hernes (1987: 32) asserts, that the challenge for welfare states is '. . . to design a gender equality policy that allows for pluralism and gender difference while guaranteeing equality'. This consensus tends to fold, however, once the question—difference with regard to what?—is contemplated. Two strands emerge: the one, advocating equality in difference via employment; the other, emphasizing equality in difference via care. Empirical attempts to gender welfare states tend to be characterized by an emphasis on one or other of these positions, but rarely both.

In engaging with the dilemma of what constitutes women's social citizenship, Cass (1994: 110–11), while supporting a view that recognition and support should be attributed to caring activities, contends: 'to do only this . . . would enshrine *care-giving work* as women's *work*. If the social welfare system legitimated and (inadequately) financially supported women as caregivers, why should activists concerned with *women's rights* insist on more *equitable participation* of women in *paid employment* . . .?' (emphasis added). Cass's association of caregiving with work, and of women's rights with equitable participation in the labour market, is central to understanding the equality in difference via employment perspective. Thus, on the one hand, the route to women's equality is employment on a par with men, largely since it has the potential to mitigate women's dependence, and, thereby, limit the control of men over them. On the other hand, the source of women's difference is their overwhelming responsibility within the family for caregiving, which, since it constrains their ability to participate in the labour market on an equal footing with men, is a barrier to their social citizenship. The provision of social rights that guarantee women equality in the labour market by recognizing their difference in condition provoked by care work is, therefore, the key to women's social citizenship.

It is hence also the key to constructing a typology that is sensitive to women and gender relations. While a number of studies fall within this genre (see e.g. Siaroff 1994; Gornick *et al.* 1997), Jane Lewis's (1992) and Lewis and Iloma Ostner's (1994) examination of welfare regimes in terms of variations in the level of adherence to a male-breadwinner–female-housewife household form, is perhaps the most significant. This is a typology based on elucidating the gendered assumptions encoded in welfare states. It is, however, firmly situated within the equality in difference via employment perspective. Thus, as Lewis (1992: 163) avers, her typology 'serves as an indicator of the way in which women have been treated in social security systems, of the level of service provision particularly in regard to child care; and of the nature of married women's position in the labour market'. In ideal-typical form, therefore, the male-breadwinner model would 'find married women excluded from the labour market, firmly subordinated to their husbands for the purposes of social security entitlements and tax, and expected to undertake the work of caring . . . at home without public support' (Lewis 1992: 162). Lewis, and Lewis and Ostner, compare Ireland, Britain, Germany, France and Sweden, classifying Britain, Ireland, and Germany as strong adherents to the male-breadwinner form, France as moderately so, and Sweden as only weakly so, tending instead towards a dual-breadwinner model.

While social rights associated with women's access to and equality in conditions of paid work are the central focus of the former approach, those associated with undertaking care form the key elements in the construction of typologies in the second approach. As a key exponent of the equality in difference via care perspective, Trudie Knijn (1994: 103) argues:

> Caring for children is a social activity as important as many other . . . women should be allowed to claim the right to an income from that activity . . . a good welfare state needs to consider the value of caring citizens—people, mostly women, who voluntarily, and perhaps in contradiction of their own interests, provide care in their immediate familial and social networks . . . care-givers should be rewarded by their welfare state because of their direct involvement in daily care. The role of 'citizen-mother' . . . should be a viable option.

Essentially, for Knijn, care is not perceived as work. She thus follows a perspective that rejects the conceptualization of care-as-labour for its simplicity, and, in contrast, points to care-as-social-relations (McLaughlin and Glendinning 1994). In the first place, care is, therefore, perceived as a social rather than as a private/family activity; and as one element of the web of activities that constitutes the social, it is as deserving of the status of citizenship as paid work is. Secondly, care is relational, and as such its character is complex: it may constitute 'caring about' and/or 'caring for' (Graham 1983; Finch 1993); it may be characterized by love and/or labour (Graham 1983; Ungerson 1990); and it entails a variety of different relationships rather than simply one of the labourer–cared-for and the dependant–non-dependant (Waerness 1984). That women undertake responsibilities for care, therefore, is not inherently detrimental to their interests and equality with men. Rather, it is the relegation of care to the sphere of private responsibility, and the privileging of paid work in the construction of citizenship rights, that are problematic for women, since it is in this context that care develops as a gendered activity. Thus, the provision of social rights that recognize the obligation and right to care as an equally valid base for citizenship as paid work has the potential to degender care, and, as such, is central to women's equality (Knijn and Kremer 1997).

From this perspective, care as opposed to paid work has been placed at the centre of attempts to develop a typology of welfare states that is sensitive to gender (see e.g. McLaughlin and Glendinning 1994; Alber 1995; Jenson 1997; Knijn and Kremer 1997; Mahon 1997; Ungerson 1997; Bussemaker 1998). The most significant empirical work to date is that of Knijn and Kremer (1997). They apply the dimension of the right to time for care, defined as the ability to choose to undertake care as opposed to paid work in respect of children and the frail elderly,[4] to an examination of the British, Danish, and Dutch welfare states. Knijn and Kremer gauge the quality of this right via an examination of the availability of labour-market-related parental-leave programmes, exemption from the obligation to work for caregivers in respect of social-security systems, payments for care and regulations in labour law and social-security systems that are favourable to part-time employees. The researchers characterize all three countries in their study as being in transition, but along different lines. Thus, in Denmark, there is judged to be a movement away from a citizen-worker model, which implied only a limited option for undertaking care rather than paid work, towards a more balanced configuration, especially in regard to care for children via parental leaves. The Netherlands is considered to be moving in the opposite direction: away from valuing women's care to emphasizing their employment. Finally, while Britain has begun to institutionalize special non-contributory payments for carers and 'benefit credits' for those choosing 'long-term' care, it is judged to have done little to value periods of 'short-term' care—for example, via parental-leave programmes.

LONE MOTHERS AND ECONOMIC WELL-BEING ❖

While the dichotomy between an approach that places paid work centre stage and one that has care as the central focus is prevalent in the literature, the contribution of such a division to the task of constructing a typology of welfare state variation sensitive to gender may be limited. This is the case since neither approach fully captures what is likely to be important in an examination of the manner in which welfare states influence the balance of gendered power within individual and societal relationships. Equality in access to and conditions of employment is a key mechanism through which women have the potential to gain a modicum of independence from men's control. The gendered division of responsibility for care is, in part, both a cause and an effect of women's unequal position in the labour market, and gendered power relations more generally. Yet, the receipt of care is vital to the meeting of human needs, and as such is an important societal rather than individual responsibility. Moreover, given the complexity of personal relationships over the life course, and the extensive time commitment that may be required to meet care needs, to undertake care is itself an activity that warrants societal support via the award of social rights of citizenship. While such rights are important for all individuals—that is, both male and female—the latter's material position in relation to care implies that the valuing of carework within the framework of citizenship rights has a particular practical salience for women. The extent of its significance, however, will be influenced by the degree to which it accords women independence from men.

It may be the case, therefore, that an examination of the manner in which welfare states structure women's relationship to paid work and care, as opposed to paid work or care, may be more appropriate if we want to gauge the degree to which social rights alter the balance of gendered power within families. The concept of 'defamilialization' developed by Lister (1994a,b) would seem to provide a useful dimension for doing so. Lister defines defamilialization as 'the degree to which individual adults can uphold a socially acceptable standard of living, independently of family relationships, either through paid work or social security provision' (1994a: 37, 1994b: 32). Lone-mother families may represent an interesting analytical category in employing this dimension cross-nationally.[5] As the sole main carer of a child or children and the sole possible breadwinner in a family, the dual responsibility of lone mothers to provide both cash and care is likely to represent an extreme in the tensions between paid work and care responsibilities. How women in such a situation are treated, therefore, may be the quintessential example of how welfare states construct the relationship between paid work and caring for all women (Cass 1992). The level of lone mothers' economic well-being, whether relying on social security or engaged in paid work, may also provide a test of the degree to which welfare states enable women to live independently of men. In this sense, the position of lone mothers *vis-à-vis* the welfare state may also be indicative of the strengths and weaknesses of social rights for women in general, for, as Hobson (1994: 176) argues: 'the kinds of state support solo mothers receive indirectly shape the equality in families. Solo motherhood is the reflector or rearview mirror for the dynamics of power and dependency—the more difficult and stigmatized solo motherhood is in a society, the greater the barriers against opting out of a bad marriage.'

❖ LONE MOTHERS: Prevalence, Employment and Poverty

The increasing prevalence of lone-mother families across industrialized countries, such that, in some countries at least, lone motherhood can be perceived as another stage in the female life cycle (Ford and Millar 1998: 19), provides the context in which the above arguments assume greater validity. Estimates[6] of the prevalence of lone-mother families as a proportion of all families with children (Table 5.1) suggest that, with the exception of Italy, the incidence of lone motherhood has increased in the countries for which data are available over the period *c.* 1980 to *c.* 1990. The extent of this increase, however, varies considerably across countries. Thus, for example, it appears to be greatest in Norway and the UK, where the proportion of lone-mother families has more than doubled, and least in Austria, where there has only been an 8 per cent increase in their prevalence. The data in Table 5.1 also suggest that the significance of widowhood as a route into lone motherhood has been decreasing. Instead, relationship dissolution and births outside married and cohabiting unions are the most important causes in most countries.[7]

Both the increase in the prevalence of lone-mother families and the proportion of lone mothers who are divorced, separated, and single-never married, might indicate that to raise children independently of men is an option that is increasingly viable for women. The mechanisms by which women are enabled to do so, that is via employment or caring, and the degree to which they are enabled to uphold a socially acceptable standard of living, however, are important factors when considering the 'quality' of this option.

There is considerable cross-national variation in the overall rates of employment among lone mothers, the balance between full-time and part-time paid work, and the degree to which lone mothers' employment patterns converge with those of their other counterparts (Table 5.2). Thus, in Australia, Ireland, the Netherlands, New Zealand, and the UK, only a

Table 5.1. Prevalence of lone-mother families and lone mothers by marital status in twenty-one countries, 1980 and 1990

Country	Lone-mother families[a] as a % of all families with dependent children		Percentage of lone-mother population widowed (W), separated (Sep.), divorced (D), and single never-married (Sing.)[a]							
	c.1980	c.1990	c.1980[b]				c.1990[b]			
			W	Sep.	D	Sing.	W	Sep.	D	Sing.
Australia[c]	11 (1980)	16 (1994)	14	30	37	20	8	34	32	25
Austria	12 (1981)	13 (1993)		64		36		19	32	49
Belgium	6 (1985)	10 (1992)	20	35	37	9	9	40	40	12
Canada	14 (1981)	16 (1991)	33	29	27	11	23	25	32	20
Denmark	11 (1980)	16 (1990)	20	15	59	6	8	22	45	25
Finland	11 (1980)	14 (1993)	••	••	••	••	7	14	48	31
France	9 (1982)	11 (1990)	30	13	40	17	19	15	43	23
Germany[d]	12 (1980)	16 (1992)	50	9	31	10	30	9	38	23
Greece	n.a.	9 (1990/91)	••	••	••	••	••	••	••	••
Ireland	6 (1981)	9 (1991)	73	24	0	3	54	35	0	11
Italy	5 (1983)	5 (1991)	42	39	7	12	34	48	7	12
Japan	8 (1980)	10 (1990)	36	10	49	5	25	4	64	5
Luxembourg	n.a.	6 (1992)	••	••	••	••	14	6	68	12
Netherlands	10 (1981)	14 (1992)	51	1	42	6	29	9	45	17
New Zealand	11 (1981)	21 (1991)	19		61	21	8		55	38

❖ MAJELLA KILKEY AND JONATHAN BRADSHAW

Norway	9 (1980)	19 (1991)	13	11	51	24	6	15	37	43
Portugal	9 (1981)	11 (1991)	56	28	6	10	51	22	16	10
Spain[e]	5 (1981)	7[f] (1991)	51	8	35	15	••	••	••	••
Sweden	14 (1985)	15 (1990)	6	24	47	39	4	9	41	46
UK[g]	10 (1980)	22 (1995)	17	28	39	20	5	22	34	39
USA	19 (1980)	25 (1991)	11	28	44	17	6	22	37	35

[a] Definitions are not consistent across countries (see sources).

[b] Precise dates are as for the lone-mother estimate for all countries, except Australia (c.1980 data are for 1982) and Japan (data are for 1983 and 1993).

[c] Data for c.1980 refer to lone parents as opposed to lone mothers.

[d] 1980 data refer to the former FRG; 1992 data refer to unified Germany.

[e] Data for Spain are based on the region of Madrid.

[f] Data refer to lone parents.

[g] Data exclude Northern Ireland.

Note: •• = not available.

Sources: Lone-mother estimates: Bradshaw *et al.* (1996a: table 2.1) and unpublished data, except UK (Haskey 1998) and Ireland (McCashin 1997). Marital-status data: Bradshaw *et al.* (1996a: table 2.2) and unpublished data, except UK (Haskey 1998) and Australia (Whiteford 1997); Canada: Lindsay (1992).

Table 5.2. Percentage of lone and other mothers employed full-time and part-time, early 1990s

Country	% of the lone mothers employed				% of other mothers employed			
	Full-time[a]	Part-time[a]	All employed	% of all employed who are full-time	Full-time	Part-time	All employed	% of all employed who are full-time
Australia (1994)	23	20	43	53	24	32	56	43
Austria[b] (1993)	43	15	58	74	28	18	46	61
Belgium (1992)	52	16	68	76	36	22	61	59
Canada (1992)	42	10	52	81	19	46	65	29
Denmark (1994)	59	10	69	86	64	20	84	76
Finland (1993)	61	4	65	94	62	8	70	89
France (1992)	67	15	82	82	49	20	68	72
Germany (1992)	46	21	67	69	29	28	57	51
Greece[c] (1992)	..	..	72	..	..	..	50	..
Ireland[d] (1993)	..	..	22	..	..	..	32	..
Italy (1993)	58	11	69	84	29	12	41	71
Japan[e] (1993)	46	27	87	63	17	20	54	46
Luxembourg (1992)	61	13	73	84	32	13	45	71
Netherlands (1994)	16	24	40	40	13	39	52	25
New Zealand (1991)	17	10	27	63	31	27	58	53

❖ MAJELLA KILKEY AND JONATHAN BRADSHAW

Norway (1991)	44	17	61	72	40	37	77	52
Portugal[f] (1991)	61	10	71	86	48	7	55	87
Spain[g] (1991)	••	••	68	••	••	••	38	••
Sweden (1994)	41	29	70	59	42	38	80	53
UK[h] (1990/92)	17	24	42	40	21	41	63	33
USA (1992)	47	13	60	78	45	19	64	70

[a] Full-time is usually greater than, or equal to, thirty hours per week, part-time is usually less than thirty hours per week. Not all countries conform to this definition (see sources).

[b] Data exclude 20% of lone mothers and 12% of other mothers who are on parental leave.

[c] Data refer to: (1) activity rate rather than employment rates; (2) age group 25–49 only; (3) widowed and divorced lone mothers only.

[d] McCashin (1997) estimates that 71% of lone parents employed in 1995 worked full-time.

[e] All-employed figure for lone mothers includes 7% working in a family business and 7% self-employed, for whom it is not possible to distinguish between full-time and part-time. All employed figure for other mothers includes 16% self-employed, for whom it is not possible to distinguish between full-time and part-time. Data for other mothers refers to all other women, even those without children.

[f] Excludes widows, since their inclusion biases results; 30% of widows are employed compared with 66, 65, 81% respectively of single, separated, and divorced women.

[g] Data are based on the region of Madrid and are activity rates.

[h] Data exclude Northern Ireland.

Note: •• = not available.

Sources: Bradshaw et al. (1996a: table 1.3) and unpublished data; Canada: Lindsay (1992).

LONE MOTHERS AND ECONOMIC WELL-BEING ❖

minority of lone mothers participate in the labour market. In Ireland and the Netherlands, less than one-third of lone mothers are in employment, while, in the other three countries, the proportion is around 40 per cent. In the remaining countries, the majority of lone mothers undertake paid work, but the rate at which they do so varies. In one group (Austria, Belgium, Denmark, Finland, Germany, Italy, Norway, Spain, and the USA) the rate is less than 70 per cent, in another (Greece, Luxembourg, Portugal, and Sweden) it is less than 75 per cent, and in France and Japan, it is over 80 per cent.

Only in the Netherlands and the UK is part-time working more prevalent among those lone mothers in employment. While in Australia there is an almost equal balance between full-time and part-time hours, in the remaining countries full-time working is the dominant pattern. Its prevalence ranges, however, from less than 70 per cent of those in employment in Germany, Japan, New Zealand, and Sweden; to less than 80 per cent in Austria, Belgium, Norway, and the USA; to over 80 per cent in Canada, Denmark, France, Italy, Luxembourg, and Portugal; and in Finland it stands at 94 per cent.

Comparing lone and other mothers' overall employment rates, countries appear to be equally divided between those in which lone mothers are more likely to work than the latter, and those in which the opposite is the case. Within each group though, distinct categories of countries are distinguishable. Thus, within the former group, both lone and other mothers have relatively high rates of employment in Belgium and France. In Austria, Germany, Greece, Italy, Japan, Luxembourg, Portugal, and Spain, however, in contrast to lone mothers, other mothers have relatively low rates of employment. In countries in which lone mothers are less likely to be in employment than other mothers, we can identify three groupings: first, that in which both groups of mothers have a low employment rate (Australia, Ireland, the Netherlands, and New Zealand); secondly, a group where both types of mother have a relatively high rate of employment (Denmark, Finland, Sweden, Norway, and the USA); and, thirdly, a group composed of Canada and the UK, where, while lone mothers' employment rate is low, that of other mothers is relatively high. In relation to the balance between full-time and part-time working, we find that in all countries except Portugal, where the difference between both groups of mothers is small, lone mothers are more likely to be in full-time employment than are other mothers.

The degree to which lone-mother families are vulnerable to poverty, how this compares with two-parent families, and the extent to which lone mothers' employment status affects their economic well-being also vary considerably across countries (Table 5.3). Thus in Australia, Austria, the

Table 5.3. Poverty rates: lone-parent and two-parent families, and lone mothers by employment status, c.1990 (%)

Country	Poverty rate		Poverty rate for lone mothers	
	Lone-parent families	Two-parent families	Not in paid work	In paid work
Australia	42	9	64	20
Austria	46	38	58	42
Belgium	11	5	29	3
Canada	43	10	73	30
Denmark	6	3	13	7
Finland	6	3	31	5
France	23	13	44	12
Germany	26	19	64	11
Greece	18	16	24	13
Ireland	24	13	40	7
Italy	18	12	22	8
Luxembourg	12	5	14	4
Netherlands	34	7	51	9
Norway	7	3	25	7
Portugal	28	21	41	23
Spain	28	10	25	17
Sweden	5	3	16	4
UK	47	11	66	28
USA	56	16	93	43
Average	25	11	42	14

Notes: Data for all countries except Greece, Ireland, and Portugal, are derived from the 'third-wave' LIS. People in poverty are defined as those whose equivalent disposable income is less than 50% of the average equivalent disposable income in their country. Data for Greece, Ireland, and Portugal are derived from national Household Budget Surveys. People in poverty are defined as those whose expenditure is less than 50% of the average expenditure in their country.

Sources: LIS data (Bradshaw and Chen: 1997; Bradshaw 1998) for all countries, except Luxembourg, the data for which are derived from Mitchell (1991). Household Budget Survey data: Eurostat (1994).

USA, Canada, and the UK lone parents [8] have the highest poverty rates: between 42 and 56 per cent. In contrast, the poverty rate among lone parents in Belgium, Denmark, Finland, Luxembourg, Norway and Sweden is around 10 per cent or less. Between these two extreme groupings, however, there is much diversity. In all countries, the incidence of poverty is higher among lone-parent families than among two-parent families.

Across all countries except Spain, the incidence of poverty among lone

LONE MOTHERS AND ECONOMIC WELL-BEING ❖

mothers not undertaking paid work is higher than that of the lone-parent population as a whole. The former have the highest rate of poverty in Canada and the USA and the lowest in Denmark and Luxembourg. The risk of poverty, however, decreases with employment: on average, across the countries, lone mothers in paid work are almost three times less likely to be poor than those not in paid work. The role that labour-market participation plays in poverty reduction varies considerably between countries. It appears to be least effective in Austria, Greece, Spain, and Portugal, where non-employed lone mothers are less than twice as likely to be in poverty than their employed counterparts; in contrast, in Belgium the incidence of poverty is reduced to a tenth of what it was as a result of labour-market participation.

The observed variations across countries in the rates of employment and poverty in relation to lone mothers would appear to suggest that welfare states differ both in the degree to which and the manner in which—that is, via paid work or social security—they defamilialize. To establish more clearly, however, whether this is indeed the case, and if so the types of mechanisms involved, it is necessary to compare more closely the social and fiscal policies that exist in each country to assist lone mothers.

❖ COMPARING THE TAX/BENEFIT SYSTEMS FOR LONE MOTHERS

All welfare states have some combination of cash benefits, tax reliefs, or services in kind that provide assistance for lone parents with the costs of raising children alone. They may take the form of cash benefits, tax allowances, housing subsidies, free or subsidized services, and/or child-maintenance arrangements. They may be paid in respect of children, in some countries at an enhanced level for a lone parent, or they may be paid in respect of the status of being a lone parent. Together they supplement or replace market income and contribute to lifting lone parents out of poverty. The policies that make up the package may not be conceived of as having the same purposes, and in neither their origins nor their current objectives may they be primarily concerned with poverty relief. Nevertheless, the package as a whole represents the effort that a nation makes to mitigate some of the (extra) costs borne by lone parents in raising children. This 'lone-parent package' is a measure of the extent to which the needs of lone parents and their children are conceived of as a collective or state responsibility, as opposed to a purely individual or family one.

A 'model-families-matrix' method has been used to allow comparisons to be made of the structure and value of the 'packages' of cash benefits, tax relief, services, and charges that contribute towards meeting the needs of lone parents.[9] The data are derived from the work of the European Observatory on National Family Policies, whose members complete a 'matrix' that summarizes what a number of selected family types, in specific circumstances, with given earnings levels would receive in each country. The results presented here relate to the situation in May 1996 and are derived from the data collected for the 1996 report of the Observatory (Ditch *et al.* 1998). The data for 1996 are available only for the countries of the EU.

The methods employed and the assumptions made are discussed and critically evaluated in the 1994 Observatory report (Ditch *et al.* 1995) and will not be repeated here. However, it is worth mentioning that what we are measuring is what ought to be received as a result of the tax and benefit system rather than what actually occurs in practice, and that this may be one reason for any mismatches that we observe later.

In this chapter the focus of the analysis is the contribution of public policy to the income of a lone-parent family both in employment and out of employment and receiving social assistance. Unfortunately we cannot cover the arrangements in social-insurance schemes to support lone parents who are unemployed, widowed, and so forth, because data on those schemes are not collected. To obtain the net income for lone parents with earnings, income tax payable by a given lone parent was deducted. Then the social-security contributions required to be paid by a given lone parent at those earnings was deducted, including all compulsory statutory contributions whether they fund social-security entitlements, health entitlements, or other things. The test is that they are required of employees by the state. This gives post-tax income. Then non-income-related and income-related cash benefits that may be made to a given family at that income level are added. These are mainly family allowances or child benefits, but in some countries social assistance may be payable to low earners, and lone parents may be entitled to child support, maintenance, or alimony, and this is included if there is a scheme for advancing at least some of the payments due from public funds irrespective of the compliance of the non-resident parent. We also make assumptions about health costs. The baseline assumption is that health care is provided free of charge and that its quality and availability are equal between countries. Then we price what families might be actually required to pay for a standard package of health care. Account is also taken of the costs or value of free or subsidized pre-school childcare provision and the costs/benefits of schooling.

Finally, account is taken of housing costs. One of the most problematic aspects of this methodology relates to the treatment of housing costs. There is no way of overcoming the fact that tenure patterns vary between countries, and that housing costs vary within countries according to a host of factors—direct and indirect subsidies, geographical location, the size and age of the dwelling, the length of occupation, and many other factors. It would be easiest to ignore housing costs altogether. However, housing costs and housing subsidies are in many countries an important element of the lone-parent package and to ignore them altogether would be to misrepresent the impact of that package. Because of the difficulties involved, results are presented both before and after housing costs. In addition, local property-based taxes used to fund local services are taken into account. Deducting net housing and local taxes—that is, the amount payable after the receipt of any relevant housing benefit or rebates—gives net income after housing costs.

In the social-assistance cases, national informants provide estimates of what a lone parent on social assistance would receive, taking account of the impact of the benefits and services and housing costs in the way described for earners. Where payments vary between local areas they are asked to nominate a 'typical' municipality and follow its guidelines (see Eardley *et al.* 1996 for a full discussion of the strengths and weaknesses of these methods).

❖ Lone Mothers with Earnings

Figure 5.1 takes a lone mother in employment earning half national average (male) earnings—that is, either working full-time in a low-paid job (or on the minimum wage if one exists) or part-time in a higher-paid job. It can be seen that earnings vary. They are lower in the south European countries than in the northern countries. They are lower in France, Finland, and Sweden than other northern European countries; in those three countries there is certainly a trade-off between earnings and the social wage. The chart then shows the impact of direct taxes (income tax and social-security contributions) on earnings. Post-tax income falls in all countries but less in the south European countries, Ireland, Luxembourg, and the UK than, for example, in Denmark, Netherlands, Finland, and Sweden. These deductions from net income as a result of taxation are offset in all countries by cash benefits paid in respect of children or, in some countries, also lone parents. The value of these benefits at this income are highest in Germany, Ireland, Finland, Sweden, and the UK and lowest in the south European countries. Indeed in Ireland and the UK the benefit package exceeds the amount deducted in direct taxes, leaving the lone mother with a net addition to her earnings. Then comes the impact of charges for health and education. In France the value of school meals actually increases net income and in Denmark, Germany, Luxembourg,

Fig. 5.1. The redistributive impact of policies for lone mothers with low earnings

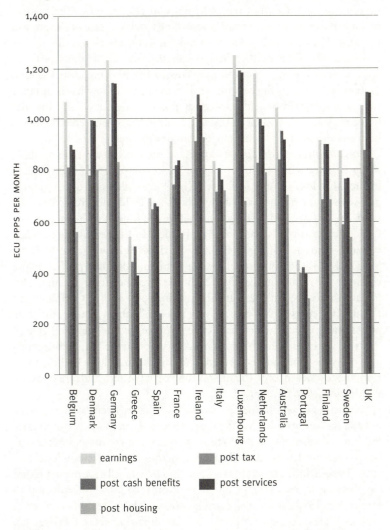

Note: Statistics are for a lone mother earning half national average earnings, with one child aged 7.

Finland, Sweden, and the UK there are no charges. Finally, there is the impact of net housing costs. These are comparatively low in Ireland (because of a differential rent scheme) and also in Italy. The relative income of this lone mother varies according to which stage of the process of redistribution is taken. The lone mother in Denmark has the highest earnings. The lone mother in Luxembourg has the highest post-tax income until the impact of housing costs. After housing costs the lone mother in Ireland is the best off—this is the result of low levels of tax, a well-targeted child-benefit package at this earnings level, and low net housing costs. The UK, Germany, and Denmark also have comparatively high post-housing-costs income for this lone mother.

However, these comparisons do not take into account any costs of child-care associated with working. In Figure 5.2 we compare the net disposable incomes of a lone mother with a pre-school-age child not requiring child-care with a lone mother with a pre-school-age child after childcare costs, again on half average earnings and before the impact of housing costs. Childcare is assumed to be the most prevalent full-time childcare in each country—thus in Denmark it is a subsidized place in a public day nursery; in the UK it is the full costs of a private childminder partly offset by the childcare disregard in Family Credit. France, Belgium, Ireland, and Finland have free childcare at this earnings level and in Germany and Portugal the costs of childcare are very low. In all other countries the costs of childcare reduce the net disposable resources of the lone mother, and the costs are particularly high in Greece, Spain, and the UK. Before child-care costs the lone mother in the UK at this earnings level had the third from highest net income (before housing costs). After childcare costs the UK drops back to ninth place.

So whether or not the lone parent needs childcare to enable her to work outside the home makes a difference to her in-work income. But so does the level of earnings of the lone mothers. Some countries have a tax-benefit system that is relatively more generous to low-earning lone par-ents. These include France, Ireland, and the UK, who all have means-tested supplements to low earnings, and in the Nordic countries it is possible to receive social assistance when earnings are low. There are other countries, notably France (again), Belgium, and Luxembourg, where there are tax allowances that are of greater value to lone mothers (and others) the higher their earnings.

❖ Lone Mothers without Earnings

So far we have looked at the tax/benefit package as it impacts on lone par-ents with income from employment. But, as we have seen, the proportion

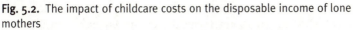

Fig. 5.2. The impact of childcare costs on the disposable income of lone mothers

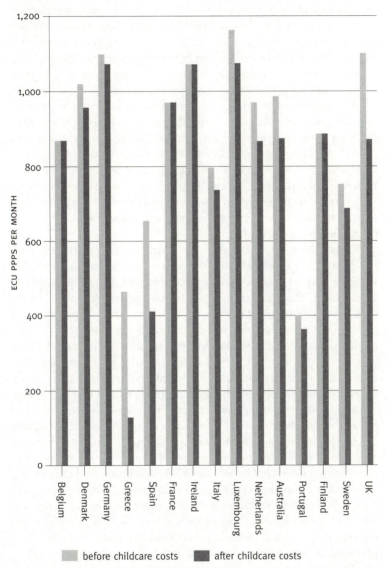

Note: Statistics are for a lone mother earning half national average earnings, with one pre-school child, before housing costs.

of lone mothers in employment varies between countries. Those lone mothers who are not in employment have to rely either on a social-security benefit or, if none exists, on income from relatives or friends. Figure 5.3 compares the net disposable income of a lone mother with one school-age child on social assistance before and after housing costs. It is important to make the comparison both before and after housing costs because in some countries lone parents have to pay some or all of their housing costs out of their social assistance, whereas in others housing costs are fully covered or free. In Greece and Spain social assistance is either non-existent or insufficient to cover (the assumed) housing costs and in the other south European countries social assistance is also very low, particularly after housing costs. This may explain the relatively high levels of employment among lone mothers in these countries. Among the north European countries it can be seen that the level of social assistance varies considerably, with the highest post-housing-costs rates payable to lone parents in Denmark, Germany, Finland, and Sweden and lower rates payable in France and Austria.

Perhaps more important than the actual level of social assistance payable is the replacement rate—the ratio of the income a lone mother would be entitled to on social assistance to her net disposable income in employment. The replacement rate is an indicator of the financial incentives facing a lone mother in choosing whether to enter employment. Of course, the replacement rate will depend on the earnings that the lone mother would be able to obtain. Furthermore, financial incentives will be only one of the factors that will determine whether or not she takes employment. Nevertheless, Figure 5.4 presents notional replacement rates (social assistance as a proportion of net disposable income at half average earnings prior to housing costs) before and after childcare costs. The higher the replacement rates, the less financial incentive there is for being in employment. Replacement rates are higher if childcare costs are deducted from in-work income. Among the north European countries replacement rates exceed 80 per cent in Belgium, Denmark, Luxembourg, and Sweden and are less than 60 per cent in France, Ireland, Austria, and the UK. It is difficult to discern a clear relationship between replacement rates and labour supply. Some of the countries with high replacement rates have high levels of labour supply (Denmark), and some of the countries with low replacement rates have low labour supply of lone mothers (the UK). This lack of association between replacement rates and labour-supply rates remains even after account is taken of housing costs. Clearly there are other factors that have an impact on labour-supply behaviour apart from purely financial incentives.

Another aspect of financial incentives is presented in Figure 5.5. This

Fig. 5.3. Net disposable income of lone mothers on social assistance and housing costs

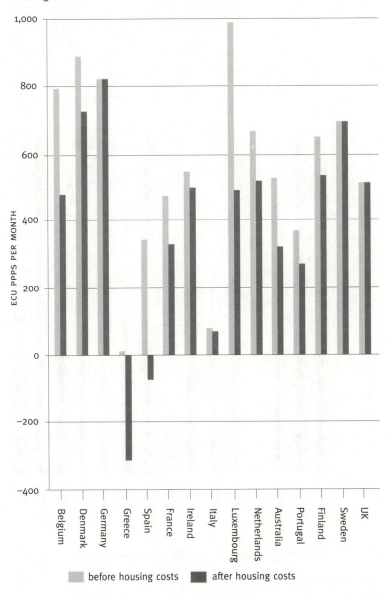

Note: Statistics are for a lone mother, with one child aged 7.

Fig. 5.4. Social assistance replacement rates

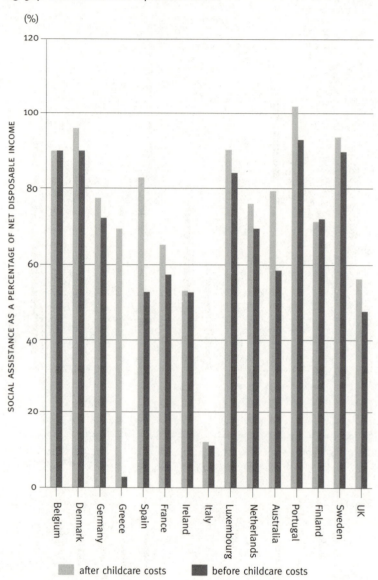

Note: Net disposable income is defined as half national average earnings before housing costs.

❖ MAJELLA KILKEY AND JONATHAN BRADSHAW

Fig. 5.5. Notional poverty trap: marginal tax rates

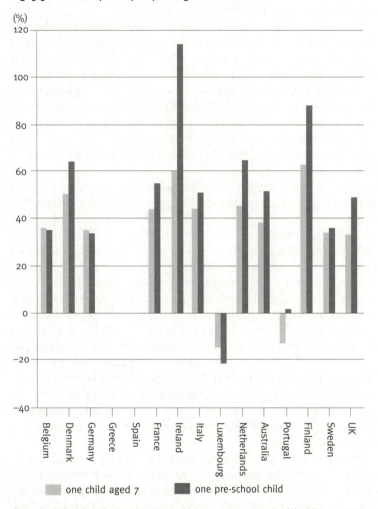

one child aged 7   one pre-school child

Note: Statistics show the increase in marginal tax rates as a result of doubling earnings from half national average to average.

presents an estimate of the notional poverty trap facing lone parents in each country. The poverty trap is the marginal tax rate faced by lone mothers in employment. Thus it may have an impact on the incentives to work more hours and/or earn more. The hypothesis is that lone mothers in countries with high marginal tax rates, as a result of the impact of income taxes, social-security benefits, the loss of means-tested child benefits, housing subsidies, and increased charges for services in kind, may have less incentive for working full-time rather than part-time.

Marginal tax rates are normally calculated over a fairly narrow band of earnings. We present average notional marginal tax rates in increasing earnings from half average to average. Within this range there may appear higher (or lower) marginal tax rates over a narrower band of earnings. The percentage increase in net disposable income as a result of doubling earnings presented in Figure 5.5 is after housing costs, on the grounds that housing costs and the withdrawal of direct housing subsidies are an important element in the poverty trap. The results for Greece and Spain are not included, because housing costs are a very high proportion of net income.

There are two countries, Luxembourg and Portugal, where doubling earnings results in a more than doubling of net disposable income, thus they have negative marginal tax rates over that range of earnings. The reason for the Luxembourg result is the very generous child tax allowance, which is of most benefit to those with higher earnings. The highest average marginal tax rate is found in Finland, where, as a result of doubling earnings, the lone mother increases her net disposable income by only 37 per cent—that is, a marginal tax rate of 63 per cent. Other countries with high marginal tax rates are Ireland (60 per cent), Denmark (50 per cent), and the Netherlands (45 per cent). The UK has a relatively low marginal tax rate of 33 per cent. The countries with income-related childcare subsidies have higher marginal tax rates than those that do not. If childcare is involved, the marginal tax rate in the UK increases to 49 per cent. It is also very high in Finland (88 per cent), the Netherlands (65 per cent), Italy (61 per cent), and Ireland (104 per cent). In the case of Ireland, a lone mother will be 4 per cent worse off as a result of doubling her earnings and having to pay childcare costs.

Again it is difficult to discern a relationship between the level of marginal tax rates and the amount of labour supplied. The Netherlands has a high proportion of lone mothers working part-time and high marginal tax rates. But so does the UK, with low marginal tax rates. Finland has high marginal tax rates with the lowest proportion of part-time workers of any country in the EU.

❖ Towards a Gender-Sensitive Typology

The data presented on employment and poverty rates among lone mothers suggest that there is a great deal of international variation in the degree and manner in which lone mothers achieve economic well-being. In the discussion below we combine the data on lone mothers' employment rate

(Table 5.2) with those on their not-in-paid-work and in-paid-work poverty rate (Table 5.3), to establish a sixfold classification of the countries. We then attempt to explain these groupings of countries on the basis of the analysis presented in the previous section of the chapter. Basically, it is an attempt to see whether or not we can explain the welfare outcomes for this particular group of women in terms of the characteristics of the welfare state covered in the matrix analysis. In addition, we have tentatively classified the non-EU countries into the groups, although there are no matrix data for them.

Two preliminary problems should be acknowledged. First, the data on employment rates and poverty rates relate to the period around the early 1990s. The matrix data relate to the policies in operation in May 1996. Thus, there is something of a disjunction in time between outcomes and inputs. Secondly, the matrix analysis does not cover the whole range of policies that may have a bearing on outcomes. In our earlier study of the factors affecting the employment rates of lone mothers, we concluded

> The employment levels of lone mothers will be influenced by their characteristics, the state of the labour market, public attitudes to mothers' employment, maternity and parental leave, the level of in-work incomes and the benefits available out of work, the rules governing labour participation, the effectiveness of the maintenance regime, the treatment of housing costs and health and education costs. However, probably the most important factor of all is the availability of good quality, flexible and affordable childcare. (Bradshaw *et al.* 1996*b*: 79)

This analysis has not looked at variations in the characteristics of lone mothers, the state of the labour market, public attitudes, or maternity and parental leave; and all these are as likely to be as relevant to the poverty rates as they were to the employment rates.

❖ Group 1: Belgium, Denmark, Finland, Luxembourg, Sweden (and Norway)

This group includes countries in which lone mothers are predominantly (that is, over 50 per cent) paid workers, and have a below-average (relative to other countries) rate of poverty whether they are in paid work or not.

Earnings are comparatively high in Belgium, Denmark, and Luxembourg, and all these countries have relatively generous child-benefit packages. Belgium and Finland have free childcare, and in Denmark, Luxembourg, and Sweden it is heavily subsidized and good quality. The Nordic countries all have systems for advancing maintenance payments. Belgium also has a (fairly ineffective) scheme. For lone mothers out of the labour market, social assistance, at least before housing costs, is comparatively generous. Also social assistance is locally administered in the Nordic countries with the expectation that a lone mother should work after parental leave, and once her child reaches the age of 6 in Luxembourg. Replacement rates are high (over 80 per cent) in each country except Finland, where they are about 70 per cent. The notional marginal tax rates are comparatively low in Belgium, Luxembourg, and Sweden, but higher in Denmark and Finland if childcare is involved.

❖ Group 2: France and Germany

This group includes countries in which lone mothers are predominantly paid workers, and have a below-average poverty rate when in employment, but an above-average rate when not in employment.

France does not have high earnings levels, but the social wage is generous. In particular, France has free pre-school childcare and lone mothers are given priority in access to public childcare places. The complexity of the child tax-benefit system makes it difficult to generalize about whether it encourages lone parents into employment. The main benefits are relatively generous and reach a long way up the income scale, but they are selective (both in terms of age and the number of children), and their time-limited nature excludes many lone parents. However, the fact that benefits are more generous for lone parents with young children may establish patterns of employment when children are young that continue regardless of the incentive structure in later years. The level of social assistance is relatively low in France. Housing costs are reduced on social assistance, and a move from social assistance into low-paid work results in a doubling of housing costs, though help with housing costs extends some way up the earnings scale. Lone mothers in France have middling replacement rates and low marginal tax rates. The latter may be an encouragement to full-time employment. The child-maintenance scheme awards low amounts and is difficult to enforce, and, though there is an advance maintenance scheme, it seems unlikely to have an impact on working activity.

Germany has comparatively higher earnings and the child-benefit package is comparatively generous. Germany has an advanced maintenance scheme for mothers in employment if they have a child under 12. Germany has a low level of childcare provision. Where daycare is available, it is largely for the purpose of developing children educationally, and not facilitating the employment of mothers—though the costs of childcare are subsidized. Social-assistance benefits are comparatively high in Germany, but lone mothers are subject to a relatively harsh work test—they are expected to seek part-time work when their youngest child is 3 and full-time work when their youngest child is 14. Social-assistance replacement rates are comparatively high, especially after child-care and housing costs. However, notional poverty traps are low. It is difficult to discern an explanation for the high poverty rates among social-assistance recipients in Germany where the level of benefits are comparatively high.

❖ Group 3: Austria (and the United States)

This group includes countries in which lone mothers are predominantly paid workers, and have an above-average rate of poverty whether in paid work or not.

Austria has relatively high earnings, although the child-benefit package is not particularly generous. Austria also has a housing-benefit scheme, but after the impact of housing costs the net income of lone mothers in employment is comparatively low. The costs of childcare are subsidized. Social assistance is comparatively very low in Austria, especially after housing costs, and lone mothers are expected to seek employment when their youngest child is 3. Social-assistance replacement rates are comparatively high, especially after childcare and housing costs. However, notional poverty traps are low. Generally it looks as though high housing costs and childcare costs explain the high poverty rates of lone mothers in employment, and low social-assistance rates after housing costs explain the high poverty rates out of employment.

❖ Group 4: Ireland

This group consists of a country in which lone mothers are predominantly undertaking care on a full-time basis, and have a below-average rate of poverty whether in paid work or not.

This circumstance must be due to three factors: first, the state of female labour demand (until recently); secondly, cultural attitudes to female labour supply—Ireland also has low levels of labour supply among couple mothers; and, thirdly, the disjunction between the date of the poverty data and the tax-benefit system. Ireland is a country that made rapid improvements in its tax-benefit system for families with children during the 1990s, and the effect of this and the impact of a growing economy may not have been picked up in increased female labour supply. Earnings in Ireland are comparatively high. There is a both a non-means-tested and a means-tested child-benefit scheme that boosts low earnings, and a differential rent scheme that means that lone mothers in public-sector housing have relatively high net incomes after housing costs. Childcare is free for low-earning lone mothers, though on higher earnings it has to be paid for and this presents a very sharp poverty trap—it would not be surprising to find a high rate of part-time employment in Ireland (the data are not available). Social-assistance rates are middling and replacement rates are comparatively low and do not explain the high level of dependence of lone mothers on social assistance in Ireland.

❖ Group 5: The Netherlands

This group consists of a country in which lone mothers are predominantly undertaking care on a full-time basis, but have a below-average poverty rate when in employment, but an above-average rate when not in employment.

While earnings are comparatively high in the Netherlands, direct taxes are also high and the child-benefit package even at low income levels is not comparatively very generous. There is an income-related housing benefit scheme which reduces housing costs, but net disposable incomes after housing costs in the Netherlands are not particularly high, especially as a lone mother has to pay some of the childcare costs. For those lone mothers out of employment, social assistance is not particularly generous comparatively, especially as they have to pay some of their housing costs. Replacement rates are middling. Notional marginal tax rates are comparatively high if childcare costs are involved, as these costs vary with earnings. However, it is difficult to establish from this evidence why the Netherlands has such low poverty rates among its mostly part-time working lone mothers. It may be due to the fact that mothers who are cohabiting with a man are still classified as lone mothers if the man is not the father of their child. Thus, the poverty rate among lone mothers may be underestimated.

❖ Group 6: The UK (Australia and Canada)

This group includes countries in which lone mothers are predominantly undertaking care on a full-time basis and have an above average rate of poverty whether in paid work or not.

The UK has comparatively high earnings, and in-work benefits, particularly for the low paid, are relatively generous. But these factors are offset by a housing-benefit system that results in sharp increases in housing costs associated with coming off social assistance and increasing income. The UK also has very high childcare costs, with (in 1996) a modest disregard in the Family Credit scheme. Thus, although social-

❖ MAJELLA KILKEY AND JONATHAN BRADSHAW

assistance rates are comparatively low, after housing costs and childcare costs, replacement rates are very high, as are marginal tax rates. There is also an ineffective maintenance regime and a liberal work test on income support—lone mothers do not have to seek employment until their youngest child reaches 16.

Some of the south European countries are able to be placed in this classification. Thus, Greece and Italy fall into the first group as countries in which lone mothers are paid workers and are not poor regardless of labour-market status. In Portugal and Spain, though, while the majority of lone mothers are in employment, they tend to be poor as paid workers, but not so as non-workers. There is reason, however, to be cautious about the groupings of the south European countries. This is the case since, while previous research (Bradshaw *et al.* 1996a, b) has identified lone mothers as paid workers, it has been unable to identify aspects of state policy, or, indeed, sociocultural norms that positively support (lone) mothers in employment. Thus, for example, all these countries have weak or non-existent social-assistance schemes; effectively there is no alternative to paid work, except familial and charitable support. Moreover, there is little to suggest that the policy framework for (lone) mothers when in employment would be conducive to the prevention of poverty: for example, cash transfers for working mothers are minimal, as are public services, such as childcare facilities. All these countries, however, have relatively high (compared with other EU countries) proportions of lone mothers living in multi-generational households (Ditch *et al.* 1998), and relatively low proportions of couple mothers in employment. It may be, therefore, that private familial support rather than public support enables lone mothers to undertake paid work. The high incidence of lone mothers living in multi-generational households also suggests that our poverty measure, which is household-based, may not be a reliable indicator of their poverty.

❖ CONCLUSION

This chapter has adopted the concept of defamilialization in an attempt to conduct a more gender-sensitive analysis of welfare state variation. We took lone mothers as a case study and investigated the degree to which welfare states permit women to uphold a socially acceptable standard of living independently of men, either as paid workers or as full-time carers. The basis of the argument is that a welfare state can really claim to provide women's social rights only if lone mothers are enabled to live independently of men, out of poverty, and also are not forced to chose between paid work or full-time care to avoid poverty.

In no country are lone mothers less likely to be poor than two-parent families. However, there is very considerable variation in the proportions of lone mothers who are in poverty in different countries. This suggests that some countries defamilialize to a greater degree than others. There is definitely an association between poverty and labour-market activity—poverty rates among lone mothers are lower in all countries if they are employed. However, among the employed there are considerable variations in poverty rates between countries. Indeed, there are some countries with low poverty rates despite low levels of employment and still others with high poverty rates despite high levels of employment. Overall the complexity is such that six groupings of countries have been identified on the basis of whether lone mothers are likely to be poor or not and whether they are predominantly in paid employment or not. An attempt was then made to relate these outcomes to the structure of the tax and benefit system using model-family-matrix analysis. A number of weaknesses in the analysis have been acknowledged, in particular the fact that the data on employment and poverty are not as up to date as the data on tax/benefit regimes. Nor are all relevant elements of welfare state activity included in the tax/benefit analysis. Nevertheless, there were reasonable 'stories' to explain the position of most of the countries. The outcomes for two countries—Germany and the Netherlands—were difficult to explain and further work needs to be undertaken to produce a more coherent explanation for why Germany has such high poverty rates among lone parents on social assistance, and why the Netherlands has such low poverty rates among lone parents in employment—given their social and fiscal policies.

The groupings of countries that have been produced on the basis of their poverty and employment characteristics are certainly different and substantially more disaggregated than found in Esping-Andersen's (1990) analysis. The Nordic countries do form a group (which includes Finland), but they are joined by Luxembourg and Belgium. The Netherlands, which Esping-Andersen located to his social-democratic group, is not part of that group. Ireland appears to be unlike the other liberal regimes and is probably changing quite rapidly. Nor is the USA like the other liberal-regime countries. While France and Germany are in the same group, the other conservative countries are in different groups. Perhaps a lesson to learn from this analysis is that welfare state institutions that have an impact on women are more varied (and volatile) than other elements of policy.

Clearly there is much more work to be done in relating social-policy inputs to an outcome such as poverty. We need better and more up-to-date data on outcomes, and need to take account of a broader range of policies. However, some countries do seem to achieve comparatively low levels of poverty among lone mothers whether or not they are in employment.

❖ MAJELLA KILKEY AND JONATHAN BRADSHAW

❖ Notes

1 We are aware that is a universal category that masks a variety of ideological perspectives. Moreover, as Daly (1994a: 102, 117) notes, some of the work that we categorize here as being within the feminist perspective is not exclusively feminist.

2 Independently of Lister (1994a and 1994b), McLaughlin and Glendinning (1994) have also proposed a dimension of defamilialization that is very similar in definition to that of Lister.

3 Orloff (1993) and Langan and Ostner (1991) note, however, that the decommodification dimension also misrepresents the situation of men to the extent that it neglects that men's dependence on women's unpaid labour facilitates men's commodification. Furthermore, to the degree that men make claims on social rights as 'fathers' and 'husbands' (Land 1993), the concept of decommodification does not fully capture men's relationship to the welfare state.

4 Knijn and Kremer also incorporate a second dimension, the right to receive care, since care is more fully defined by them as caregiving and care-receiving.

5 We adopt but also narrow the scope of Lister's concept of defamilialization. A precise employment of defamilialization would require among other things an examination of the unit and conditions of benefit entitlements, since whether or not benefits are linked to family and marital status is a key measure of the degree of independence from family relationships permitted by welfare states. In this chapter, however, we assume that, since lone mothers are already living independently of men, the key question is one of the degree and manner in which they are enabled to achieve economic well-being.

6 Establishing reliably comparable, both temporally and spatially, estimates of the prevalence of lone-mother families is a difficult task, not least because of the absence of an internationally harmonized definition of a lone-mother family. The estimates provided here, therefore, should be treated with some caution. Readers are referred to Ditch *et al.* (1998) for a detailed discussion of the problems inherent in arriving at estimates of the prevalence of lone-mother families, and a presentation of estimates derived from a variety of sources.

7 These data on routes to lone motherhood suffer from similar problems as the prevalence data, and should be taken as estimates. See Bradshaw *et al.* (1996a, b) for a discussion.

8 Much of this data on poverty rates actually refer to lone *parents* as opposed to lone mothers. In all countries, the majority of lone parents are mothers, however. We might expect the data, though, to underestimate the prevalence of poverty among lone mothers, since lone fathers tend to be less poor than their female counterparts (Mitchell 1991).

9 The 'model-families-matrix' approach has been used for a number of comparative studies at York. It was initially developed for a comparative study of child-benefit packages (in 1992) in fifteen, later eighteen, countries (Bradshaw *et al.* 1993a, b; Bradshaw and Uzuhashi 1994; Stephens and Bradshaw 1995). It was later adapted to compare the incentive structures facing married women engaged in housework (Shaver and Bradshaw 1995), lone parents (Whiteford and Bradshaw 1994), and social-assistance schemes in OECD countries (Eardley *et al.* 1996). It was used in the 1994 report of the European Observatory on National Family Policies (Ditch *et al.* 1995) and in the 1995 report (Ditch *et al.* 1996) in the chapters on family incomes and tax/benefit policy, and in the special study of lone parents' labour supply undertaken alongside the 1994 report (Bradshaw *et al.* 1996*b*).

❖ REFERENCES

ALBER, J. (1995), 'A Framework for the Comparative Study of Social Services', *Journal of European Social Policy*, 5/2: 131–49.

BALDWIN, S., AND FALKINGHAM, J. (1994) (eds.), *Social Security and Social Change: New Challenges to the Beveridge Model* (Hemel Hempstead).

BRADSHAW, J. (1998), 'International Comparisons of Support for Lone Parents', in Ford and Millar (1998*b*), 154–68.

——AND CHEN, J. R. (1997), 'Poverty in the UK: A Comparison with Nineteen Other Countries', *Benefits*, 18: 13–17.

——AND UZUHASHI, T. (1994), 'Child Support in Japan', *Japanese Journal of Household Economy*, 24, 52–62.

——DITCH, J., HOLMES, H., AND WHITEFORD, P. (1993*a*), 'A Comparative Study of Child Support in Fifteen Countries', *Journal of European Social Policy*, 3/4: 255–71.

—————— (1993*b*), *Support for Children: A Comparison of Arrangements in Fifteen Countries*, Department of Social Security Research Report No. 21 (London).

——KENNEDY, S., KILKEY, M., HUTTON, S., CORDEN, A., EARDLEY, T., HOLMES, H., AND NEALE, J. (1996*a*), *The Employment of Lone Parents: A Comparison of Policy in 20 Countries* (London).

———————————— (1996*b*), *Policy and the Employment of Lone Parents in 20 Countries: The EU Report* (York).

BRYSON, L, BITTMAN, M., AND DONATH, S. (1994), 'Men's Welfare State, Women's Welfare State: Tendencies to Convergence in Practice and Theory?', in Sainsbury (1994*b*), 118–31.

BUSSEMAKER, J. (1998), 'Rationales of Care in Contemporary Welfare States: The Case of Childcare in the Netherlands', *Social Politics*, 5/1: 70–96.

——AND VAN KERSBERGEN, K. (1994), 'Gender and Welfare States: Some Theoretical Reflections', in Sainsbury (1994*b*), 8–25.

CASS, B. (1992), 'Caring Work and Welfare Regimes: Policies for Sole Parents in Four Countries', in Shaver (1992*b*), 93–106.

—— (1994), 'Citizenship, Work and Welfare: The Dilemma for Australian Women', *Social Politics*, 1/1: 106–24.

DALY, M. (1994*a*), 'Comparing Welfare States: Towards a Gender Friendly Approach', in Sainsbury (1994*b*), 101–17.

❖ MAJELLA KILKEY AND JONATHAN BRADSHAW

—— (1994*b*), 'A Matter of Dependency: Gender in British Income Maintenance Provision', *Sociology*, 28/3: 779–97.

DITCH, J., BARNES, H., AND BRADSHAW, J., COMMAILLE, J., AND EARDLEY, T. (1995), *A Synthesis of National Family Policies 1994*, European Observatory on National Family Policies (York).

—————— (1996), *A Synthesis of National Family Policies 1995*, European Observatory on National Family Policies (York).

—————— AND KILKEY, M. (1998), *A Synthesis of National Family Policies 1996*, European Observatory on National Family Policies (York).

EARDLEY, T., BRADSHAW, J., DITCH, J., GOUGH, I., AND WHITEFORD, P. (1996), *Social Assistance in OECD Countries: Synthesis Report*, Department of Social Security Research Report No. 46 (London).

ESPING-ANDERSEN, G. (1990), *The Three Worlds of Welfare Capitalism* (Cambridge).

EUROSTAT (1994), *Poverty Statistics in the Late 1980s: Research based on Micro-Data* (Luxembourg).

—— (1997), 'Family Responsibilities: How are They Shared in European Households?', *Statistics in Focus/Population and Social Condition, Series No. 5* (Luxembourg).

FINCH, J. (1993), 'The Concept of Caring: Feminist and Other Perspectives', in Twigg (1993), 5–22.

—— AND GROVES, D. (1983) (eds.), *Labour and Love: Women, Work and Caring* (London).

FLORA, P., AND HEIDENHEIMER, A. J. (1981) (eds.), *The Development of Welfare States in Europe and America* (New Brunswick).

FORD, R., AND MILLAR, J. (1998*a*), 'Lone Parenthood in the UK: Policy Dilemmas and Solutions', in Ford and Millar (1998*b*), 1–21.

—— (1998*b*) (eds.), *Private Lives, Public Responses: Lone Parenthood and Future Policy in the UK* (London).

FRASER, N., AND GORDON, L. (1994), 'Civil Citizenship against Social Citizenship?', in Van Steenbergen (1994), 82–100.

FURNISS, N., AND TILTON, T. (1977), *The Case for the Welfare State: From Social Security to Social Equality* (Bloomington, Ind.).

GORNICK, J. C., MEYERS, M. K., AND ROSS, K. E. (1997), 'Supporting the Employment of Mothers: Policy Variation across Fourteen Welfare States', *Journal of European Social Policy*, 7/1: 45–70.

GRAHAM, H. (1983), 'Caring: A Labour of Love', in Finch and Groves (1983), 13–30.

GUSTAFSSON, S. (1994), 'Childcare and Types of Welfare States', in Sainsbury (1994*b*), 45–61.

HANTRAIS, L., AND MANGEN, S. (1994) (eds.), *Family Policy and the Welfare of Women*, Cross-National Research Papers, 3rd Series, Cross-National Research Group, European Research Centre (Loughborough).

HASKEY, J. (1998), 'One-Parent Families and their Dependent Children in Great Britain', in Ford and Millar (1998*b*), 22–41.

HERNES, H. (1987), *Welfare State and Woman Power* (Oslo).

HOBSON, B. (1990), 'No Exit, No Voice: Women's Economic Dependency and the Welfare State', *Acta Sociologica*, 33/3: 235–50.

—— (1994), 'Solo Mothers, Social Policy Regimes, and the Logics of Gender', in Sainsbury (1994*b*), 170–87.

HOLTER, H. (1984) (ed.), *Patriarchy in a Welfare Society* (Oslo).

JENSON, J. (1997), 'Who Cares? Gender and Welfare Regimes: A Commentary', *Social Politics*, 4/2: 182–7.

KNIJN, T. (1994), 'Fish without Bikes: Revision of the Dutch Welfare State and its Consequences for the (In)dependence of Single Mothers', *Social Politics*, 1/1: 83–105.

—— AND KREMER, M. (1997), 'Gender and the Caring Dimension of Welfare States: Towards Inclusive Citizenship', *Social Politics*, 4/3: 328–61.

KORPI, W. (1980), 'Social Policy and Distributional Conflict in the Capitalist Democracies: A Preliminary Comparative Framework', *West European Politics*, 3: 296–316.

LAND, H. (1993), 'The "Public" and the "Domestic": Changing Boundaries or Changing Meanings?', paper presented at the International Sociological Association Conference on Poverty, Social Welfare and Social Policy, Oxford, 9–12 Sept.

LANGAN, M., AND OSTNER, I. (1991), 'Gender and Welfare', in Room (1991), 127–50.

LEIRA, A. (1993), 'Mothers, Markets and the State: A Scandinavian Model?' *Journal of Social Policy*, 22/3: 329–47.

LEWIS, J. (1992), 'Gender and the Development of Welfare Regimes', *Journal of European Social Policy*, 2/3: 159–73.

—— (1993) (ed.), *Women and Social Policies in Europe: Work, Family and the State* (Aldershot).

—— AND OSTNER, I. (1994), 'Gender and the Evolution of European Social Policies', Working Paper No. 4/94, Centre for Social Policy Research, University of Bremen.

LINDSAY, C. (1992), *Lone Parent Families in Canada* (Ottawa).

LISTER, R. (1994*a*) ' "She has other Duties": Women, Citizenship and Social Security', in Baldwin and Falkingham (1994), 31–44.

—— (1994*b*), 'Dilemmas in Engendering Citizenship', paper presented at the Crossing Borders Conference, Stockholm, 27–9 May.

McCASHIN, A. (1997), *Employment Aspects of Lone Parenthood in Ireland* (Dublin).

McLAUGHLIN, E., AND GLENDINNING, C. (1994), 'Paying for Care in Europe: Is There a Feminist Approach?', in Hantrais and Mangen (1994), 52–69.

MAHON, R. (1997), 'Child Care in Canada and Sweden: Policy and Politics', *Social Politics*, 4/3: 382–418.

MARSHALL, T. H. (1950), *Citizenship and Social Class* (Cambridge).

MEYER, T. (1994), 'The German and British Welfare States as Employers: Patriarchal or Emancipatory?', in Sainsbury (1994*b*), 62–81.

MISHRA, R. (1977), *Society and Social Policy: Theoretical Perspectives on Welfare* (London).

——(1990), *The Welfare State in Capitalist Society: Policies of Retrenchment and Maintenance in Europe, North America and Australia* (Hertfordshire).

MITCHELL, D. (1991), *Income Transfers in Ten Welfare States* (Aldershot).

O'CONNOR, J. (1993), 'Gender, Class and Citizenship in the Comparative Analysis of Welfare State Regimes: Theoretical and Methodological Issues', *British Journal of Sociology*, 44/3: 501–18.

OLDFIELD, N., AND YU, A. (1993), *The Cost of a Child: Living Standards for the 1990s* (London).

ORLOFF, A. (1993), 'Gender and the Social Rights of Citizenship: The Comparative Analysis of Gender Relations and Welfare States', *American Sociological Review*, 58/3: 303–28.

PASCALL, G. (1997), *Social Policy: A New Feminist Analysis* (London).

PATEMAN, C. (1989), *The Disorder of Women: Democracy, Feminism and Political Theory* (Cambridge).

ROOM, G. (1991) (ed.), *Towards a European Welfare State?* (Bristol).

SAINSBURY, D. (1994*a*), 'Women's and Men's Social Rights: Gendering Dimensions of Welfare States', in Sainsbury (1994*b*), 150–69.

——(1994*b*), *Gendering Welfare States* (London).

——(1996), *Gender, Equality and Welfare States* (Cambridge).

SHAVER, S. (1992*a*), 'Body Rights, Social Rights and the Liberal Welfare State', paper presented at the Workshop in Comparative Welfare State Development, University of Bremen, Bremen, 2–5 Sept.

——(1992*b*), 'Comparative Perspectives on Sole Parents Policy: Work and Welfare', Proceedings of a Seminar, Social Policy Research Centre, University of New South Wales, 7 Apr.

——AND BRADSHAW, J. (1995), 'The Recognition of Wifely Labour by Welfare States', *Social Policy and Administration*, 29/1: 10–25.

SIAROFF, A. (1994), 'Work, Welfare and Gender Equality: A New Typology', in Sainsbury (1994*b*), 82–100.

STACEY, M., AND PRICE, M. (1981), *Women, Power and Politics* (London).

STEPHENS, B., AND BRADSHAW, J. (1995), 'The Generosity of New Zealand's Assistance to Families with Dependent Children: An Eighteen Country Comparison', *Social Policy Journal of New Zealand*, 4: 53–75.

TAYLOR-GOOBY, P. (1991), 'Welfare State Regimes and Welfare Citizenship', *Journal of European Social Policy*, 1/2: 93–105.

TITMUSS, R. M. (1974), *Social Policy: An Introduction* (London).

TWIGG, J. (1993) (ed.), *Informal Care in Europe* (York).

UNGERSON, C. (1990), *Gender and Caring: Work and Welfare in Britain and Scandinavia* (Hemel Hempstead).

—— (1997), 'Social Politics and the Commodification of Care', *Social Politics*, 4/3: 362–81.

VAN DER LIPPE, T., AND ROELOFS, E. (1995), 'Sharing Domestic Work', in Van Doorne-Huiskes *et al.* (1995), 90–105.

VAN DOORNE-HUISKES, A., VAN HOOF, J., AND ROELOFS, E. (1995) (eds.), *Women and the European Labour Markets* (London).

VAN STEENBERGEN, B. (1994) (ed.), *The Condition of Citizenship* (London).

VOGEL, U. (1991), 'Is Citizenship Gender-Specific?', in Vogel and Moran (1991), 1–23.

—— AND M. MORAN (1991) (eds.), *The Frontiers of Citizenship* (Basingstoke).

WAERNESS, K. (1984), 'Caring as Women's Work in the Welfare State', in Holter (1984), 67–87.

WALBY, S. (1990) *Theorizing Patriarchy* (Cambridge).

—— (1994), 'Is Citizenship Gendered?', *Sociology*, 28/2: 379–95.

WHITEFORD, P. (1997), 'Patterns of Benefit Receipt Among Lone Parent Families: A Comparison of Australia, New Zealand, the United Kingdom and the United States', paper for the conference 'Beyond Dependency: A Watershed for Welfare', Auckland, New Zealand, 16–19 Mar.

—— AND BRADSHAW, J. R. (1994), 'Benefits and Incentives for Lone Parents: A Comparative Analysis', *International Social Security Review*, 47/3–4: 69–89.

WILENSKY, H. L. (1975), *The Welfare State and Equality: Structural and Ideological Roots of Public Expenditure* (Berkeley and Los Angeles).

—— (1981), 'Leftism, Catholicism, and Democratic Corporatism: The Role of Political Parties in Recent Welfare State Development', in Flora and Heidenheimer (1981), 345–82.

❖ MAJELLA KILKEY AND JONATHAN BRADSHAW

6 ❖ Taxation, Family Responsibilities, and Employment

Diane Sainsbury

In most discussions on types of welfare states, taxation has been neglected. Taxation and tax benefits, for example, are undertheorized in Gøsta Esping-Andersen's welfare state regimes (1990). This lack of attention to taxation may stem from his focus on stratification and decommodification, which crowds out redistribution. In critiquing Esping-Andersen's regime typology, Francis Castles and Deborah Mitchell (1993) argue for the inclusion of taxation as an instrument of redistribution. They make progressive taxes a variation and a defining property of welfare states. While progressivity in the tax system is a crucial aspect in the analysis of welfare state types, the place of taxation in welfare state regimes is more complex and requires further elaboration.

Feminist scholars have emphasized the importance of the tax system as an instrument for promoting preferred types of families and relationships within the family (Land 1983; Bergmann 1986). This emphasis is hardly surprising, since a long-standing goal of many feminists has been the married woman's right to control her own money and a vision of financial independence and equality within marriage. The repercussions of the taxation system are not limited to the family but extend to the market, because secondary earners have often been treated less generously. This negative treatment can influence expectations about women's and men's wage work, disadvantaging women's job opportunities and pay scales (McCaffery 1997; Kessler-Harris, forthcoming). In short, *the tax system is a crucial nexus of the state, the family, and the market.* Through tax regulations the state can privilege certain types of families and provide incentives to enter or leave the labour market. These incentives usually differ for women and men in influencing their access to paid work. The structure of incentives and disincentives and their influence on work decisions affect power relations and the gender division of labour within the family and society.

While recognizing its importance in specific national contexts, feminist research has less frequently considered the tax system as a welfare state variation. Comparative frameworks based on the male-breadwinner model have referred to taxation (Lewis 1992), and I make it a dimension of variation in her analytical scheme (Chapter 3, this volume). To date the few empirical comparisons have tended to examine either how tax systems vary in supporting single earner families (Shaver and Bradshaw 1995; Hantrais and Letablier 1996; Sainsbury 1996) or how they vary in promoting married women's employment (Gustafsson 1990, 1992; OECD 1990; Gustafsson and Bruyn-Hundt 1991).

This chapter brings together these two empirical concerns, focusing on the encodement of family responsibilities in taxation in fourteen countries (Australia, Austria, Belgium, Canada, Denmark, France, Finland, Germany, Italy, the Netherlands, Norway, Sweden, the UK, and the USA). The examination of family responsibilities in the tax system concentrates on standard tax relief for a dependent spouse and minor children.[1] Initially the chapter compares income taxation of the fourteen countries over time to determine the extent to which the tax privileges of the married man have eroded. Of additional interest is whether the encodement of family responsibilities in taxation cuts across or corresponds to welfare state regimes. The second concern of this chapter is the gender impact of tax benefits—how taxation penalizes or rewards married women's and men's employment. To assess this, I examine (1) the unit of taxation (the family or the individual), and (2) the generosity in tax relief for a dependent spouse or what I call the housewife bonus. From the outset, it needs to be stressed that individual taxation cannot be equated with the disappearance of family obligations in the tax system. As we shall see, many countries have combined separate taxation with tax relief for dependants and in some instances with unequal tax treatment of earners in dual-breadwinner families. The discussion reveals three trajectories of recognition of family responsibilities in taxation. The final section attempts to explain the growing variation in the tax treatment of family responsibilities by examining the politics of tax reform.

❖ A Decline in Family Responsibilities in Taxation?

During the 1950s male-breadwinner families were much more prevalent than dual-earner families. The tax systems of that period reflected and reinforced the norm of a single-earner family in all our countries. Joint taxation of married couples was the rule, and the family provider enjoyed tax deductions to compensate for support obligations. Generally, the married man received either a tax allowance or a tax credit for a dependent

❖ Diane Sainsbury

wife. The family provider was also granted tax relief for children in most of the countries. Married women have joined the workforce in large numbers, and the dual-earner family is now either common or predominant in all our countries—with the exception of Italy. How have policy-makers adjusted tax systems to these changing realities?

Since the 1950s many countries have switched from joint taxation to individual taxation. A second long-term trend until the 1990s was that child allowances replaced tax exemptions for children.[2] In countries where child allowances are paid to the mother, the elimination of tax exemptions transferred benefits from the father to the mother. Tax benefits for a dependent wife have been much less susceptible to erosion. In fact, until around 1990 the tax systems of all fourteen countries—irrespective of whether the unit of taxation was the individual, the married couple, or the family—retained some form of tax relief for a dependent spouse.

Despite similar reforms in several countries, which would lead one to expect convergence, greater diversity characterizes the tax treatment of maintenance obligations in the 1990s compared to previous decades. Drawing on the data of the Social Citizenship Indicator Program (SCIP) at the Swedish Institute for Social Research, Ingalill Järensjö Montanari has tracked variations in the tax relief for a dependent spouse in eighteen OECD countries during the period 1950–90. She found a trend towards cross-national convergence until the 1970s. During that decade a process of differentiation set in; some countries decreased marital tax relief and others increased it (Järensjö Montanari 1998). This trend has continued during the 1990s. Now a few countries have fully individualized tax systems that no longer recognize support obligations, while others approximate the male-breadwinner model and have increased tax benefits to compensate for maintenance responsibilities.

As a summary measure of family privilege in taxation, Table 6.1 presents the family tax benefit ratio. This measure consists of the taxes paid by the male breadwinner with a dependent wife and two children as a percentage of the taxes paid by a single person with the same earnings—the average earnings of production workers in manufacturing. The lower the percentage, the larger is family privilege. Conversely, a figure of 100 per cent indicates that there are no differences in the taxes of single persons and family providers. To demonstrate the importance of the tax structure, I have calculated the ratio for all direct taxes (social-insurance contributions and personal income tax) and income taxes. Data from 1985 and the latest available data (1996) are used in order to capture the changes in the 1990s.

Two shortcomings in the calculations based on the 'model' family ought to be mentioned. First, tax relief is calculated for a family with two

Table 6.1. The family tax benefit ratio in fourteen countries, 1985 and 1996 (%)

1985

Country	All direct taxes	Country	Income taxes
Canada	61	France	—
France	67	Canada	53
USA	75	Germany	60
Norway	76	USA	67
Australia	78	Belgium	71
Germany	79		
		Netherlands	74
Italy	80	Italy	74
Belgium	81	Austria	74
Finland	84	Norway	75
UK	86	Australia	78
Denmark	86		
		UK	80
Austria	90	Finland	83
Netherlands	92	Denmark	86
Sweden	95	Sweden	95

1996

Country	All direct taxes	Country	Income taxes
Germany	53	Germany	8
Canada	64	France	31
USA	70	Canada	55
Belgium	73	Austria	56
France	79	USA	57
		Belgium	60
Austria	81		
Norway	83	Netherlands	77
Denmark	84	Norway	78
Italy	87	Italy	79
Netherlands	89	Denmark	80
UK	93	UK	85
Australia	95	Australia	95
Finland	100	Finland	100
Sweden	100	Sweden	100

Note: a dash = magnitude nil.

Source: calculated from OECD (1986, 1998).

❖ DIANE SAINSBURY

children. Thus Table 6.1 does not reflect whether the tax system privileges larger families. Perhaps the best-known example of the privileged treatment of families with three or more children is the French tax system. Besides making the household the unit of taxation, family tax exemptions (*quotient familial*) are weighted so that parents are counted as one unit and children as a half unit. To ease the tax burden of large families, the third child and subsequent children are each counted as one unit (Hantrais and Letablier 1996: 54). In addition to France, the tax systems of Belgium, Austria, and Germany (formerly also Finland) have larger exemptions as the number of children increases. A second limitation is that the calculations are based on a family provider with average earnings, but several tax systems are biased in favour of higher earners. In progressive systems, exemptions are often of more value to high-income earners.

An inspection of the column for all taxes reveals that the following countries cluster together in generosity in total tax relief for families in 1985: Canada, France, the USA, Norway, Australia, and Germany. The least generous were Austria, the Netherlands, and Sweden. The countries do not cluster according to welfare state regimes. The clusters are combinations of welfare state types.

Upon closer scrutiny, however, traits related to the three welfare state regimes are discernible. Characteristically, the tax systems of countries representing the liberal welfare state regime have provided generous tax relief for a dependent wife, while the USA and Canada also have generous exemptions for children. As reflected in all direct taxes, familialism was stronger in these tax systems—except for the UK—than in those of many continental European countries. Canada ranked first, the USA third, and Australia fifth. Australia's ranking is quite remarkable given the fact that there was no tax relief for children. These high rankings have to do with the heavy reliance on income taxation in the liberal welfare state regime. Social-security taxes were virtually non-existent in Australia, and they ranged between 5 and 7 per cent of earnings in the other three countries. In Canada tax exemptions for family responsibilities at the national level also influence the provincial income tax. Apart from Quebec (which has even more generous family deductions), the provincial tax is a percentage of the federal tax.

The tax systems of the social-democratic welfare states also rely heavily on income taxation, but they have higher tax rates than the liberal welfare states. The Scandinavian countries also have a proportional income tax levied by local and regional governments. In the mid-1980s Norway and Finland offered extensive tax relief for families. Moreover, this relief affected both national and local income taxes as well as social-insurance contributions. Even so the family tax privilege in relation to the single earner without maintenance responsibilities was rather moderate—with the exception of Norway. Tax relief for family responsibilities substantially reduced national income tax, but its effect on local income taxes was blunted by proportionality and high tax rates. The availability of low-cost childcare and generous parental benefits, however, offset the modest effects of family tax relief.

If we look at income tax alone, the picture changes considerably. In the mid-1980s the French family with two children and average earnings paid little or no income tax, whereas the single individual paid several thousand francs in income tax. The family tax privileges of German, Dutch, Austrian, and Belgian breadwinners also change dramatically for income taxation compared to all taxes. The deflated level of generosity towards families in several of the conservative welfare states with respect to total direct tax burden is the result of the Bismarckian insurance model. Social-insurance contributions make up a larger proportion of the direct taxes and in some cases dwarf income taxes. Insurance contributions in these countries ranged from roughly 10 to 20 per cent of earnings, while in the Netherlands the figure approached an extraordinary 40 per cent (OECD 1986). Furthermore, social-insurance contributions are deductible and thus eat away at the tax base of income taxation. Despite tremendous income-tax relief, the French male breadwinner still paid 67 per cent of the total direct taxes of the single earner without family responsibilities.

Comparing the family tax benefit ratios for all direct taxes in 1985 and 1996 we can see that the divergence in encoding family responsibilities in tax systems has grown. Several countries have increased tax relief for families. Contrary to the past trend of eliminating tax exemptions for children, Austria reintroduced them in 1993. In the same year the Canadians converted their universal child allowance into an income-tested refundable tax credit. Canada has always taxed married couples on an individual basis. But this reform constituted a move towards more familialism in the tax system because eligibility for the tax credit is based on family income. In 1996 Germany replaced cash transfers with children with tax credits, resulting in a major tax cut for families with children. The USA has recently enlarged tax credits for families with children, and Belgium has substantially increased the tax credit of the head of the family (*chef de famille*) (OECD 1986, 1995, 1998).

By contrast, reforms in Sweden and Finland abolished the standard tax benefits related to family obligations, making the taxation of income fully individualized. As part of 'the tax reform of the century', which eliminated national income tax for most Swedish taxpayers, the tax allowance for a dependent spouse disappeared in 1991. Finnish reforms were much more sweeping in doing away with the influence of family obligations on taxes; as recently as 1985 the Finnish tax system ranked fairly high in its tax relief for both wife and children. In the late 1980s Finland abolished the house-wife bonus, and in 1994 tax exemptions for children were replaced by more generous child allowances. Australia converted its tax benefit for support of a spouse into a cash allowance for the caring parent in 1995.

The lower half of Table 6.1 ranks the countries according to generosity in tax benefits for families in the mid-1990s. Now the most generous cluster includes Germany, Canada, the USA, Belgium, and France. An intermediate cluster consisted of Austria, Norway, Denmark, Italy, and the Netherlands. The least generous countries were the UK, Australia, Finland, and Sweden. Even though several conservative welfare states have introduced familialist tax reforms, the clusters of countries still do not coincide with Esping-Andersen's welfare state regimes. Trends to ease the tax burden of families in the 1990s have occurred in countries belonging to both the liberal and conservative welfare state regimes, while other countries in these regimes have cut family tax benefits. The value of family-related exemptions has declined in the UK, Australia, and Italy. The social-democratic regime is also fragmented. Denmark has increased tax relief for support obligations, Norway has retained family tax benefits, while Sweden and Finland have eliminated them.[3] The encodement of family responsibilities in the tax system and its impact on taxation largely cut across welfare state regimes.

❖ TAXATION AND EMPLOYMENT

Taxation creates incentives or disincentives to engage in paid work in a variety of ways. In the popular mind, taxation is associated with disincentives to work. High taxes discourage greater involvement in paid employment, whereas low taxes operate in the opposite direction. Tax benefits, however, may serve as incentives. In his seminal discussion on welfare, Richard Titmuss (1958) distinguished between social welfare (public provision of benefits in cash and kind), occupational welfare (benefits distributed through the employment system), and fiscal welfare (benefits distributed through taxation). A feature of fiscal welfare that promotes employment is that these benefits presuppose a taxable income through either labour-market or capital earnings. Especially in countries where there are few or no social benefits in the form of government cash transfers, tax benefits and in particular refundable tax credits may increase the attractiveness of employment. Tax benefits have also often been constructed so that they are of disproportionate value to high-income groups, thus encouraging their work efforts.

In terms of the state–family–market nexus, taxation can prioritize or marginalize the earning opportunities of family members. The design of both social-security taxes and income taxation is of importance. Among the key factors are the ceilings and lower limits of social-insurance contributions, the income-tax threshold, the unit of taxation, and marital tax relief. The housewife bonus for the male breadwinner is an employment penalty for the married woman.

Both the amount and the construction of social-security contributions can influence employment decisions. Social-insurance contributions vary in the bite they take out of an employee's pay cheque. In the mid-1990s social-security contributions ranged from zero to over 30 per cent of earnings in our fourteen countries. Ceilings and lower limits for paying contributions may make it more advantageous for a husband to work extra or for a wife to take a part-time job. It may be more lucrative for a husband to increase his earnings if they are higher than the contributions ceiling. He would not have to pay more in contributions, but a wife earning the same amount would have to pay social-security contributions at the full rate. Conversely the lower limit of contributions may encourage a wife to work limited part-time hours (under 10–12 hours per week) to avoid paying contributions. If the threshold of income tax coincides with that of contributions, it creates quite a strong incentive to work fewer hours. A high income-tax threshold or wide zero tax bracket has a similar effect. In such instances, the incentives of the tax system promote married women's peripheral position in the labour market.

An added disincentive related to social-security taxes is derived rights, such as medical and pension benefits. These rights are based on the contributions of the family provider but do not entail extra contributions. Family members without an income are covered for benefits by the male breadwinner's contributions to medical insurance schemes in most European continental countries. Generous spouse benefits in the UK and US pension systems are also derived rights. The two-earner couple is disadvantaged when it pays more contributions than the male-breadwinner couple but both couples have the same social rights.

Turning to the unit of taxation, joint taxation is often advantageous to the traditional male-breadwinner family or the dual-earner couple when the wife has small earnings. In many instances the family provider enjoys three advantages: double exemptions, income splitting, and preferential tax rates. Under joint taxation, the personal exemptions of husband and wife are usually double those of the single taxpayer, although they may be more or slightly less. The second advantage—income splitting—is especially beneficial when there is a single earner and progressive tax rates. In Germany the marital unit is the basis of income splitting. The joint earnings of the married couple are divided in two, the tax rate is applied to half of the income and then multiplied by two. France is the most extreme example of income splitting. Instead of dividing the income by two, it is split according to the number of family members. Thirdly, preferential tax-rate schedules often benefit married couples in joint-taxation systems. In Germany the married couple has received the same tax rate for twice the income of a single taxpayer. For example, if the taxable income of the earner without family responsibilities was DM20,000 and the tax rate was 14 per cent, the tax rate for the married couple would be 14 per cent for a taxable income of DM40,000.

Favourable treatment of the married couple can make joint taxation an attractive option for many two-earner couples, even though it disadvantages the working wife. Her earnings increase taxable income, and progressivity in the tax rates and the breadth of tax bands determine the marginal effects on her income. In the worst scenario she must earn a substantial amount before her earnings contribute to family income. Couples in most countries with joint taxation can choose separate taxation. If they opt for separate taxation, personal exemptions are used by the individual taxpayer. The taxable income of the husband is increased by the loss of a deduction for his wife, and the earnings of both partners are subject to higher tax rates.

In systems with separate taxation, tax relief for a dependent spouse often imposes an employment penalty upon a married woman. Since the allowance for a dependent wife is reduced or totally vanishes depending on her earnings, a wife's earnings are pitted against the husband's. The same is true when a wife's exemptions can be transferred to her husband to reduce his tax liability. More generally, the larger the deduction and the wider its application, the larger the employment penalty of the married woman.

Figure 6.1 presents an overview of the income-tax systems of the fourteen countries in the mid-1990s with regard to the generosity of marital tax relief and whether they provide for joint or individual taxation. The vertical axis represents the size of the housewife bonus as a percentage of paid taxes. The horizontal axis is a continuum between separate or fully individualized taxation and mandatory joint or household taxation.

Most of the countries tax labour-market income on an individual basis, but they differ on three important counts. The first is the absence of a housewife tax bonus, and no possibility of transferring tax relief. Only tax systems of this sort fulfil the criterion of separate taxation. The second is whether the taxpayer receives a tax allowance or credit for a dependent wife. The third difference is whether tax allowances or credits of the husband and wife can be transferred. In both the second and third cases tax

Fig. 6.1. Separate/joint taxation and marital tax relief in fourteen countries

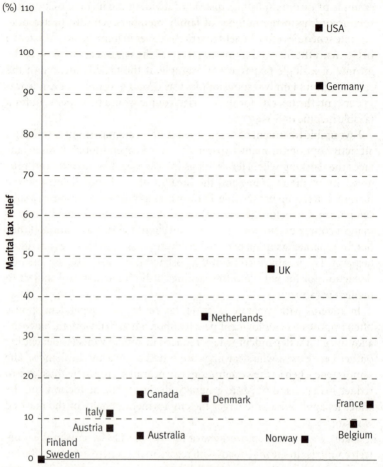

Note: Marital tax relief refers to the percentage of paid tax. Separate taxation is fully individualized with no exemptions for a dependent spouse nor transferability of tax benefits between spouses, whereas the opposite end of the continuum is mandatory joint taxation. For a fuller explanation of the placement of countries along the horizontal axis, see the text.

Source: OECD (1998).

❖ DIANE SAINSBURY

regulations can be a disincentive to a wife's employment because her husband must forgo tax benefits. In plotting the countries' positions along the horizontal axis, the transferability of tax benefits is considered closer to joint taxation than individual tax deductions. The size of the transferable deduction and the tax rate determine the strength of the remaining element of joint taxation. The larger the deduction and the higher the tax rate, the stronger is the element of joint taxation (Gustafsson and Bruyn-Hundt 1991: 35).

Only one country—France—has retained mandatory joint taxation, and it is located at the opposite end of the horizontal axis. Several others— Germany, Belgium, the USA, and Norway—have made separate taxation an option, but joint taxation is still important. In the USA, Germany, and Belgium most couples file joint returns because of more favourable tax schedules for married persons compared to single individuals. More Norwegian dual-earner couples are taxed individually because the preferential tax rates for married couples are not as generous compared to the other countries.

To what extent does the tax system affect women's employment? The answer offered here is quite speculative. It consists of pointing out how patterns of employment coincide with the expected effects of the tax systems. Table 6.2 presents labour-market-participation rates and the percentage of women who work part-time (defined as less than thirty hours per week).

The encodement of family responsibilities in the tax system may help account for women's decisions to enter the labour market in several conservative welfare states. Table 6.2 reveals women's relatively low employment rates in the conservative or social-capitalist countries. The tax systems of Germany, Belgium, and the Netherlands contain strong employment disincentives for married women. Of the fourteen countries, the German tax system imposes the most severe penalties on a working wife; the tax burden jumps from 22 per cent of gross earnings for the male-breadwinner family to 29 per cent for a family where the working mother has modest earnings, to 36 per cent when a working wife has the same earnings but no children. Belgium follows suit; the corresponding Belgian tax increases are from 30 per cent to 35 per cent and 37 per cent respectively (OECD 1998: 26). In the Belgian case, the tax system provides an explanation for the puzzle of women's low rate of employment despite ambitious policies supporting mothers' employment (Meyers *et al.*, Chapter 4, this volume). The structure of taxes is less helpful in understanding employment patterns in the liberal and social-democratic countries. In particular, women's labour-market participation rates in the USA and Denmark run counter to expectations. In the liberal welfare states the tax burden is

TAXATION AND FAMILY RESPONSIBILITIES ❖

Table 6.2. Women's labour-market participation rates and part-time employment in fourteen countries, 1996 (%)

Country	Labour-market-participation rate	Part-time employment[a]
Sweden	76.3	23.5
Denmark	74.0	24.2
Norway	72.3	**46.3**
USA	72.0	19.1
Finland	70.6	11.2
Canada	68.7	••
UK	68.4	**38.9**
Australia	64.4	**46.1**
Austria	62.4	21.7
France	60.7	22.1
Germany	60.4	29.1[b]
Netherlands	59.8	**55.4**
Belgium	52.3	30.0
Italy	43.7	20.9

[a] Part-time employment is defined as working less than thirty hours per week.
[b] 1995.

Note: •• = not available.

Source: OECD (1997: 165, 178).

generally lower than the other countries, so that incentives and disincentive may be weaker. Also the tax systems of the two liberal countries with the highest employment rates—the USA and Canada—provide tax credits to help cover the costs of childcare.

Table 6.2 also shows that part-time employment is unusually high in Australia, the Netherlands, Norway, and the UK. These high rates are partially due to the prevalence of short part-time employment (OECD 1990: 26–7). In three countries, features of the tax system serve as powerful incentives for married women to work part-time. Australia, for example, has a very wide zero bracket for income tax. A wife could earn up to $ A 5,400 without paying tax. In the UK, insurance contributions have a lower limit; neither workers nor employers are liable for payment of contributions on earnings below the limit. The income tax threshold (£72 per week in 1996) has often been very close to lower contributions limit (slightly over £60 per week in 1996) so that small earnings have not been subject to direct taxation. Marital tax relief has existed irrespective of a wife's employment encouraging married women to work. An additional incentive in both Australia and the UK is that the tax burden for dual-earner

❖ DIANE SAINSBURY

families is less than for a single earner as long as the income of the wife is less than her husband. The Dutch tax system entitles a wife to transfer her entire tax allowance or part of it to her husband. Nor is she required to pay contributions if she works fewer hours per week than the minimum, which varies according to the insurance scheme. The Norwegian tax incentives for part-time employment are less obvious. The preferential tax rates for married couples allow a wife to earn an amount corresponding to around 20 per cent of average earnings before individual taxation would be more advantageous to the dual-earner family (OECD 1998: 26, 148, 276, 289, 341–2). Of the four countries, the UK and Norwegian tax systems permit wives to earn a larger tax-free sum relative to average earnings.

❖ A MALE-BREADWINNER VERSUS A DUAL-BREADWINNER TAX REGIME

So far I have mainly discussed how taxation privileges the male breadwinner and the negative implications for working wives, but tax systems have also moved to accommodate dual-breadwinner couples. Three major trajectories are evident in the fourteen countries. The first is little or no change in the male-breadwinner model, and even a strengthening of the tax benefits of the family provider. The second trajectory is that tax systems have introduced measures to aid the second earner, while leaving the tax prerogatives of the family provider intact. Under joint taxation, for example, two-earner couples with minor children have received special tax allowances in some countries. Another variant has been to grant dual-breadwinner couples a special tax allowance for the earner with the lower income. The rationale behind these allowances has been to compensate for extra costs because women were no longer doing domestic work at home, and these couples must purchase services. Several countries have also introduced tax deductions for childcare expenses, but they differ in whether this tax relief is allotted to the male breadwinner or the principal carer. In Belgium the taxpayer with the higher income is entitled to the deduction (Bradshaw *et al.* 1993: 104), while other countries grant it to the earner with the lower income. Tax rules that assign exemptions and credits to the taxpayer with the highest earnings are vestiges of the male-breadwinner regime.

Perhaps the most important step has been the introduction of individual taxation, because it explicitly granted working wives personal exemptions in their own right. Furthermore, individual taxation, in theory, emphasizes the production of income and thus may act as an inducement to enter the labour market. By contrast, joint taxation stresses the family as a unit of consumption (Hantrais and Letablier 1996: 53). All individual taxation systems originally retained some form of tax relief for a dependent wife, representing a compromise with the male-breadwinner model.

The third trajectory involves a transition to a tax system that more fully reflects the dual-breadwinner model—one that is characterized by individual taxation with equal and non-transferable exemptions.[4] The tax systems of Finland and Sweden have evolved along these lines most clearly. The Swedish tax system had already replaced joint taxation of labour-market earnings in 1971 with individual taxation. The 1971 reform did not eliminate the housewife bonus, but it was reduced. At the same time the working wife received a much larger tax allowance, and importantly her tax allowance was not transferable. The construction of tax exemptions, together with progressive tax rates, created incentives for married women to enter the labour market. Because of the progressive income tax and separate taxation, a wife's earnings were taxed at a lower rate until her earnings equalled her husband's.

It is instructive to compare the German and Swedish tax systems as alternatives of family taxation: the male-breadwinner regime versus the dual-breadwinner or individual regime. The Swedish system has prioritized not the male breadwinner's earnings but those of the second earner. If the earner with the larger income increased his earnings, they were taxed at a higher rate than the earnings of the partner who entered the labour market. Since the employer—not the employee—paid social-security taxes, they did not enter the employment calculations of husband and wife. The situation was the opposite in Germany. Under joint taxation the married woman's earnings were subject to high marginal tax rates, and both earners paid sizeable social-insurance contributions. Disposable family income would often be increased more, when the male breadwinner increased his earnings (Wallberg *et al.* 1996: 75). If the dual-breadwinner family opted for individual taxation, the income of both earners was taxed at twice the rate it would have been under joint taxation. At the same time, the male breadwinner lost the housewife bonus. Thus his taxable income was larger, and it was taxed at a much higher rate. Nor was tax relief equal for both earners. The male breadwinner received generous tax exemptions for children. Finally, the two tax systems affected the wife's and husband's contributions to family income differently. Gustafsson and Bruyn-Hundt (1991: 49, 51) show that the average contribution to family income of Swedish women in two-earner couples increased after taxation, whereas it dropped for German women in dual-breadwinner couples.

In conclusion, economists have pointed to the effects of taxation on women's entry into the labour market. Studies have estimated that a tax system tailored to dual-breadwinner couples can increase women's labour-market participation rate by as much as 20 per cent (OECD 1990; Gustafsson 1992). The design of the tax system is important in enhancing women's financial independence in the family in two ways. The tax system provides incentives and disincentives for paid income; it also has redistributive effects on the disposable income earned by family members.

❖ THE POLITICS OF TAX REFORM

Since the mid-1980s the diversity in family taxation has increased. In three countries—Finland, Sweden, and Australia—reforms struck major blows to the housewife bonus. Reforms also weakened the tax privileges of the male breadwinner in the Netherlands and the UK. By contrast, the broad contours of the family-centred French tax system and joint taxation in the USA have changed little. More strikingly, however, familialism has experienced a resurgence in the income-tax systems of several countries—Germany, Austria, Belgium, and Canada. Some clues to this diversity may be gained from studying the politics of tax reform. Here I examine Australia and the Netherlands as cases of reforms that weakened male tax privileges and the USA and Germany as opposite cases.

What are the factors that have led to the national differences in family taxation? A closer examination of the politics of tax reform in these four cases reveals the significance of the demands and strategies of the women's movements, the partisan composition of governments and their tax and family policy goals, the policy legacy, and institutional arrangements. First, a crucial cross-national variation has been the reform agenda of the women's movement and whether it made the tax system a target of reform. Gender ideologies have shaped movement demands and strategies as well as divisions within the movement. Contrasting visions of the desired gender order have influenced demands, while attitudes towards the state and the appropriateness of entering the state arena have major implications for the movement's strategy. Secondly, the partisanship of government has been decisive in setting the tax policy agenda. Changes in family taxation have been intermeshed with other tax-reform battles in most countries. These conflicts have revolved around proposals to flatten the rate of progressivity in income taxes and to broaden the tax base. The coalitions supporting and opposing the reforms opened and restricted opportunities for women's organizations entering alliances. Thirdly, policy legacies have constrained certain alternatives and prioritized others. Fourthly, institutional arrangements have furnished veto sites for the opponents of reform and have raised the thresholds required for a winning coalition. Conversely, innovations in state institutions, such as women's policy agencies, have provided new points of access. Our four cases illustrate the variation in the interplay between these factors and reform outcomes.

❖ Australia

The term 'femocrat' is associated with the Australian women's movement and its efforts to influence policy through positions in the state bureaucracy. More than in the other liberal welfare states, Australian feminists have viewed the state as a vehicle for woman-friendly reforms. Entering the bureaucracy generated controversy and divisions within the women's movement. Early successes, however, convinced many activists of the merits of this channel of influence, and they worked to create women's policy units at all levels of government.

The location of women's policy agencies in the bureaucracy is critical to their claims and strategies. Except for a period during a conservative government (1978–83), the Australian women's office has been attached to a central policy coordinating department with access to the cabinet (the Department of the Prime Minister and Cabinet). From this position, femocrats sought to create a 'gender audit' of all government policies and programmes. The gender audit made the budget a centrepiece of concern. Eventually the office developed a women's budget statement requiring all federal departments and agencies to account for how their spending proposals impacted on women. With this concentration on the budget, it is not surprising that femocrats' attention gravitated towards taxation.

The tax battles of the 1980s and 1990s have centred on the progressive income tax versus a general goods and service tax. From the mid-1980s the femocrats gendered the tax issue. Not only have Australian feminists had the advantage of strong women's machinery; the consultative aspects of the policy process have also offered a useful platform. At the 1985 tax summit, the office's feminist economists argued in favour of progressive taxes, emphasizing that they benefited women, who were generally low-income earners. They closed ranks with the unions and ministers who opposed a proposal for a retail sales tax, which was later retracted. During the 1987 income-tax cuts the office succeeded in modifying the initial proposal so that it included cuts for women. In the 1993 election taxes were a major issue, and the Labor Party campaigned against the opposition's proposal for a general goods and services tax. Part of the Labor Party's tax package, at the suggestion of the women's office, was to replace the tax allowance for a dependent spouse with payment of a home childcare allowance (Sawer 1995).[5] At crucial points a gender gap against labour and the desire to win the votes of women have prompted the party to accept policy proposals promoted by the women's office. In the late 1990s taxation was politicized along gender and partisan lines. The alternative of the non-labour parties, which formed a government after the 1996 election, has been a return to the housewife tax bonus with the family as the *de facto* unit of taxation.

❖ The Netherlands

The Dutch women's movement was not quite as fortunate in achieving a policy agency at the very hub of policy-making, but the head of the policy unit was initially a state secretary in the cabinet. The policy unit, however, was located in a specific ministry—first the Ministry of Culture and from 1981 the more powerful Ministry of Employment and Social Affairs (Outshoorn 1995). The unit's position in a ministry curtailed its powers to initiate policy in other areas, but it was well placed to pursue issues related to women's fiscal and social welfare.

Equally important were the EC directives on equal treatment of the sexes and blatant gender inequalities in Dutch taxation and social-insurance benefits. The Netherlands had introduced separate taxation in 1973, but the standard tax allowance of the family provider was nearly five times larger than his wife's.[6] Clearly reform was necessary to make the Dutch tax system comply with the EC directive. Legislation introduced in 1984 equalized the tax allowances of husband and wife, but allowed the wife to transfer her exemption to her husband. In effect, the tax situation of a single-earner family was scarcely altered. Feminist economists have pointed to the continued existence of tax disincentives for married women to engage in paid work—the transferable allowance and ceilings on social-insurance contributions. A reform to simplify taxation merged income-tax and social-security contributions into one system in 1990, producing both negative and positive consequences for married women. The reform lowered standard tax allowances, and hence reduced the employment penalty for married women. It also extended the applicability of the allowance to social-insurance contributions. The impact of the 1984 and 1990 reforms has been to remedy the gross injustices in the taxation of husband and wife as well as to reduce the housewife tax bonus.

❖ The USA

Liberal feminists have been the most reform-oriented section of the US women's movement, believing in the potential of legislation to secure change. They have attempted to influence policy through a network of lobby organizations (Gelb and Palley 1996) and to secure appointed and elected positions of power at all levels of government. In the 1970s liberal feminists worked for economic independence. They called for the treatment of women as economic equals and the removal of inequities in employment, social-security benefits, the banking system, and taxation. While joint taxation has remained intact, two tax reforms eased the burden of dual-breadwinner couples. The first was tax credits for childcare costs in 1976. The second reform in 1981 introduced a special tax allowance for the secondary earner in dual-breadwinner couples, which reduced the marriage penalty for many working couples. The second reform, however, was relatively short lived.

Women's policy units with direct access to the executive have been *ad hoc* bodies in the form of special commissions or task forces and presidential conferences. The women's task force in the Carter administration wanted to introduce individual taxation in two stages. Its proposal would have abolished the principle of community property that underpins joint taxation—a controversial venture with little hope of passage. Instead President Carter submitted a proposal to remove or reduce the two-earner marriage penalty through a tax allowance that could be claimed by the partner with the lower earnings. Congress rejected the proposal on the grounds that it would cost too much.

In the 1980 presidential election the Republican candidate, Ronald Reagan, campaigned on welfare state roll-back and tax cuts. The first bill of the Reagan administration proposed a massive cut in the income-tax rates. When finally passed by congress, the 1981 legislation contained a 25 per cent tax cut, along with deductions and tax incentives amounting to an incredible $US750 billion. Among the new tax benefits was an allowance nearly identical to the one that had been proposed by the Carter administration (Leader 1983: 144; Steinmo 1993: 161–3). The allowance reducing the marriage penalty was swept away by the tax reform of 1986. Most of the newly legislated tax benefits were eliminated, and the progressive tax scale was compressed into two brackets. Critics have noted that the 1986 reform did not compensate dual-breadwinner couples. Their former tax allowances were used to finance a reform that benefited all married couples—including traditional male-breadwinner families (McCaffery 1997).

In summary, issues related to family taxation have been subordinate to a larger tax policy agenda and concerns about fiscal constraints. The Reagan administration gave priority to slashing taxes, creating the political opportunity to pass a tax allowance benefiting dual-earner couples. Later the allowance was a victim in the process of radically restructuring

❖ DIANE SAINSBURY

income taxation. Tax credits for childcare expenses survived, however, because they fitted into the Reagan administration's blueprint for welfare state change—a shift from publicly provided services to fiscal welfare.

❖ Germany

The German women's movement has been ridden with deep divisions, and reunification has increased the divisions. Women have been divided over involvement with the state and organizations connected with the establishment. The autonomous women's movement of the 1970s emerged from the New Left and initially rejected any such involvement. This separatist stance discouraged coalition building with women activists in political parties, unions, and other organizations. Policy agendas also differed, reflecting divergent gender ideologies. A distinctive feature of German feminism has been a reluctance to equate independence with employment. Instead these feminists have wanted the valuation of domestic work and care through legislation. Quite ironically, then, their views have been attuned with state policies (Ostner 1993: 94–5). Innovations in social policy during the 1980s and 1990s have centred on entitlements based on the principle of care.

An alternative feminist agenda has focused on employment policy. The EC directives on equal treatment have primarily given impetus to improving employment opportunities. There is little indication that feminists have linked employment and taxation. Instead they gave priority to affirmative-action programmes, training programmes, and recruitment campaigns to enter male-dominated occupations.

Women's policy machinery was slow in developing, and at the federal level it remains weak. Policy units on women were first established in the Ministry of Family Affairs, and the visibility and direction of women's policy in the ministry have depended upon who has been appointed minister. In the mid-1980s at the insistence of the first woman minister, the name of the ministry was changed to include women. At the state and local levels the creation of women's affairs offices has flourished but with mixed results. The strongest women's policy machinery has been at the state level, especially in *Länder* whose governments are social-democratic and green coalitions. The principal mandate of these offices has been the promotion of women's employment through affirmative action in the civil service. At the local level the offices have extended this mandate to outreach programmes in other policy areas (Ferree 1995). In short, the most dynamic women's policy units are at the state and local levels, while taxation issues are settled at the federal level, where women policy's machinery is weak and located in the Ministry of Family Affairs.

The policy legacy has also posed serious constraints to changing the marital privileges in taxation. Both the constitutional status of marriage and court rulings on family taxation enhance the legitimacy of the existing tax system. The 1949 constitution enshrines marriage as the foundation of the family, and it specifically declares that marriage and the family are to be protected and promoted by the state (Hantrais and Letablier 1996: 26–7). In the early 1950s the constitutional court handed down a decision that led to the current tax arrangements. After the court ruled that the constitution required equal treatment of married and unmarried taxpayers, income splitting was introduced (Pechman 1987: 16).

The right-centre (Christian Democratic–Liberal) coalition government that took office in late 1982 had tax reform high on its agenda. During the decade, this government introduced the largest tax cuts during the post-war period and simultaneously broadened the tax base (Mangen 1991: 111–12). In three waves of cuts from 1986 to 1990 the rates of progressivity were reduced. The first wave of legislation, billed as 'the law on incentive stimulating tax reductions and on relief of families', tax exemptions for children were increased sixfold (from DM432 to DM2,484). This tax package combined the neo-liberal aspirations and the social conservatism of the two coalition parties.

The Social Democrats and the unions opposed both lower progressivity in tax rates and larger child tax exemptions because of their redistributive effects 'from the bottom to the top'. In countering criticisms, the government argued that greater relief for taxpayers with higher incomes was justified because they had borne the brunt of the excessive marginal tax rates. It also emphasized that low-income groups and large families would benefit from the reform (Dengel 1987: 286–9), and the size of the increase in exemptions for children lent credence to the claim. The increased familialism of German taxation may have resulted from efforts to counter the opposition's criticism, but it is also in line with the long-standing policy of the Christian Democrats.

In sum, a major redistributional shift in support of families occurred from cash transfers to tax benefits during the 1980s and 1990s. Income limits for receipt of child allowances were reintroduced, and the benefit levels of cash transfers to families were first reduced and then more or less frozen. Tax exemptions were increased, and they were constructed so that taxpayers with higher incomes derived a larger tax advantage from them (Wallberg *et al.* 1996: 69). This shift also reversed a trend towards universalized family benefits.[7] In 1996 child allowances were replaced by tax exemptions for children. Family taxation has been politicized in terms of class much more than gender.

❖ DIANE SAINSBURY

❖ CONCLUSION

The examination of these four cases points to several preconditions for and barriers to the introduction of woman-friendly policies. Although it is much disputed whether women's activism is a prerequisite for policies that benefit women (e.g. Adams and Winston 1980; Ruggie 1984; Gelb 1990), the argument here is that women's political mobilization and their demands are significant to policy formation. Their demands or failure to voice claims can shape the policy agenda, their criticism of policy proposals can alter final legislation, and their entering alliances can contribute to the adoption or rejection of policy proposals. In all four countries, sections of the women's movement equated independence with paid work, but in Germany this position was contested. Only in three countries did feminists incorporate taxation in their agenda for reform. Women's varying success in bringing about reforms is related to state structures and the nature of the policy process, the tax policy inheritance, and the partisan composition of governments.

State structure is particularly relevant in understanding the successes and failures in changing the tax system in the USA. Institutional fragmentation—federalism and the separation of powers—offers multiple points of access. Since these points of access are also veto sites, they increase the difficulties of securing passage of legislation. This structure of the state encourages outsider tactics and downplays insider tactics because the payoff is uncertain. The possibilities for a policy unit in the executive to influence policy is not the same as in a parliamentary system. Because of the separation of powers, executive adoption of a proposal from a women's policy unit does not ensure its approval by the legislature. Federalism can further limit a proposal's implementation. The difficulties posed by institutional fragmentation are compounded by the weakness of women's policy machinery in the USA. Policy units are not yet institutionalized at the cabinet level, although there is a women's bureau in the Department of Labor. Women's direct access to the executive has been through *ad hoc* arrangements whose existence has depended on the politics of the president. Institutional fragmentation turns into an advantage by providing alternative arenas of activism, however, when an administration is hostile to feminist politics and public policy claims.

A state with a parliamentary system and majority governments structures opportunities quite differently. Insider tactics and women's policy units with direct access to the cabinet or specific ministers are of paramount importance in initiating and securing desired legislation. In Australia and the Netherlands these agencies were well placed. The consultative policy process in these two countries also offered femocrats additional playing fields to influence policy. The ministerial location of women's policy machinery is also indicative of the thrust of feminist politics and the political culture of women's issues. The Dutch policy unit has been located in the Ministry of Employment and Social Affairs. In the German case the placement of the women's unit in the Ministry of Health, Family, and Youth has reinforced a traditional view of women and the types of policies that are in their interest.[8]

The policy legacy in countries with family and marriage-centred tax schemes makes change more difficult. In France and Germany taxation was part of a post-war settlement. Taxation is interwoven with other policy goals, the privileging of specific types of families. France has prioritized large families, and Germany the family based on marriage. The constitutional enshrinement of the family and marriage provides opponents of individual taxation with a powerful weapon. Such proposals can be discredited as contrary to the spirit of the constitution.

The policy legacy is important in other respects. Among the limitations to further reform of family taxation is the unusual tax structure of the Netherlands. The huge proportion of earned income going to social-security taxes makes abolition of ceilings unlikely. In the USA the policy legacy constrained attempts to change joint taxation but aided the success of the Tax Reform Act of 1976, which extended the availability of childcare tax credits. In this case the policy was already in place but it benefited few families. The Reagan administration increased the credits; its preferences for tax expenditures rather than budget outlays for childcare contributed to this development.

Finally, left governments have generally sponsored pro-women legislation and initiatives (Norris 1987; Wennemo 1994), and partisanship has been important concerning issues of family taxation.[9] Left parties either in a coalition government or as the party of government have initiated the most radical reforms—those that abolished or weakened the housewife tax bonus. Likewise, the task force of a Democratic president contemplated an assault on joint taxation. While the Republicans introduced a tax allowance benefiting dual-breadwinner couples, they were reluctant to tamper with the marital unit of taxation. In many of the countries that have strengthened family responsibilities in their tax systems since the mid-1980s, the Christian Democrats are a major political force. However, the Australian and the US cases (along with the Norwegian case (see Chapter 3, this volume)) make it clear that parties advocating family privileges in taxation are not limited to Christian Democratic parties. These other parties help determine the cluster of countries providing generous family tax benefits, and they explain why this cluster spans types of welfare state regimes.

❖ DIANE SAINSBURY

❖ Notes

1 The analysis does not include tax relief for alimony or temporary support of relatives, although many tax systems allow exemptions for such expenditures. Nor does it consider tax relief for elderly parents.

2 Australia and Sweden had already abolished tax exemptions for children in the 1940s when they introduced cash benefits for families with children (Wennemo 1994).

3 The decline in the impact of Norwegian family tax relief compared to the mid-1980s was related to the reform that eliminated national income tax for most taxpayers in the early 1990s.

4 The criterion of equal and non-transferable exemptions can be met by eliminating family-related deductions or dividing the exemptions equally among the two earners. Finland and Sweden have eliminated family tax benefits, while in Italy exemptions for children are divided when both parents work.

5 This account relies heavily upon Sawer (1995).

6 On the eve of the Dutch equalization reform in the mid-1980s, the husband's tax allowance was 13,516 guilders and the wife's 2,709 guilders (Grift and Siegers 1992: 151).

7 Family benefits were targeted to families whose income was below a certain level until 1974 in Germany. Then the Social Democratic–Liberal coalition government eliminated the income test, making cash transfers available to all families. At the same time tax exemptions for children were abolished. This trend towards universalized family benefits did not, however, encroach upon the special system of lavish benefits for civil servants.

8 There is a parallel in the Swedish and Norwegian cases. In Sweden gender equality issues were assigned to the Ministry of Labour, while in Norway they came under the Ministry of Consumer Affairs.

9 Left governments have also been more supportive of the establishment of women's policy agencies (Stetson and Mazur 1995: 311–14). The political mobilization of women and competition among parties have operated to ensure the continued existence of women's policy units and sometimes even their expansion under governments of non-left partisanship.

❖ References

Adams, C., and Winston, K. (1980), *Mothers at Work: Public Policies in the United States, Sweden and China* (New York).

Bergmann, B. (1986), *The Economic Emergence of Women* (New York).

Bradshaw, J., Ditch, J., Holmes, H., and Whiteford, P. (1993), *Support for Children: A Comparison of Arrangements in Fifteen Countries*, Department of Social Security Research Report No. 21 (London).

Castles, F. (1993) (ed.), *Families of Nations: Patterns of Public Policy in Western Democracies* (Aldershot).

——AND MITCHELL, D. (1993), 'Worlds of Welfare and Families of Nations', in Castles (1993), 93–128.

DENGEL, A. (1987), 'Federal Republic of Germany', in Pechman (1987), 265–95.

DIAMOND, I., AND SHANLEY, M. L. (1983) (eds.), *Families, Politics and Public Policy* (New York).

ESPING-ANDERSEN, G. (1990), *The Three Worlds of Welfare Capitalism* (Cambridge).

FERREE, M. M. (1995), 'Making Equality: The Women's Affairs Offices in the Federal Republic of Germany', in Stetson and Mazur (1995), 95–113.

GELB, J. (1990), *Feminism and Politics* (Berkeley and Los Angeles).

——AND PALLEY, M. L. (1996), *Women and Public Policies* (Charlottesville, Va.).

GLENNERSTER, H., AND MIDGLEY, J. (1991) (eds.), *The Radical Right and the Welfare State* (Hemel Hempstead).

GRIFT, Y. K., AND SIEGERS, J. J. (1992), 'The Effect of the Tax and Social Premium System on the Income Distribution between Dutch Couples', *Bevolking en Gezin*, 1: 141–68.

GUSTAFSSON, S. (1990), 'Labor Force Participation and Earnings of Lone Parents: A Swedish Case Study Including Comparisons with Germany', in *Lone-Parent Families* (Paris), 151–72.

——(1992), 'Separate Taxation and Married Women's Labor Supply: A Comparison of West Germany and Sweden', *Journal of Population Economics*, 5: 61–85.

——AND BRUYN-HUNDT, M. (1991), 'Incentives for Women to Work: A Comparison between the Netherlands, Sweden and West Germany', *Journal of Economic Studies*, 18: 5–6: 30–65.

HANTRAIS, L., AND LETABLIER, M. T. (1996), *Families and Family Policies in Europe* (London).

JÄRENSJÖ MONTANARI, I. (1998), 'The Marriage Subsidy: From Natural Wage to Gender-Biased Taxation Strategy', paper presented at the European Social Science History Conference, Amsterdam, 5–7 Mar.

KESSLER-HARRIS, A. (forthcoming), *What's Fair? Gender and the Search for Economic Citizenship* (Oxford).

LAND, H. (1983), 'Who Still Cares for the Family? Recent Developments in Income Maintenance, Taxation and Family Law', in Lewis (1983), 64–85.

LEADER, S. G. (1983), 'Fiscal Policy and Family Structure', in Diamond and Shanley (1983), 139–47.

LEWIS, J. (1983) (ed.), *Women's Welfare, Women's Rights* (London).

——(1992), 'Gender and the Development of Welfare Regimes', *Journal of European Social Policy*, 213: 159–73.

❖ DIANE SAINSBURY

—— (1993) (ed.), *Women and Social Policies in Europe: Work, Family and the State* (Aldershot).

McCaffery, E. J. (1997), *Taxing Women* (Chicago).

Mangen, S. (1991), 'Social Policy, the Radical Right and the German Welfare State', in Glennerster and Midgley (1991), 100–23.

Norris, P. (1987), *Politics and Sexual Equality: The Comparative Position of Women in Western Democracies* (Brighton).

OECD (1986), Organization of Economic Cooperation and Development, *The Tax/Benefit Position of Production Workers 1981–1985* (Paris).

—— (1990), *Employment Outlook* (Paris).

—— (1995), *The Tax/Benefit Position of Production Workers 1991–1994* (Paris).

—— (1997), *Employment Outlook* (Paris).

—— (1998), *The Tax/Benefit Position of Employees 1995–1996* (Paris).

Ostner, I. (1993), 'Slow Motion: Women, Work and the Family in Germany', in Lewis (1993), 92–115.

Outshoorn, J. (1995), 'Administrative Accommodation in the Netherlands: The Department for the Coordination for Equality Policy', in Stetson and Mazur (1995), 168–85.

Pechman, J. A. (1987) (ed.), *Comparative Tax Systems: Europe, Canada and Japan* (Arlington).

Ruggie, M. (1984), *The State and Working Women* (Princeton).

Sainsbury, D. (1996), *Gender, Equality and Welfare States* (Cambridge).

Sawer, M. (1995), ' "Femocrats in Glass Towers": The Office of the Status of Women in Australia', in Stetson and Mazur (1995), 22–39.

Shaver, S., and Bradshaw, J. (1995), 'The Recognition of Wifely Labour by Welfare States', *Social Policy and Administration*, 29/1: 10–25.

Steinmo, S. (1993), *Taxation and Democracy* (New Haven).

Stetson, D. M., and Mazur, A. G. (1995) (eds.), *Comparative State Feminism* (Thousand Oaks, Calif.).

Titmuss, R. M. (1958), *Essays on 'The Welfare State'* (London).

Wallberg, E., Medelberg, M., and Strömqvist, S. (1996), *Samhällets stöd till barnfamiljerna i Europa*, Ministry of Finance, Ds 1996: 49 (Stockholm).

Wennemo, I. (1994), *Sharing the Costs of Children: Studies on the Development of Family Support in the OECD Countries* (Stockholm).

7 ❖ Gender Equality in the Labour Market

Janet C. Gornick

Feminist critics of mainstream welfare state theory have argued persuasively, that a core dimension along which welfare states have been compared, that of decommodification—the extent to which social rights eliminate dependence on the labour market—applies poorly to women's social circumstances and needs (O'Connor 1992; Orloff 1993). These critics have countered that decommodification is not emancipatory for those with restricted ties to paid work in the first place; persons must be commodified before they benefit from a loosening of their commodity status. These and other feminist critics argue, in contrast, that comparisons of welfare states that reflect the reality of women's lives must highlight the extent to which state policies promote women's opportunities to engage, and advance, in paid work.

Ann Orloff (1993) argues that access to paid work should constitute an independent dimension in any model of welfare state variation. Julia O'Connor (1992, 1996) suggests supplementing, or even replacing, the concept of decommodification with that of autonomy, or insulation from dependence more broadly, including dependence on family members. Barbara Hobson (1990), and Suzanne Bianchi, Lynne Casper, and Pia Peltola (1996), recast earnings differentials between spouses as economic dependency within marriage, and argue that dependency in this form is embedded in gender differentials in labour-market engagement; Hobson (1990: 247) thus calls for 'bringing economic dependency into welfare state research'. Carole Pateman (1988), Ruth Lister (1990), and others contend, furthermore, that freedom from economic dependency is a prerequisite for full citizenship status. Despite remaining conceptual disagreements, much recent scholarship on gender and the welfare state concludes that public policies that support gender equality in the labour market form the core of the woman-friendly welfare state.

Although feminist welfare state theorists have substantially altered the mainstream model, they share with their more traditional colleagues a burgeoning interest in policy outcomes. A new consensus finds that research on women's well-being across welfare states must make central the study of gender inequality in labour-market outcomes, with a focus on the effects of policy on those outcomes and their consequences.

One of the most entrenched and consequential components of gender differentiation is in the provision of unpaid care for children and other dependent family members (Bryson *et al.* 1994; Baxter and Kane 1995). In the industrialized countries, the primary responsibility for dependent care work remains delegated to women. The gendered nature of standard patterns of unpaid work affects women throughout the life cycle, since adult work roles are long anticipated and have enduring consequences. The sexual division of unpaid labour, in turn, shapes gender-linked patterns of labour-market investments and attachments, and consequently claims on welfare resources as well.

This chapter presents a cross-national portrait of gender equality in the labour market in the early 1990s, based on Luxembourg Income Study (LIS) data from fifteen countries. Cross-country comparisons are analysed in the context of variation both across, and within, the three welfare state regime types that have dominated recent theoretical and empirical scholarship on the welfare state. The *social-democratic* welfare states are represented in this analysis by Denmark, Finland, Norway, and Sweden; the *conservative* (or corporatist) welfare states by Belgium, France, Germany, Italy, Luxembourg, the Netherlands, and Spain; and the *liberal* (or residual) welfare states include, here, Australia, Canada, the UK, and the USA. The question as to whether these three regime types shape gendered labour-market outcomes—in other words, the extent to which variation across the regime types is greater than variation within them— anchors the presentation of empirical findings.

In the next section, three central concerns about the meaning of gender equality in the labour market are raised, and resolutions discussed. The following section traces major trends in gendered labour-market patterns since 1960. Two subsequent sections present empirical results for the 1990s on gender differences across various labour-market outcomes. Policy implications are presented in the final section, followed by conclusions.

❖ Gender Equality in the Labour Market

The question of what constitutes gender equality in the labour market remains surprisingly thorny. There are a range of conceptual and empirical concerns, and three are addressed in this section.

First, gender differences take a variety of forms, and the interplay of multiple aspects of gender difference complicates the task of comparing countries' relative performances. Because the different employment outcomes do not co-vary consistently—and some may even vary inversely (for example, employment levels and full-time employment)—a complete cross-national comparison must include several outcomes and, ideally, a composite indicator that aggregates multiple aspects of gender difference.

Empirical findings reported in this chapter address this issue by describing gender differences in several outcomes, including employment levels, rates of part-time work, and labour-market earnings. Earnings differentials are also presented using multiple indicators, including an indicator of women's overall integration into the labour market. 'Women's share of total labour market earnings' is a composite indicator of the share of each country's earnings taken home by women. This measure aggregates gender differences in employment rates, hours worked, and wages, and shifts the perspective from gender discrimination within the labour market to the overall distribution of labour-market returns between women and men.

A second substantial challenge is offered by traditional economists who place little significance on observed gender differences in labour-market outcomes. Neo-classical economists have attributed differences in outcomes to the fact that women's 'tastes' for paid work lag behind men's, albeit to varying degrees in different places and at various times (Mincer and Polachek 1974; Becker 1985; Polachek 1995). The traditional claim is that women simply prefer time spent outside paid work more than men do, or readily accept the advantages of specializing in unpaid work at home. As a result, women accumulate less education and fewer skills (Becker 1981), and they are less likely to seek paid work, especially full-time; some argue that women prefer a subset of occupations and jobs (Polachek 1995), which explains workplace segregation. Thus, substantial gender differences in employment outcomes are seen as reflecting women's underlying tastes, rather than indicating the presence of social or institutional constraints on women's labour-market involvement.

However, women's 'tastes' in the absence of existing social expectations and institutional limitations constitute a classic counterfactual; they cannot be measured. It is clear that much gender differentiation, particularly in activity rates and hours, is located on the supply-side of the labour market; in other words, women *are* less likely to seek work, especially full-time work, than are men. However, feminist labour-market scholars have challenged the premise that women's underlying tastes for time spent in market work are distinct from men's (Bergmann 1986; Folbre and Hartmann 1988; Reskin and Padavic 1994), and/or have argued that women's tastes 'are undoubtedly influenced by social attitudes and norms' (Blau and Ferber 1992: 87). Given the methodological difficulties of explaining gendered outcomes by gender-differentiated tastes or preferences, the approach taken here is to equate 'gender inequality in the labour market' with observed gender differences in all labour-market outcomes.

A third complication in the conceptualization of gender equality in the world of work comes from feminists. Fraser (1994) suggests that the convergence of women's and men's involvement in paid work, if achieved, would not constitute full gender equality if it were not accompanied by a breakdown of the sexual division in caregiving that persists in all Western countries. Concomitantly, promoters of women's employment—those envisioning what Fraser calls 'a universal-breadwinner model'—must bear in mind possible disadvantages for women, such as the potential for increasing their time spent in paid work without any reduction in their duties on the 'second shift'.

Fraser is clearly correct that fully realized gender equality with respect to work must include gender equality in caregiving and other unpaid work, and that an integrated picture of paid and unpaid work would be ideal. Unfortunately, cross-nationally comparable data on the sexual division of unpaid work are very limited. At the same time, there is no clear evidence that the achievement of gender equality in *paid* work in the shorter term will do other than accelerate the breakdown of the sexual division of labour in unpaid work in the longer term. As Heidi Hartmann has observed (personal communication), when women achieve more parity in the labour market, many will reduce their disproportionate responsibilities in the home by 'voting with their feet'—meaning, they will go to their jobs, leaving more unpaid work to the men with whom they live. Nevertheless, the potential costs of increasing and strengthening women's labour-market ties—without achieving gender parity in unpaid work—must be considered.

❖ The Changing Labour Market

During the post-war period, the industrialized countries have seen a dramatic increase in the participation of women, especially of married women with children, in the paid labour market. Yet, despite the rapid increase in women's employment, substantial gender gaps persist in all industrialized labour markets. As of the early 1990s, throughout the industrialized countries:

- women are still less likely to be employed than are men;
- employed women are less likely to hold full-time jobs than are employed men;
- women and men are employed in different industries and in different occupations and, within those, in different jobs—i.e. substantial segregation pervades the workplace;
- women receive lower hourly wages than do men, even after a host of worker and job characteristics are controlled for; combined with women's fewer hours, the gender gap in annual earnings is even greater;
- women contribute the majority of household labour and maintain primary responsibility for child-rearing; the sexual divisions in the paid labour market are paralleled in unpaid work.

Change with respect to these critical indicators has been uneven since 1960. Between 1960 and 1990, women's *labour-force participation* increased in every OECD country, with the sharpest rise seen among mothers; in some countries, women's participation rates more than doubled. Because male participation rates fell steadily throughout the same period—though from much higher base levels—the female share of the labour force increased sharply (OECD 1992).

Change in the percentage of women *employed part-time* showed more variation. Between 1960 and 1990, the percentage of employed women working part-time increased, sometimes dramatically, in two-thirds of the OECD countries; and decreased, usually modestly, in one-third. At the same time, the percentage of employed men working part-time increased—although from much lower base levels—in all industrialized countries. As a result of the two trends, the female share in part-time work has remained fairly stable, at a high level in most countries (OECD 1991).

Change with respect to *occupational and industrial segregation* by gender presents a mixed picture. Cross-national data are not widely available, and methodological difficulties limit comparability across countries. Nevertheless, between 1960 and the middle 1980s, occupational segregation by gender appears to have declined in most countries (OECD 1984; Jacobs and Lim 1992). However, the decline has been slow and levels of segregation remain high; in most countries, women remain concentrated in a few occupations. Industrial segregation by gender, while less pronounced, shows no clear pattern of change since the early 1970s. Structural effects—that is, changes in the size of female-dominated sectors—appear to play little role in the moderate decline of occupational segregation. There is, however, some evidence that structural shifts are working in the direction of increasing industrial segregation, possibly explaining the overall absence of decline (OECD 1985).

Considerable empirical research in recent years has been carried out on the *gender earnings gap*, and a substantial cross-national literature exists (Treiman and Roos 1983; Rosenfeld and Kalleberg 1990, 1991; Blau and Kahn 1992). Gross (unadjusted) female/male hourly earnings differentials in the OECD countries averaged between 15 and 45 per cent in the late 1980s, with an overall trend in the industrialized countries towards a narrowing of the gap during the preceding two decades (OECD 1988). Single- and multi-country studies that have attempted to adjust for worker characteristics, job characteristics, or both, typically report smaller but always positive unexplained wage differentials. The factors that drive the gender earnings gap are complex and varied. Nevertheless, a consensus has emerged that, in most countries, a primary factor underlying the persistent earnings gap is the high level of occupational segregation (Gunderson 1989; Reskin and Padavic 1994)—specifically, women's continued over-representation in low-wage occupations. Until substantial desegregation of the labour force takes place, the goal of equal earnings for men and women will remain elusive.

❖ Gender Inequality in Employment and Hours Worked

As a whole, we see a picture in the industrialized world of a rapidly growing female labour force, but one that remains distinct, in several ways, from the male labour force. In this section and the next, employment, hours, and earnings differentials are presented, for the early 1990s, with a focus on the question of variation across welfare state types.

❖ Data and Sample Selection

Empirical results presented here on employment and earnings are based on data from the LS, an archive of comparable micro-datasets from a large number of industrialized countries. The LIS datasets, primarily based on household surveys, contain demographic, labour-market, and income data at the individual and household level. This study uses fifteen datasets from the third, and most recent, wave (1989–92) of LIS data.[1]

The selected sample, in each country, includes all adults aged 20–59, excluding the agricultural and military sectors. Individuals were coded as employed if they reported current employment, including self-employment, at the time of the survey.[2] In the ten LIS countries for which data on hours were available, employed individuals were further coded as part-time versus full-time, based on their reported usual hours during the prior year, using a thirty-five-hour cut-off, the cross-national standard.[3] Most findings are presented for the population (age 20–59) as a whole— that is, persons in all family types (married or single; with or without children)—and then separately for women and men who are married and the parents of children under age 6.[4]

❖ Employment

Table 7.1 presents women's and men's employment rates and female/ male employment ratios. Table 7.1 reveals, first, that women's overall employment rates in the early 1990s varied considerably, ranging from 85 per cent in Sweden to 31 per cent in Spain, a spread of over 50 percentage points. Men's overall employment rates varied much less, falling within a ten percentage point range (89 to 79 per cent); Canada was an exception, with somewhat lower male employment rates reported (74 per cent). The near uniformity in men's employment rates suggests that the sources of the variation in women's outcomes are gender specific. Cross-national variation in women's employment rates is not simply traceable to fundamental differences—for example, in unemployment rates—in the overall labour markets in these countries. The relatively invariant male rates also mean that the cross-national picture of women's overall employ- ment rates parallels the portrait indicated by the ratios, and thus the two indicators can be used fairly interchangeably (compare the first and third columns).

That caregiving responsibilities are a powerful source of gender differ- entiation in employment can be seen in the comparison of persons in all family types with the subgroup of married parents. Table 7.1 reveals that mothers of young children are less likely to work for pay than are women overall in nearly all countries; the exceptions are Belgium, Italy, Denmark, and Sweden. (Note that, because controls for adults' ages are not included in this comparison, the generally lower employment rates among mothers of young children are found despite the likelihood that they are younger, on average, than women in the larger sample.)

In contrast, Table 7.1 indicates that fathers of young children—that is, the husbands of these mothers—are *more* likely to be employed than are men overall, in all fifteen countries. While mothers in only two countries (Denmark and Sweden) have employment rates exceeding 70 per cent, fathers' employment rates are 80 per cent or higher in all fifteen countries, and 90 per cent or higher in twelve. The general patterns of reduced employment among mothers and greater employment among fathers combine to produce the result that female/male employment ratios are

❖ Janet C. Gornick

Table 7.1. Employment rates and employment ratios in fifteen countries

Country	Persons in all family types			Married parents with a child under age 6		
	Female (%)	male (%)	Female/male ratio	Female (%)	Male (%)	Female/male ratio
Sweden (1992)	85	87	0.98	86	92	0.93
Finland (1991)	77	83	0.93	68	94	0.72
Denmark (1992)	74	80	0.93	77	89	0.87
UK (1991)	68	82	0.83	53	87	0.61
USA (1991)	68	83	0.82	55	90	0.61
Norway (1991)	67	84	0.80	62	95	0.65
Canada (1991)	66	74	0.89	61	83	0.73
Australia (1989)	63	86	0.73	49	91	0.54
Germany (1989)	61	88	0.69	38	96	0.40
France (1989)	60	83	0.72	55	94	0.59
Belgium (1992)	57	83	0.69	62	95	0.65
Netherlands (1991)	51	83	0.61	37	90	0.41
Luxembourg (1991)	49	89	0.55	42	95	0.44
Italy (1991)	42	79	0.53	42	97	0.43
Spain (1990)	31	79	0.39	26	90	0.29

Note: Data are for persons aged 20–59; employment rates include the self-employed; the countries are ordered in relation to the first column of the table.

Source: LIS.

GENDER, EQUALITY IN THE LABOUR MARKET ❖

substantially lower—that is, the gender differences are larger—among parents. In twelve countries (Belgium, Denmark, and Sweden are exceptions), the female/male employment ratios fall by ten or more points as we shift from the population that includes all family types to the parents' subgroup; in Germany, the female/male employment ratio falls by over thirty points. Clearly, the presence of young children is a powerful source of gender differentiation, and more so in some countries than in others.

Do the welfare state types have distinct employment patterns? Esping-Andersen (1990) posited that each welfare state model would be associated with a distinct labour-market trajectory for women—in particular, that regime types would shape female employment levels. He argued that women's employment rates would be highest in the social-democratic countries, where both supply and demand are increased by the extensive provision of public services. Moderate levels of female employment were predicted in the liberal countries, where workers—including women—are less decommodified and alternatives to labour-market income are limited. The lowest levels of women's employment would be expected in the conservative countries, as a result of a slow-growth service sector and policies that encourage mothers to remain in the home.

The results in Table 7.1 largely conform to these predictions. Cross-national variation in gender equality in activity rates can be seen both within and across the dominant welfare state clusters; however, by and large, the clusters do have corresponding employment levels. Women's overall employment rates, relative to men's, are highest in the social-democratic countries (0.93 to 0.98), with the exception of Norway. Slightly lower employment ratios are reported in Norway and in the four liberal countries (0.80 to 0.89, with Australia lagging at 0.73).[5] Women's employment rates are most different from men's, consistently, in the conservative countries. Variation among the conservative countries, however, is substantial; whereas ratios approaching those in the liberal countries are seen in Belgium, France, and Germany (0.69 to 0.72), women in Spain are only 30 per cent as likely as men to be employed.

When attention is focused on parents, gender differences are sharper everywhere, but the cross-national comparative portrait is largely upheld. Among adults raising young children, women's employment patterns most resemble men's in three social-democratic countries (Denmark, Finland, and Sweden) and in Canada, where mothers are more than 70 per cent as likely to be employed as the fathers of these young children. The remaining liberal countries follow, joined by Norway, Belgium, and France, with employment ratios ranging from 0.54 to 0.65. The countries in which mothers' and fathers' employment rates are most sharply differentiated include the remaining conservative countries—Germany, Italy,

Luxembourg, the Netherlands, and Spain—in which mothers of young children are less than half as likely as their husbands to work for pay.

❖ Part-Time Employment

Women's employment rates indicate the likelihood that they are engaged in paid work, but they mask the intensity of that engagement. Many women in these countries—especially those with young children—work part-time, most of them 'voluntarily' (OECD 1990), meaning that they have sought part-time hours. Table 7.2 indicates the percentage of employed women and men whose employment is part-time, and the female/male ratios in part-time rates; again, results are presented separately for persons in all family types and for the subgroup of parents. Figure 7.1 presents women's employment rates (for persons in all family types) and indicates the breakdown of employment into part-time versus full-time.

Table 7.2 reveals that part-time employment as a share of women's employment varied widely in the early 1990s, ranging from a high of 59 per cent in the Netherlands, to a low of 10 per cent in Finland and Italy. As with their overall employment rates, the share of men's employment that is part-time varied much less, nowhere reaching as high as 12 per cent. Clearly, part-time work remains women's work throughout the welfare states of the 1990s.

As with activity rates, the strong effect of caregiving responsibilities can be seen when we shift our attention to the married parents of young children. In all countries, employed women's likelihood of part-time employment increases, in many cases dramatically; in contrast, in none of the ten countries for which we have data are fathers more likely to work part-time than are men as a whole. With three exceptions (Finland, Canada, and the USA), approximately half or more of employed mothers with young children hold part-time jobs; remarkably, in two countries, Germany and the Netherlands, more than four out of five employed mothers are employed part-time.

Figure 7.1 reveals that high levels of female part-time work cut across the three welfare state models and that the regime types show substantial variation within. While a large share of employed women (38–48 per cent) in three Nordic countries (Denmark, Norway, and Sweden) hold part-time jobs, the pattern in Finland (10 per cent) is sharply different. Rates of female part-time work in the UK (45 per cent) are double what they are in the USA (22 per cent), and part-time work in Australia and the UK is as common as it is in the Nordic countries. And among the conservative countries (the seven countries on the right half of the figure), while

Table 7.2. Part-time employment as a share of employment in fifteen countries

Country	Persons in all family types			Married persons with a child under age 6		
	Female (%)	Male (%)	Female/male ratio	Female (%)	Male (%)	Female/male ratio
Netherlands (1991)	59	9	6.6	89	8	11.1
Norway (1991)	48	9	5.3	••	••	••
UK (1991)	45	4	11.3	74	3	24.7
Sweden (1992)	40	5	8.0	54	5	10.8
Australia (1989)	39	5	7.8	63	3	21.0
Denmark (1992)	38	11	3.5	••	••	••
Belgium (1992)	36	6	6.0	47	6	7.8
Germany (1989)	36	3	12.0	81	1	81.0
Canada (1991)	30	9	3.3	38	5	7.6
Luxembourg (1991)	30	2	15.0	57	1	57.0
France (1989)	24	4	6.0	••	••	••
USA (1991)	22	7	3.1	32	2	16.0
Spain (1990)	12	2	6.0	••	••	••
Finland (1991)	10	4	2.5	16	3	5.3
Italy (1991)	10	3	3.3	••	••	••

Note: Data are for persons aged 20–59; employent rates include the self-employed; the countries are ordered in relation to the first column of the table; •• = not available.

Sources: France, Italy, Spain, Denmark, and Norway: OECD (1994a: 194, table C); all other data: LIS.

❖ JANET C. GORNICK

Fig. 7.1. Women's employment, part-time and full-time

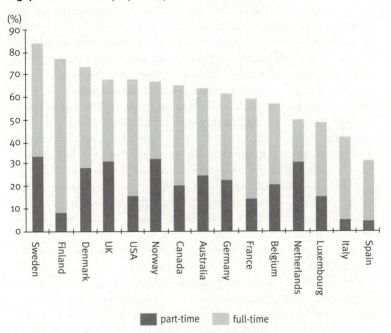

Note: Statistics are for persons aged 20–59 in all family types.
Source: LIS.

women in the Netherlands report the highest rates of part-time employment (59 per cent), part-time employment in Italy and Spain (10–12 per cent) is as rare as it is in Finland.

With the exception of the relatively homogeneous results seen in Denmark, Norway, and Sweden, the extent to which women engage in part-time employment does not clearly vary by regime type. That is not surprising, in part because there is little correlation between rates of part-time work and overall employment rates. The relationship between the two indicators is positive, but weak ($r = +0.29$), a finding that counters a widespread perception that high rates of part-time work among women, as seen in the Nordic countries, are necessary for high rates of employment.[6]

❖ GENDER GAPS IN EARNINGS

The pattern of gender differences in unadjusted earnings—meaning, when there are no controls for gender differences in worker or job characteristics—indicates a surprising degree of similarity across these coun-tries.[7] As reported in the first column of Table 7.3, women in the full-time labour market reported earning between 77 per cent (in Belgium and Finland) and 65 per cent (in Germany) of what men earn—a relatively narrow spread.[8] Within that narrow spread, however, countries fall into two loose groups that cross-cut welfare state types. Earnings ratios lie between 0.77 and 0.74 in four countries—Australia, Belgium, Finland, and Sweden—and between 0.71 and 0.65 in the other six. The countries with the higher level of gender equality include both of the social-democratic exemplars (Finland and Sweden), but also one liberal and one conserva-tive country. The countries where women's relative earnings lag somewhat include a mix of the remaining conservative and liberal countries.[9]

A crucial question is the extent to which this pattern of gender inequal-ity in earnings—both within and across countries—is explained by gender differences in either *worker-* or *job-*related characteristics. In other words, do women earn less than men earn, across these countries, simply because they work fewer hours or because they are less educated or younger than men are? If so, then women's lower earnings, presumably, would reflect lower productivity, and less financial value to the employer. Likewise, do women earn less than men do because they work in different occupations? If substantial gender differences exist in hours, education, age, and occupation, then we can infer that the observed gender gaps in earnings would disappear if, over time, employed women assumed men's characteristics and those of their jobs. Moreover, to the extent that gender differences in earnings are explained, statistically, by these kinds of differ-ences, the dominant explanation for the gender gap in earnings must be rooted in factors other than direct discrimination in pay based on gender.

To approach this question, a multivariate regression analysis was con-ducted to control statistically for gender differences in hours worked (within the full-time workforce), workers' age and education, and occupa-tion.[10] Data limitations allowed the inclusion of only broadly grouped education and occupation variables; education was coded into low, medium, and high (where medium corresponds to completion of sec-ondary school), and occupation was coded as professional/administra-tive, service/sales/clerical, and blue collar. The results presented in Table 7.3 (columns 2–4) indicate what the gender earnings ratios would be—hypothetically—if women had the characteristics of men in their own countries, in particular, their hours worked, age, education, and occupation.

Table 7.3 indicates that, in all of the liberal and conservative countries included here, controlling for these differences in worker and job charac-teristics shrinks the gender gap in earnings somewhat, but never by more

Table 7.3. Gender earnings differentials in the full-time labour force in ten countries

Country	Female/male earnings ratio (means)				Percentage of the gender gap explained by compositional differences
	Unadjusted	Adjusted for Hours	Adjusted for Hours, Age, and Education	Adjusted for Hours, Age, Education, and Occupation	
Belgium (1992)	0.77	0.79	0.82	0.78	4
Finland (1991)	0.77	0.70	0.69	0.65	−53
Australia (1989)	0.74	0.77	0.79	0.78	17
Sweden (1992)	0.74	0.74	0.73	0.71	−10
Luxembourg (1991)	0.71	••	••	••	••
USA (1991)	0.70	0.72	0.72	0.71	2
Canada (1991)	0.68	0.68	0.70	0.70	6
Netherlands (1991)	0.68	0.69	0.82	0.80	36
UK (1991)	0.67	0.72	0.74	0.74	21
Germany (1989)	0.65	0.66	0.73	0.72	21

Note: Data are for persons aged 20–59; self-employed workers are not included; the countries are ordered in relation to the first column of the table; •• = not available.

Source: LIS.

GENDER, EQUALITY IN THE LABOUR MARKET ❖

than about one-third. A portion of the gender gap—from 2 per cent in the USA to 36 per cent in the Netherlands—is explained by compositional differences between women and men in the full-time labour force (that is, by gender differences in worker characteristics and occupation). First, controlling for gender differences in hours worked, alone, explains a slight portion of the gender gap in six of these seven countries (Canada excluded). The largest effect is seen in the UK, where the gender difference in hours worked explained 15 per cent of the unadjusted gap. Secondly, controlling for 'human-capital' differences—age and education—diminishes the gaps further everywhere, except in the USA. The most substantial narrowing is seen in Germany and the Netherlands, where the pattern of labour-market exit at marriage results in marked age differences between the female and male labour forces. Thirdly, the introduction of occupational controls tends to increase the earnings gap—largely because of women's over-representation in the professional/administrative sector. The broad categories used here, however, limit the explanatory power of these controls.

In contrast, in both of the social-democratic countries included here, controlling statistically for gender differences in worker and job characteristics actually *increases the gap*. This indicates that if women, hypothetically, had men's characteristics and occupations, they would earn *less* than they actually do.[11] Thus the relatively high earnings ratios in these countries overstate the extent to which similar women and men, doing broadly similar work, take home the same pay. The results in the social-democratic countries are seen most tellingly in column 4 (the earnings ratios adjusted for hours, age, education, and occupation), where the cross-national rankings of both Finland and Sweden, with respect to gender equality in earnings, fall markedly.

These results, taken together, indicate that systematic variation across countries in gendered compositional differences do not explain the cross-national variation in earnings ratios within the full-time labour force. That is, the gender gaps in earnings across these countries are not primarily due to gender differences in worker attributes, or in job-related characteristics, at least not as captured in these measures of occupation.

❖ BEYOND THE EARNINGS GAP: WOMEN'S SHARE OF TOTAL LABOUR-MARKET EARNINGS

Nearly all studies of the gender earnings gap limit their analyses to the full-time labour market, and most gender-gap researchers make direct wage *discrimination* based on gender their primary analytic concern. Undoubtedly, these analyses are crucial for uncovering the extent to which women with strong attachments to the labour market are paid less than are men. Moreover, studies that decompose the gap into the portion explained by compositional differences versus the portion that is not—the discrimination component—are crucial for identifying the determinants of earnings differentials.

There are, however, two serious limitations of the traditional focus on discrimination within the full-time labour market. First, some portions of the gender earnings gaps in these countries may be explained by compositional differences between women and men—as they are in the liberal and conservative countries (see Table 7.3)—but those explanations leave intact the actual earnings differences and the economic, social, and political consequences of those differences. If women's status or opportunities, in the public or private sphere, are shaped by actual earnings levels, then earnings comparisons that net out substantial portions of the gender gap will beg the question.

Secondly, large numbers of women—those employed part-time or not at all—are excluded from these analyses altogether. In twelve of these fifteen countries, the full-time labour force excludes more than half of the country's working-age women altogether; in the Netherlands, measures of earnings equality within the full-time labour force concern one woman in five.

Table 7.4 presents a broader picture, one that captures the distribution of labour-market returns between women and men more broadly. It shows women's aggregate earnings levels, relative to the men with whom they live and work. Column 1 presents the standard earnings ratios reported in Table 7.3; column 2 presents earnings ratios across the employed population as a whole (that is, part-time workers are included), and column 3, earnings ratios for the working-age population as a whole (i.e. the non-employed are included).

Consider Australia, for example, where the standard earnings measure indicates that employed women earn a comparatively impressive 74 cents on the male dollar. When we shift our attention to all employed Australian women (column 2), women take home a somewhat less substantial 61 cents on the male dollar. When we widen the lens to include all working-age adults (employed or not), Australian women take home only 45 cents in labour-market earnings for each dollar earned by a man. In Australia, as elsewhere, the broader perspective reminds us that women *overall* earn considerably less 'on the male dollar' than the standard indicator reveals.

Column 4 (a transformation of column 3) presents *women's share of total labour-market earnings*, a composite index of women's overall integration into the labour markets of the industrialized countries. This index

Table 7.4. Earnings ratios and women's share of total earnings in fifteen countries

Country	Female/male earnings ratios (means) (all family types)			Women's share of total labour-market earnings	
	Full-time labour force	Employed labour force (includes part-time)	Working-age population (includes non-employed)	All family types (includes non-employed) (%)	Married-parents with a child under 6 (includes non-employed) (%)
Finland (1991)	0.77	0.75	0.71	41	33
Denmark (1992)	••	0.71	0.66	40	35
Sweden (1992)	0.74	0.67	0.65	39	30
Canada (1991)	0.68	0.62	0.55	35	27
Norway (1991)	••	0.67	0.53	35	27
USA (1991)	0.70	0.64	0.53	34	25
France (1989)	••	0.71	0.51	34	29
Australia (1989)	0.74	0.61	0.45	31	20
Belgium (1992)	0.77	0.67	0.46	31	29
Italy (1991)	••	0.79	0.41	29	26
UK (1991)	0.67	0.49	0.41	29	18
Germany (1989)	0.65	0.54	0.38	27	12
Luxembourg (1991)	0.71	0.62	0.34	25	18
Netherlands (1991)	0.68	0.50	0.31	23	13
Spain (1990)	••	0.68	0.27	21	18

Note: Data are for persons aged 20–59; self-employed workers are not included; the countries are ordered in relation to the fourth column of the table; •• = not available.

Source: LIS.

❖ JANET C. GORNICK

compounds gender differentials in activity rates, in hours worked, and in earnings per hour, providing a parsimonious measure that combines multiple aspects of gender inequality. Women's share of total earnings *indicates the extent to which women command a share of labour-market earnings in proportion to their numbers.* The shift to the 'share' measure reveals substantially more cross-national variation in women's relative levels of labour-market remuneration than the standard earnings measures allow us to see (see Figure 7.2).

Among working-age adults, women's share of earned income is lowest in Spain, where women take home only one-fifth of their nation's earnings, and highest in Finland, where women claim two-fifths of all earned income. Women in Finland and in two other social-democratic countries (Denmark and Sweden) command the largest share of their countries' earnings (39–41 per cent); the combination of high employment ratios and high earnings ratios drives the composite result upwards. Remarkably, Denmark and Sweden are ranked second and third, of fifteen, despite the high incidence of female part-time work.

In a second tier of countries, women command approximately one-third of total labour-market earnings (31–35 per cent). This diverse group includes Norway—consistently a laggard among the social-democratic countries—as well as three liberal countries (Australia, Canada, and the USA), and Belgium and France as well.

The UK and five conservative countries—Germany, Italy, Luxembourg, Netherlands, and Spain—form a lower tier, in which women command less than 30 per cent of their countries' total labour-market earnings. The conservative countries, by and large, are ranked lowest on this composite measure of gender equality, owing to a combination of marked gender differentials in employment rates and sizeable gender earnings gaps as well.

Column 5 indicates mothers' shares, across countries, in the total labour-market income earned by the parents of young children. Figure 7.2 clearly indicates that caregiving responsibilities sharpen gender inequality in all countries, dramatically in some. Although these cross-sectional data do not allow an analysis of the long-term economic consequences for women, it is clear that mothers of young children, as a rule, are economically dependent on their husbands during their children's early years. In Germany and the Netherlands, mothers earn just over one-tenth of the earned income of parents of young children, primarily as a result of their extraordinarily low rates of full-time employment; in one-third of the fifteen countries, mothers take home less than one-fifth of total parental earnings. These findings indicate that throughout these countries, albeit to varying degrees, the economic security of mothers with young children is largely in the hands of their husbands.

GENDER, EQUALITY IN THE LABOUR MARKET ❖

Fig. 7.2. Women's share of total labour-market earnings

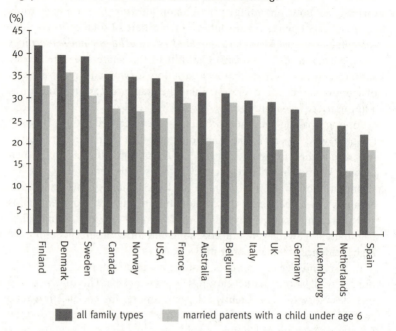

■ all family types   ▨ married parents with a child under age 6

Note: Statistics are for persons aged 20–59.
Source: LIS.

❖ WELFARE STATES, PUBLIC POLICIES, AND GENDER EQUALITY

Much recent research supports the conclusion that public policies shape labour-market outcomes, especially women's employment patterns, which are known to be quite responsive to an array of institutional factors. A multitude of policies—individually and in combination—influence employment levels, and an overlapping set of policies affects gender earnings gaps. Taken together, the effects of a complex array of policies can be seen in the marked variation across countries in the women's share of total earnings. This section briefly discusses policy explanations for the employment and earnings patterns described in this chapter, and lays out policy implications.

❖ *Policy Determinants of Variation in Employment Patterns*

The cross-national employment results presented in this chapter largely conform to Esping-Andersen's predictions: the most gender-equalized

❖ JANET C. GORNICK

employment rates are seen in the social-democratic countries (Norway is an exception), followed by the liberal welfare states; women's employment most lags behind men's in the conservative countries. Among women rearing young children, the clusters are upheld for the most part, except that Canadian mothers 'move up'—there is more gender equality in activity levels than in the other liberal countries—as do Belgian and French women *vis-à-vis* their conservative neighbours.

Cross-national variation in employment supports for mothers explains some of the pattern reported here, in particular the regime 'breakdowns'. In a study of state supports for maternal employment in the middle 1980s, Meyers, Gornick, and Ross (Chapter 4, this volume) found that public provisions were strongest in the social-democratic countries, with the exception of Norway. Employment supports for mothers in the conservative countries followed—with the exception of Belgium and France (and to some extent, Italy), where caregiving work is socialized as extensively as in the Nordic countries. Employment supports lagged in the liberal countries, with the exception of Canada, where they resembled those in the conservative countries. This policy variation is remarkably consistent with the intra-regime variations reported here (see Table 7.1): mothers are employed less in Norway—and more in Belgium, France, and Canada—than are their counterparts in relatively similar welfare states. Furthermore, since the reported policy variation precedes the employment variation reported in this chapter, by five to seven years, it is reasonable to infer that the policies have shaped the employment patterns, at least to some extent, rather than the other way around.

Perhaps the question least resolved is: why are female employment rates (and ratios) in the liberal countries consistently higher than those seen in the conservative countries, given the more extensive policy supports for mothers' employment generally provided in the conservative countries? Clearly, non-policy factors such as sex role expectations and attitudes towards work and family vary across countries, creating a complex and multidirectional interplay among private beliefs, policy arrangements, and employment patterns (Alwin *et al.* 1992). The combination of women's movements in the liberal countries whose strategies have focused on emancipation through paid work, combined with political cultures that emphasize the value of markets, may explain a substantial portion of their higher employment rates. However, a diverse set of other policies may depress women's employment in some conservative countries, such as tax features that discourage second earners (Norregaard 1990; Gustafsson 1991); public-school schedules that conform poorly to standard employment hours (Gornick *et al.* 1997); and a historical reliance on immigrant workers (Gustafsson 1994).

GENDER, EQUALITY IN THE LABOUR MARKET ❖

Furthermore, as Esping-Andersen's predictions suggest, low income transfers in the liberal countries—both means-tested and universal—may have an 'employment-forcing' effect; in the USA, employment pressures are reinforced by the link between employment and health insurance. The employment-forcing effects of social-welfare features may be further exacerbated by men's lagging wages in the liberal countries. Men's real wage growth in the USA, Canada, and Australia has been well below that found in most other OECD countries in recent years (OECD 1994*b*). Yet the extent to which liberal welfare state features force women into paid work remains an open question. Indeed, the women's movements in the English-speaking countries have made important legislative gains that would increase employment opportunities for women. The anti-discrimination apparatus has clearly opened doors for women, in particular, by desegregating some occupations, and reducing barriers to women's upward advancement.[12] High levels of women's employment in the liberal countries probably result from a combination of forces that are both employment forcing and employment facilitating.

Variation in rates of female part-time employment is less easily traced to underlying policy factors. Recent research has linked levels of female part-time employment to supply and demand effects of both social-security rules (Euzeby 1988) and statutory protections for part-time workers (Maier 1991); childcare and public-school schedules that are inconsistent with the full-time working week (OECD 1988); marginal tax rates (Rosenfeld and Birkelund 1995); and public-sector hiring patterns (Rein 1985). The effects of policy factors on gender differentiation in hours of employment demands further study; the existence of substantial variation among relatively similar countries provides a useful framework for analysis.

❖ Public Policy and the Earnings Gap

The results in Table 7.3 indicate that the gender earnings gap is somewhat more attenuated in four countries—Australia, Belgium, Finland, and Sweden—and the multivariate results suggest that cross-national variation in compositional differences does not explain this finding. What, then, does explain the reported variation? Recent work by Francine Blau and Lawrence Kahn (1992) suggests that two competing explanations for cross-national variation in the gender earnings gap need to be considered. One possibility is that the variation across countries is rooted in variation in overall wage structures, especially in the magnitude of the earnings spread. A second is that gender gaps vary across countries because women's labour-market 'positions', relative to men's, vary across countries. These competing explanations provide a valuable framework for policy analysis because they have distinct policy implications.

The central insight in this work—adapted from Juhn, Murphy, and Pierce's analyses of US race differentials (Blau and Kahn 1992)—is that cross-national variation in the magnitude of the gender earnings gap might be explained, in part or in full, by cross-country variation in the overall level of earnings inequality; in other words, wage structures matter. That hypothesis can be grasped intuitively: consider two countries in which women are equally disadvantaged, owing for example, to their lower levels of human-capital acquisition (relative to men) or to labour-market discrimination directed against them as women. If one country has a compressed earnings distribution and the other a dispersed distribution, the gender earnings ratio will be higher in the former, because, in the compressed earnings spread, the earnings of the lowest paid are closer to the middle. In visual terms, it is the length of the earnings 'ladder' that determines the gender earnings ratio—in particular, the distance between the bottom and middle rungs, more than the rung (the 'position') on which the median female worker sits.

Using a variety of data sources, Blau and Kahn (1992) conclude that variation in wage structure accounts for some cross-national variation in gender gaps, in particular, the USA's relatively low female/male earnings ratios. They reported that the higher degree of earnings inequality that characterizes the USA—where returns to skill are high—fully accounts for the larger gender earnings gap in the USA in comparison to several apparently more woman-friendly European countries, and to Australia.

Results based on the LIS data also suggest that *both* factors—the overall earnings spread (the length of the ladder) and women's position in the earnings distribution (the rung on which the median woman sits)—play a role in shaping the pattern of gender inequality in earnings across these ten countries. The left and right boxes in Figure 7.3 divide the ten countries into those with a more equal earnings spread and those with a less equal earnings spread, as captured by the '90/10' ratio—that is, the ratio of the earnings of the 90th percentile earner to those of the 10th percentile earner—with men and women combined. In eight countries, the 90/10 ratio falls between 2.5 and 4; in Canada and the USA, the 90th percentile worker earns over five times what the 10th percentile worker earns. The upper and lower quadrants indicate the position of women in the earnings distribution—that is, where the median female worker's earnings fall in the male earnings distribution. Again, the position of women in the earnings distribution is an indicator of how well women are doing within the ranks of their country's labour market—in other words, how far up the ladder, on average, they have moved. In six countries, the median woman

Fig. 7.3. Earnings dispersion, women's position in the male earnings distribution, and the gender earnings ratio

Median woman's earnings in men's earnings distribution	Earnings dispersion (based on 90/10 ratios)				
	90/10 ratio = 2.5 – 4 (more equal earnings spread)		90/10 ratio = 5+ (less equal earnings spread)		
		Female/male earnings ratio		Female/male earnings ratio	
Median woman's earnings are equal to men's in the third decile from the bottom (higher position)	Australia	0.74	Canada	0.68	
	Belgium	0.77	USA	0.70	
	Finland	0.77			
	Sweden	0.74			
	Average earnings ratio in this quadrant	**0.76**	Average earnings ratio in this quadrant	**0.69**	
Median woman's earnings are equal to men's in the second decile from the bottom (lower position)	Germany	0.65			
	Luxembourg	0.71			
	Netherlands	0.68			
	UK	0.67			
	Average earnings ratio in this quadrant	**0.68**			

Women's labour-market 'position'

Note: Includes only persons aged 20–59 employed full-time. The '90/10 ratio' is the ratio of the earnings of the 90th percentile earner to those of the 10th percentile earner (men and women combined). The 'position' indicates where the median female worker's earnings fall in the male earnings distribution. The figures in the quadrants indicate the unadjusted gender earnings ratios (as reported in Table 7.3).
Source: LIS

❖ JANET C. GORNICK

worker's earnings fall somewhere between the earnings of the 23rd and 30th percentile male's—that is, her earnings fall in the range of men's in the third decile (meaning, the third tenth from the bottom). In four countries, the median woman's earnings fall at or below those of the 20th percentile male—that is, her earnings are equal to those of men in the second decile of male earners (meaning, the second tenth from the bottom).

The four countries in the upper-left quadrant (Australia, Belgium, Finland, and Sweden)—the countries where women's position is higher *and* the earnings spread is more equal—are precisely the four countries with the higher gender earnings ratios (see Table 7.3, column 1). This suggests that both factors are at work—in other words, that gender earnings ratios lag for different reasons in different countries. In two liberal countries, the USA and Canada, the earnings ratios lag behind those in the top four countries primarily because of the unequal wage structure; the low end of the earnings distribution lies far below the middle. In line with Blau and Kahn's findings, the US women's position in the labour market— where the median woman falls in the male distribution—is higher than in all four countries with higher earnings ratios. In three conservative countries (Germany, Luxembourg, and the Netherlands) and in the UK, the gender earnings differentials lag behind the top four countries largely because women are falling further behind their male counterparts—that is, they are positioned on lower rungs on their countries' earnings ladders.

That multiple factors are at work in shaping the cross-national pattern of gender gaps is seen easily in the contrast between the Netherlands and Canada. In both countries, women in the full-time labour force earn 68 per cent of what men earn—trailing their Finnish counterparts by nearly ten percentage points. Dutch women hold the lowest position across these ten countries—their median earner is paid what the 18th percentile male worker earns—but the entire distribution in the Netherlands is relatively compressed (the 90/10 ratio is 2.9). Canadian women, in sharp contrast, are substantially more positively situated within their home labour market—the median earner is paid what the 27th percentile male earns (nearly the same as in Finland)—but the highly unequal Canadian wage structure (the 90/10 ratio is 5) acts as a lever and widens the gender earnings gap.

The policy implications, then, vary across countries. In the conservative countries of Germany, Luxembourg, and the Netherlands, and to some extent in the UK, policy measures aimed specifically at raising *women's* pay should be most effective for narrowing the gender gap. Gender-specific policy approaches include: (1) anti-discrimination and positive action policies aimed at breaking down entrenched patterns of female exclusion in many higher-paid occupations (Reskin and Padavic 1994); (2) state-supported training programmes, both pre-employment and on the job, aimed at reducing vertical labour-market segregation (OECD 1994a); (3) equal pay strategies, focused on reducing earnings differentials between men and women for both equal and/or comparable work (Gunderson 1989); and (4) state actions aimed at alleviating employment-family conflicts (OECD 1994a) in order to lessen the downward pressure that rearing children exerts on mothers' wages (Korenman and Neumark 1991).

In the liberal countries, exemplified by the USA and Canada, it may be that policy measures aimed at narrowing the overall earnings distribution—that is, policies not specifically focused on women or gender differentials—would be the most effective in reducing the gender earnings gap. However, reducing earnings inequality, which is rising in most welfare states (Gottschalk and Smeeding 1997), is a complex economic and political task, because the determinants of wage inequality are varied and difficult to alter. Nevertheless, a range of policy strategies can be identified, including policies aimed at: (1) shoring up the strength of unions and/or centralized wage-setting institutions (Freeman 1997); (2) tightening regulations on minimum (Bazen and Benhayoun 1992) or even maximum wages (Hacker 1997); (3) reducing inequalities in public education (Gramlich and Long 1996); and (4) regulating elements of international trade and production that are exerting downward pressure on low wages (Sachs and Shatz 1994).

❖ CONCLUSIONS

The results presented in this chapter point toward three interrelated conclusions. *First, when we focus our attention on gendered policies and outcomes, the applicability and usefulness of the standard welfare state regime typology is partially challenged.* One of the central questions addressed in this chapter is whether levels of gender equality in the labour market vary systematically across the three welfare models. These results indicate that women's employment patterns (in particular, their rates of employment) do indeed vary across the three welfare state types, as expected. The highest female rates, and ratios, are reported in the social-democratic countries, Norway excepted, followed by the liberal countries. Lower, though widely varying, employment rates are reported throughout the conservative countries.

In contrast, the extent to which women are employed part-time—a crucial indicator of the strength of market attachment—does not clearly vary by regime type. While part-time work is very common in Denmark, Norway, and Sweden, it is rare among Finnish women. Rates of female part-time work in the UK, which are more than double those reported in the USA, actually exceed part-time employment rates in Sweden. And among the conservative countries, while women in the Netherlands report the highest overall rates of part-time employment, part-time work in Italy and Spain is as rare as it is in Finland.

Gender earnings ratios, in the full-time labour force, also cut across welfare state-regimes, with all three regime types represented among the four countries (Australia, Belgium, Finland, and Sweden) that report somewhat higher earnings ratios. On the other hand, part of the explanation for the inter-country variation in earnings ratios is the variation in the overall degree of earnings dispersion. On that score, countries are distinguished largely as the regime typology would predict; that is, two liberal countries (Canada and the USA) report markedly more unequal wage structures than those found in the social-democratic and conservative countries. Clearly, a range of economy-wide factors—which may be better predicted across the regime types—also affect gender equality; these factors—for example, centralization of wage setting—work in complex conjunction with gender-specific factors.

Finally, cross-national variation in women's share in total labour-market earnings—the measure that compounds gender differences in employment rates, rates of part-time employment, and earnings—reveals a picture of both inter- and intra-regime variation. Women command the largest shares of their nation's earned income (approximately 40 per cent) in three social-democratic countries: Finland, Denmark, and Sweden; it is interesting and somewhat surprising that Denmark and Sweden remain in the top grouping, given their high rates of female part-time employment. The second tier of countries—in which women earn 31–35 per cent of total earnings—is a diverse group that cuts across all three regime models: Australia, Canada, and the USA, and Norway, Belgium, and France. Using this composite measure of gender equality, Norway lags behind its social-democratic neighbours, while Belgium and especially France reveal more gender equality than their conservative counterparts. The lowest-tier countries, where women claim less than 30 per cent of national earnings, is, again, more homogeneous; it includes the UK, and the five remaining conservative countries (Germany, Italy, Luxembourg, the Netherlands, and Spain.)

Secondly, high levels of economic dependency within the family are evident everywhere, although there is considerable variation across countries. The results here establish that married women's caregiving responsibilities, as indicated by the presence of young children in the home, sharpen the overall gender inequality seen in all countries, dramatically so in some countries. These findings indicate that married women with young children are, for the most part, economically dependent on their husbands. In *none* of these fifteen countries—including the three with the highest level of gender equality on the composite measure, that is, Denmark, Finland, and Sweden—do women directly claim more than approximately one-third of the earnings taken home by parents. Remarkably, in five countries—Germany, Luxembourg, Netherlands, Spain, and the UK—mothers command less than one-fifth of all parental earnings.

Both the high levels of women's economic dependency seen in the welfare states of the 1990s, and the extent of the variation across countries, suggest that feminist welfare state scholars are right to call for more theory and research concerning women's economic dependency within the family. As Hobson (1990), Orloff (1993), O'Connor (1996), and others have argued, the ways in which states enhance women's access to paid work and ultimately reduce their economic dependence—including dependence on family members—need to be accounted for more fully in models of welfare state variation. More comparative research is needed on both the factors affecting women's decision-making and on the long-term consequences of the high levels of women's economic dependency seen throughout the industrialized countries in the early 1990s.

Thirdly, the results presented here suggest that 'policy matters' in shaping women's labour-market outcomes and, in turn, in influencing levels of economic dependency. Mounting evidence suggests that both overarching welfare state designs and individual policies—which vary across as well as within regime types—influence both the extent to which women have access to paid work, and also the nature and intensity of their attachment to paid work. Women's labour-market outcomes, in turn, shape both overall gender equality and the degree to which women are economically dependent on the men in their lives. The links between policy and outcomes, especially women's employment patterns, are increasingly well understood, although an appreciation of the consequences of available policy options has thus far outpaced policy development in most industrialized countries.

Public policies that support maternal employment appear to play a role in increasing the economic independence of mothers during their children's early years, relative to their counterparts in relatively similar welfare states—an effect that spills over to the population as a whole. In Belgium, France, and Italy, for example, where employment supports for mothers with children under age 6 are as highly developed as they are in Denmark, Sweden, and Finland (see Meyers, Gornick, and Ross, Chapter 4, this volume), mothers command a larger share of labour-market earnings than in the other conservative countries, and more than in most of the liberal countries as well. Likewise, Norway provides less extensive public

❖ JANET C. GORNICK

support compared with its social-democratic neighbours; the weaker supports for maternal employment probably explain a portion of the lagging labour-market attachment reported by Norwegian women.

In closing, two unanswered questions ought to be placed at the top of the research agenda on the relationship between women's labour-market integration and public policy The first concerns the direction and magnitude of policy shifts during the early years of the twenty-first century, as the post-industrial transformation continues. The combination of ongoing labour-market restructuring, high male unemployment rates (especially in Europe), and welfare state retrenchment suggests that policy supports for women's labour-market integration will face heightened scrutiny. It remains to be seen whether demands for men's employment opportunities and/or welfare state reversals will overwhelm the economic, social, and political imperatives of women's labour-market integration.

A second question concerns the possibility of policy expansion in the direction of measures aimed *directly* at reducing the sexual division of labour in unpaid work; so far, those waters are largely uncharted. Fraser (1994) suggests that an ideal outcome, in the long term, is one of convergence of women's and men's work patterns; she envisions an arrangement in which both women and men work for pay *and* care for their families. Yet the progress towards gender equality in the labour market may level off, limited by the intransigence of gendered patterns in caregiving. If so, policy formation aimed directly at altering gender inequalities in *un*paid work may constitute the next wave of woman-friendly welfare state development.

❖ NOTES

1 For more information on LIS and on the individual datasets, see de Tombeur (1997).

2 In one country, the Netherlands, data limitations required that employment be coded differently. Individuals were coded as employed if they reported positive wages in the prior year, a coding scheme that would be expected to bias employment rates upwards.

3 In Table 7.2 and Figure 7.1, LIS data are supplemented by OECD data (OECD 1994a). Because LIS data on hours worked are unavailable in five of the included countries—France, Italy, Spain, Denmark, and Norway—OECD data on part-time employment rates are included for these countries. Although data from LIS and OECD sources should be combined with caution, there is a high correspondence between the two sources on rates of women's part-time work in the ten countries for which data on hours are available from both sources. Exceptions, however, are Belgium and Luxembourg, where the LIS microdata indicate substantially higher rates of part-time work than do the OECD data—38% versus 27% in Belgium, and 30% versus 18% in Luxembourg. One source of discrepancy is that, a consistent thirty five-hour cut-off is used in the LIS results, while, in the OECD findings, part-time employment rates in some countries are based on the thirty five-hour cut-off, but in others are based on either a thirty-hour cut-off, or on employees' self-definition (as in both Belgium and Luxembourg). Furthermore— a caveat—the part-time classification based on either source includes a varied group of workers who hold diverse jobs (i.e. their employment ranges from one to thirty or more hours per week); a closer look at differences among part-time workers would be useful.

4 Married parents with children under age 6 are referred to hereafter as 'mothers' and 'fathers', or as 'parents' (or 'married parents'). Single parents—who are overwhelmingly mothers—were excluded from the analysis of parents because the focus is on gender differentiation and there were two few single fathers to constitute a comparison group. Analyses of this subgroup illuminate gender differences among adults who have both child-rearing responsibilities as well as another adult in the home with whom to share the work.

5 Canada's employment ratio indicates a somewhat higher level of gender equality, but it is the relatively low male employment rate reported that drives that result.

6 Others report little or no relationship between employment rates and rates of part-time work, over time or across countries (OECD 1994a; Rosenfeld and Birkelund 1995.)

7 The data and sample selections underlying the earnings results are the same as in the analysis of activity rates. The only exception is that self-employed workers were excluded in the analysis of earnings, because both their hours worked and their earnings are difficult to measure. The exclusion of the self-employed is likely to narrow the gender differentials in pay (Reskin and Padavic 1994). Furthermore, five of the fifteen countries had to be eliminated from the earnings analysis, owing to the absence of data that would allow the identification of full-time workers from among the employed labour force.

8 The gender earnings ratios in Table 7.3 are ratios of means. While there are advantages to presenting ratios of medians—they are less sensitive to extreme values—ratios of means are presented here so that the analysis of unadjusted ratios (column 1) could be integrated with an analysis of adjusted earnings ratios (columns 2–5)—i.e. ratios after worker and job controls are introduced. Adjusted ratios were constructed using ordinary least squares (OLS) estimations, which are structured around the comparison of means. Results (not shown) indicate that the cross-national portrait based on a comparison of medians is largely similar.

9 Note that these earnings data do not include parental-leave benefits. Parental-leave benefits were not included in the earnings data, because data on parental benefits are available only at the household level and cannot be linked to individual adults. To the extent that leave benefits replace women's earnings, not including them in this analysis may overstate gender gaps in earnings-related income—especially in the Nordic countries with the most generous benefits.

❖ JANET C. GORNICK

10 In the multivariate analysis, standard two-stage semi-log wage equations were estimated, separately for men and women. In the first stage, logistic regressions estimated the probability that persons were full-time employed. In the second stage, wage equations were estimated using OLS regression; full-time employed persons were selected and a transformation of each worker's predicted employment probability was added to the list of regressors (see Killingsworth and Heckman 1986). Independent variables in the wage equations included hours worked, age and its square, three education categories, and three occupation categories. Full regression results are available from the author. (Note that Luxembourg was excluded from the multivariate analysis because data were not available on all of the worker and job controls included in the regression models).

11 These results are consistent with those reported by Treiman and Roos (1983), based on data from the late 1970s. They also found that compositional differences—in particular, age—explain the largest share of the gender gap in Germany and the Netherlands, and that compositional controls increased the gender gaps in the Nordic countries.

12 On the other hand, in a cross-national study, Whitehouse (1992) finds no association between the presence of equal-pay or equal-employment-opportunity legislation, and women's labour-force participation.

❖ REFERENCES

ALWIN, D. F., BRAUN, M., AND SCOTT, J. (1992), 'The Separation of Work and the Family: Attitudes towards Women's Labour-Force Participation in Germany, Great Britain, and the United States', *European Sociological Review*, 8/1: 13–37.

ASHENFELTER, O. C., AND LAYARD, R. (1986) (eds.), *Handbook of Labor Economics*, i (New York).

BAXTER, J., AND KANE, E. (1995), 'Dependence and Independence: A Cross-National Analysis of Gender Inequality and Gender Attitudes', *Gender and Society*, 9/2: 193–215.

BAZEN, S., AND BENHAYOUN, G. (1992), 'Low Pay and Wage Regulation in the European Community', *British Journal of Industrial Relations*, 30/4: 623–38.

BECKER, G. (1981), *A Treatise on the Family* (Cambridge, Mass.).

—— (1985), 'Human Capital, Effort, and the Sexual Division of Labor', *Journal of Labor Economics*, 3/1: 33–58.

BERGMANN, B. R. (1986), *The Economic Emergence of Women* (New York).

BIANCHI, S., CASPER, L., AND PELTOLA, P. K. (1996), 'A Cross-National Look at Married Women's Economic Dependency', Luxembourg Income Study Working Paper No. 143 (Luxembourg).

BLAU, F. D., AND FERBER, M. A. (1992), *The Economics of Women, Men, and Work* (Englewood Cliffs, NJ).

—— AND KAHN, L. M. (1992), 'The Gender Earnings Gap: Learning from International Comparisons', *American Economic Review*, 82: 533–8.

BRYSON, L., BITTMAN, M., AND DONATH, S. (1994), 'Men's Welfare State, Women's Welfare State: Tendencies to Converge in Practice and Theory?', in Sainsbury (1994), 118–31.

DE TOMBEUR, C. (1997), 'LIS/LES Information Guide, Revised Edition', Luxembourg Income Study Working Paper No. 7 (Luxembourg).

ESPING-ANDERSEN, G. (1990), *The Three Worlds of Welfare Capitalism* (Princeton).

EUZEBY, A. (1988), 'Social Security and Part-Time Employment', *International Labour Review*, 127: 545–57.

FOLBRE, N., AND HARTMANN, H. (1988), 'The Rhetoric of Self-Interest and the Ideology of Gender', in Klamer *et al.* (1988), 184–203.

FRASER, N. (1994), 'After the Family Wage: Gender Equality and the Welfare State', *Political Theory*, 22/4: 591–618.

FREEMAN, R. B. (1997), 'Solving the New Inequality', *Boston Review* (on-line publication).

GORNICK, J., MEYERS, M., AND ROSS, K. (1997), 'Supporting the Employment of Mothers: Policy Variation across Fourteen Welfare States', *Journal of European Social Policy*, 7/1: 45–70.

GOTTSCHALK, P., AND SMEEDING, T. (1997), 'Cross-National Comparisons of Levels and Trends in Inequality', Luxembourg Income Study Working Paper No. 126 (Luxembourg).

GRAMLICH, E. M., AND LONG, M. (1996), 'Growing Income Inequality: Roots and Remedies', the Urban Institute (on-line publication).

GUNDERSON, M. (1989), 'Male–Female Wage Differentials and Policy Responses', *Journal of Economic Literature*, 27: 46–72.

GUSTAFSSON, S. (1991), 'Separate Taxation and Married Women's Labor Supply: A Comparison of West Germany and Sweden', *Journal of Population Economics*, 5: 61–85.

—— (1994), 'Child Care and Types of Welfare States', in Sainsbury (1994), 45–61.

GUTMANN, A. (1988) (ed.), *Democracy and the Welfare State* (Princeton).

HACKER, A. (1997), *Money: Who Has How Much and Why?* (New York).

HOBSON, B. (1990), 'No Exit, No Voice: Women's Economic Dependency and the Welfare State', *Acta Sociologica*, 33/3: 235–50.

JACOBS, J. A., AND LIM, S. T. (1992), 'Trends in Occupational and Industrial Sex Segregation in 56 Countries, 1960–1980', *Work and Occupations*, 19/4: 450–86.

KILLINGSWORTH, M. R., AND HECKMAN, J. J. (1986), 'Female Labor Supply: A Survey', in Ashenfelter and Layard (1986), 103–204.

KLAMER, A., MCCLOSKEY, D., AND SOLOW, R. (1988) (eds.), *The Consequences of Economic Rhetoric* (New York).

KORENMAN, S., AND NEUMARK, D. (1991), 'Marriage, Motherhood, and Wages', *Journal of Human Resources*, 27/2: 233–57.

❖ JANET C. GORNICK

Kuiper, E., and Sap, J. (1995) (eds.), *Out of the Margin: Feminist Perspectives on Economics* (New York).

Lister, R. (1990), 'Women, Economic Dependency and Citizenship', *Journal of Social Policy*, 19/4: 445–67.

Maier, F. (1991), 'Part-Time Work, Social Security Protections and Labour Law: An International Comparison', *Policy and Politics*, 19/1: 1–11.

Mincer, J., and Polachek, S. (1974), 'Family Investments in Human Capital: Earnings of Women', *Journal of Political Economy*, 82/2: 79–108.

Norregaard, J. (1990), 'Progressivity of Income Tax Systems', *OECD Economic Studies*, 15: 83–110.

O'Connor, J. (1992), 'Citizenship, Class, Gender, and the Labour Market: Issues of Decommodification and Personal Autonomy', paper presented at the ISA Conference on Comparative Studies of Welfare State Development, Bremen, Germany, 3–6 Sept.

——(1996), 'From Women in the Welfare State to Gendering Welfare State Regimes', *Current Sociology*, 44/2: 1–130.

OECD (1984), Organization for Economic Cooperation and Development, *The Employment and Unemployment of Women in OECD Countries* (Paris).

——(1985), *The Integration of Women into the Economy* (Paris).

——(1988), *Employment Outlook* (Paris).

——(1990), *Employment Outlook* (Paris).

——(1991), *Employment Outlook* (Paris).

——(1992), *Employment Outlook* (Paris).

——(1994a), *Women and Structural Change: New Perspectives* (Paris).

——(1994b), *The OECD Jobs Study: Facts, Analysis, Strategies* (Paris).

Orloff, A. S. (1993), 'Gender and the Social Rights of Citizenship: The Comparative Analysis of Gender Relations and Welfare States', *American Sociological Review*, 58: 303–28.

——(1996), 'Gender in the Welfare State', *Annual Review of Sociology*, 22: 51–78.

Pateman, C. (1988), 'The Patriarchal Welfare State', in Gutmann (1988), 231–60.

Polachek, S. (1995), 'Human Capital and the Gender Earnings Gap: A Response to Feminist Critiques', in Kuiper and Sap (1995), 61–79.

Rein, M. (1985), 'Social Policy and Labor Markets: The Employment Role of Social Provision', paper presented at the International Political Science Association Meeting, Paris.

Reskin, B., and Padavic, I. (1994), *Women and Men at Work* (Thousand Oaks, Calif.).

Rosenfeld, R. A., and Kalleberg, A. L. (1990), 'A Cross-National Comparison of the Gender Gap in Income', *American Journal of Sociology*, 96/1: 69–106.

————(1991), 'Gender Inequality in the Labor Market: A Cross-National Perspective', *Acta Sociologica*, 34: 207–25.

ROSENFELD, R. A., AND BIRKELUND, G. E. (1995), 'Women's Part-Time Work: A Cross-National Comparison', *European Sociological Review*, 11/2: 111–34.

SACHS, J. D., AND SHATZ, H. J. (1994), 'Trade and Job in US Manufacturing', *Brookings Papers on Economic Activity 1*, 1–84.

SAINSBURY, D. (1994) (ed.), *Gendering Welfare States* (Thousand Oaks, Calif.).

TREIMAN, D. J., AND ROOS, P. A. (1983), 'Sex and Earnings in Industrial Society: A Nine-Nation Comparison', *American Journal of Sociology*, 89/3: 612–50.

WHITEHOUSE, G. (1992), 'Legislation and Labour Market Gender Inequality: An Analysis of OECD Countries', *Work, Employment, and Society*, 6/1: 65–86.

❖ Part Three

Gender Regimes and Welfare State Regimes

8 ❖ Gender, Policy Regimes, and Politics

Diane Sainsbury

Part One of this book centred on countries representing the same type of welfare policy regime. The chapters examined the interplay between the basic features of the conservative or social-capitalist, liberal and social-democratic regimes and gender inequalities. In addition Part One mapped out variations in the construction of gender in the policies of countries representing each welfare state regime. Part Two broadened the analysis by studying the gender consequences of policies across the three welfare state regimes.

To tie together the analyses in Parts One and Two, this concluding chapter initially addresses two questions posed in the Introduction. The first question is the extent to which gender cuts across and fragments welfare state regimes. The second concerns the dynamics between the policy logics of gender regimes and welfare state regimes. Subsequently the chapter turns to policy design and politics. Drawing on the earlier chapters, important issues in the design of policies and their impact on gender inequalities are teased out. Lastly the prospects of introducing woman-friendly policies are considered. What political conditions are conducive or alternatively pose obstacles to policies reducing gender inequalities?

❖ GENDER AND THE FRAGMENTATION OF WELFARE STATE REGIMES

Feminists have criticized mainstream research for its preoccupation with paid work and income-maintenance programmes and its failure to bring care and provision of services into the domain of comparative welfare state research. Perhaps not surprisingly, it is precisely in the area of care and the provision of childcare services that the countries do not cluster

246

into distinct groups corresponding to welfare state regimes. Instead France, Denmark, Italy, Sweden, Belgium, and Finland formed the cluster of countries with the most ambitious childcare provision and policies to support mothers' employment policies. Only the liberal welfare states clustered together because of low provision and few supportive policies. It was not purely a liberal cluster, however; the liberal countries were joined by the Netherlands, Germany, and Norway. Countries representing the conservative welfare state regime displayed the widest range of variation in the public provision of childcare. France has one of the highest coverage rates, and the Netherlands and Germany have among the lowest. Although not as pronounced, provision of childcare in the social-democratic regime also varied, with Norway trailing behind Denmark, Finland, and Sweden (Meyers *et al.*, Chapter 4, this volume).

The conservative or social-capitalist countries differ dramatically in the provision of services for children and the elderly. The countries that are the leaders in providing childcare are the laggards in care of the elderly—and vice versa. In the provision of services for the elderly, the Netherlands has one of the highest levels of coverage and Italy one of the poorest. This asymmetry in provision of services for children and the elderly leads Anneli Anttonen and Jorma Sipilä (1996: 94, 97) to suggest that two models of social care are found in these countries. The clustering of countries in their analysis is presented in Figure 8.1.

The two models reflect different notions of *family obligations* and the appropriateness of state involvement in helping families cope with their responsibilities in providing care. France and Belgium have adopted inter-

Fig. 8.1. Social care services in ten European countries

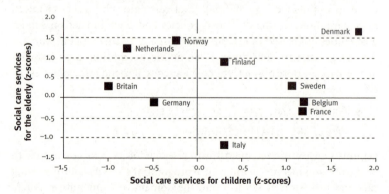

Note: The clustering of countries is based on z-scores.
Source: Anttonen and Sipilä (1996: 94).

❖ DIANE SAINSBURY

ventionist policies for the childcare of pre-schoolers, and these two countries are clustered together with Denmark, Sweden, and Finland on this policy dimension. On the other hand, French and Belgian policies assume that the family is responsible for the support and care of its elderly members. This is reflected in underdeveloped services for the elderly.

Family obligations of another sort—the widespread belief that it is the duty of the mother to stay at home and care for infants and small children—affect the availability of childcare in the Netherlands and Germany. For the most part, existing services are intended to support family care in these countries. However, Dutch social policies have eroded the responsibility of adult children to care for their ageing parents. The National Assistance Act grants aid as a right of citizenship, and a universal health insurance scheme (the AWBZ) covers exceptional medical expenses—including long-term care. In this respect, the Netherlands resembles the Scandinavian countries in displaying a clear state responsibility with no legal obligations between adult family members to care (Millar and Warman 1996: 35–6).

Another instance of gender cutting across welfare state regimes is the encoding of family responsibilities and gender biases in taxation. The most generous cluster in granting tax relief to the family provider was comprised of Germany, Canada, the USA, Belgium, and France in the mid-1990s. The least generous countries were Italy, the Netherlands, the UK, Australia, Finland, and Sweden. Moreover, as we saw in Chapter 6, there have been wide variations within all three regimes. Extensive family tax benefits have characterized the taxation of at least two countries in each regime: France and Germany among the conservative welfare states, Canada and the USA among the liberal welfare states, and Norway and formerly Finland among the social-democratic welfare states. In the 1990s Denmark has taken Finland's place.

The punitive effects of taxation on married women's employment also differed within and across welfare state regimes. Germany's tax system contains the most severe employment penalty for wives, followed by Belgium, Canada, Denmark, the USA, the Netherlands, and Norway. In all these countries the tax burden of the single-earner family is less than dual-breadwinner families, while the tax systems of Finland, Sweden, the UK, and Australia did not penalize two-earner families in the mid-1990s (see Figure 8.2). In fact, the construction of exemptions and progressive tax rates ought to encourage married women to enter paid employment, because their earnings are taxed at a lower rate until they equal the earnings of the husbands.

Nor do countries with policies that allow solo mothers to form an autonomous household with little risk of poverty crystallize into a cluster

❖ DIANE SAINSBURY

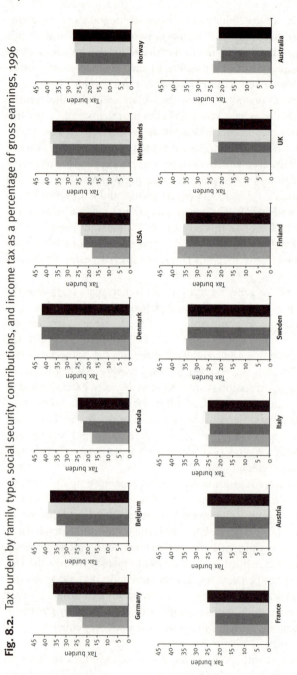

Fig. 8.2. Tax burden by family type, social security contributions, and income tax as a percentage of gross earnings, 1996

■ Male-breadwinner family with two children and average earnings (100%).

□ Dual-breadwinner family with two children where the working mother has a modest income (total gross wages are 133% of average earnings).

□ Dual-breadwinner family with two children where the mother has a larger income (total gross wages are 167% of average earnings).

□ Two-earner couple without children and the second earner has a modest income (total gross wages are 133% of average earnings).

Source: OECD (1998: 26).

corresponding to a particular welfare state regime. In the 1990s solo mothers experienced a low risk of poverty in Sweden, Italy,[1] Finland, Denmark, Belgium, and Norway. The range of variation has been very wide in the conservative and liberal welfare state regimes. In the mid-1980s solo mothers in Italy, the Netherlands, and Belgium had low poverty rates (under 10 per cent), whereas they were at a much higher risk of poverty (20–26 per cent) in Germany and France. The most recent data disclose growing variation among the conservative countries, as the poverty rates of solo mothers in the Netherlands and Germany have risen (Kilkey and Bradshaw, Chapter 5, this volume). Prior to the Thatcher era the greatest disparity in the poverty rates of solo mothers was in the liberal welfare states. Around 1980 the poverty rates of mother-headed families were the highest in the USA, Canada, and Australia, ranging from approximately 40–45 per cent; but in the UK the rate was under 20 per cent (Mitchell 1991; OECD 1997b: 160). Largely as victims of welfare state retrenchment, British solo mothers' situation has deteriorated and their poverty rate has climbed (Bradshaw 1998: 161; Kilkey and Bradshaw, Chapter 5, this volume). In the 1990s the four liberal countries appeared to be moving towards a distinct cluster whose policies were least likely to prevent poverty among solo mothers.

There have also been pronounced policy differences in the treatment of solo mothers as earners, carers, or earners-carers. In the early 1990s the income packages of solo mothers across countries revealed three distinct patterns, reflecting dissimilar gender policy regimes. The main source of income of solo mothers in the USA, Germany, Italy, Denmark, Canada, and Belgium was earnings; policies encouraged or compelled mothers to engage in paid work. By contrast, social benefits were the key component of the income package of solo mothers in the Netherlands, the UK, and Australia. In these countries, policies have provided a social wage or a mother's wage that acknowledges the worth of caring. Nor were mothers required to be available for work. In a third group of countries—Sweden, France, and Finland—benefits and earnings in roughly equal portions composed the income package of solo mothers. The policies of these countries have represented a earner–carer regime that has supported single parents as mothers and as workers. Benefits related either to the status of the single parent or to caring responsibilities supplement earnings, and public provision of childcare enables mothers to become earners. In summary, these policy differences in the treatment of solo mothers cut across welfare state regimes. The liberal regime splits in two with respect to how policies recognize care responsibilities. The UK and Australia provide a social wage for solo mothers who care for their children, while the USA and Canada have moved towards treating mothers as workers through the introduction of severe work tests (O'Connor *et al.* 1999; Evans 1997: 100–1, 105–6). The conservative and social democratic regimes unravel even more, with countries falling into each of the three gender policy regimes.

On the dimension of women's access to paid work, the countries largely cluster according to regime type (see Figure 8.3). Patterns of part-time employment, however, exhibit more diversity across welfare states, producing intra-regime variations. Within the conservative or social-capitalist regime the Netherlands has the highest rate of female part-time employment (nearly 60 per cent) and Italy the lowest (10 per cent). Nearly as wide variations are found in the social-democratic regime: the Norwegian rate was nearly 50 per cent, while the Finnish rate was 10 per cent. In the liberal countries, women's part-time employment ranged from 45 per cent in the UK to slightly over 20 per cent in the USA. The group of countries where women typically held full-time jobs consisted of Finland, Italy, Spain, the USA, and France (Gornick, Chapter 7, this volume). The cluster where short part-time work was most widespread consisted of the Netherlands, Norway, Australia, and the UK (OECD 1997a: 178).

The regimes start to break down when we examine women's earnings, and fragmentation increases when we consider mothers' earnings (Figure 8.3). Women's share of earnings provides a rough gauge of their economic independence, and the earnings of married mothers with pre-school children offer quite a rigorous test. Looking at all women's share of labour-market earnings reveals a pattern where three of the social-democratic welfare states rank highest, and several conservative countries rank lowest. None the less there are some surprises. France, Belgium, and Italy do much better than one would expect on the basis of women's labour-market-participation rates, while the USA and the UK do more poorly. Most strikingly, the UK plummets from a fourth position in terms of women's access to work to a very low ranking on mothers' share of earnings—third from the bottom. In summary, the countries do not fall into neat clusters that correspond to the welfare state regimes with regard to mothers' earnings. The countries where mothers' earnings are highest ranked are, in the following order, Denmark, Finland, Sweden, Belgium, France, Canada, and Norway. Among the countries where mothers' earnings are particularly low and their economic dependency greatest are the UK, the Netherlands, and Germany (Gornick, Chapter 7, this volume).

This brief summation of the results of Part Two illustrates how gender cuts across welfare state types and sheds light on the extent of intra-regime variations. It corroborates the initial formulations of the male-breadwinner model on two scores. First, the meagre earnings and high dependency levels of mothers with small children in the UK, the Netherlands, and

Fig. 8.3. Women's labour-market participation and share of earnings in thirteen countries

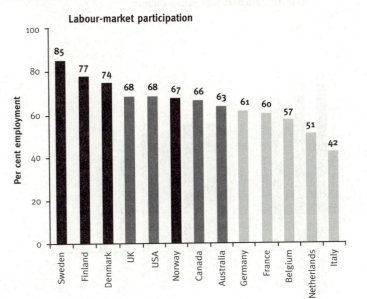

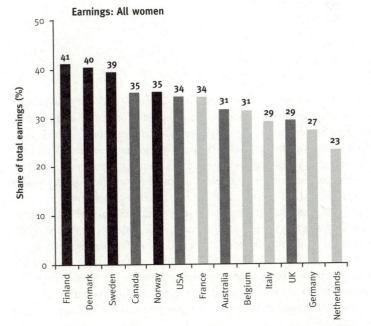

Fig. 8.3. *(Continued)*

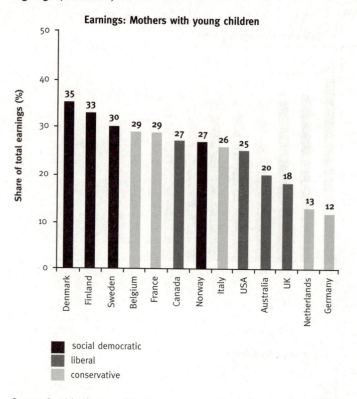

Earnings: Mothers with young children

social democratic
liberal
conservative

Source: Gornick, Chapter 7 this volume.

Germany vindicate Jane Lewis and Ilona Ostner's (1991) original categorization of these three countries as exemplars of strong male-breadwinner
countries. Secondly, they rightly flagged the distinctiveness of the French
policies as a 'modified' variant of the male-breadwinner model.

Gender cuts across welfare state regimes on specific policy dimensions,
but do countries form new clusters on the basis of their gender policy
regimes? That is, do they cluster according to ideologies that specify actual
or preferred relations between women and men, principles of entitlement,
and policy constructions? With respect to the male-breadwinner policy
regime, the countries do form a new cluster. The male-breadwinner
regime is not limited to the social-capitalist welfare states. Despite the
growing numbers of dual-breadwinner couples in the liberal countries,
policies reflect the male-breadwinner regime. Within both the conservative and liberal clusters, however, there is an uneven development. Policies

❖ DIANE SAINSBURY

of specific countries appear to be moving towards a separate gender roles regime, where social rights are allocated on the basis of the traditional division of labour among the sexes: to the male family provider *and* the female caregiver.

Chapters 4 and 7 point to another possible cluster. The policies of France and Belgium were grouped with those of Denmark, Sweden, and Finland in their support of mothers' employment and less economic dependency of women in the family. In France and Belgium mothers were as likely to be in paid employment as women without children, and the contributions of mothers with young children to total family earnings were roughly on a par with those of Swedish mothers.

At the same time it is difficult to argue that these five countries form a coherent gender policy regime because of dissimilar ideologies and policy constructions. In France the paternal authority of the head of the household persisted into the late 1960s,[2] whereas Scandinavian family-law reforms initiated the process of equalizing the rights of family members in the 1920s or earlier. Furthermore, as brought out in Chapter 6, the French income-tax system is the quintessence of familialism, with the Belgian system not far behind. This contrasts with taxation in the Scandinavian countries, which has moved towards individualization. Likewise, married women's social rights differ in that they still enjoy 'derived' rights based on their husband's entitlement in France and Belgium, while individualized rights are the rule in Scandinavia. Finally, if we were to consider the wider policy context—the type of welfare state regime—French and Belgian policies and those of Scandinavia would diverge even further.

In conclusion, gender regimes and welfare state regimes do not always coincide. The preceding chapters indicate that the welfare state regime typology breaks down at several points when gender is brought into the analysis. New and often unlikely combinations of countries crystallize along policy dimensions, such as employment-enabling measures for mothers, taxation, programmes benefiting single parents, or equal-employment policies. On the other hand, gender regimes also fragment when welfare state types are included (cf. Bussemaker 1997: 188). Therefore we need to consider how gender regimes interface with welfare state regimes and how principles of eligibility intersect.

❖ THE POLICY LOGICS OF WELFARE STATE REGIMES AND GENDER REGIMES

It is necessary to unpack the interlocking effects of principles of entitlement, gender regimes, and welfare state regimes to understand the gendered outcomes of policies. In the construction of welfare state policies

five principles of entitlement have been central: the principle of maintenance, the principle of care, need, work performance, and citizenship/
residence. These principles have major consequences for gender relations
and how claim structures for benefits are gendered.

The policy logics of gender regimes and welfare state regimes privilege
specific principles of entitlement and policy constructions. Furthermore,
as noted earlier, the male-breadwinner regime and the separate gender
roles regime extend across welfare states. The patterning of gender in policies is different depending on the type of welfare state regime and how a
specific country deviates from the regime. To explore this, we look at the
interplay between the policy logics of gender regimes and each welfare
state regime.

❖ The Conservative Regime and Gender

The policy logic of the conservative or social-capitalist regime operates
to temper the ill effects of the market but without undermining the ethos
of the market; it privileges the social-insurance model based on work
performance and the distributional principle of equivalence prescribing
that benefits should correspond to contributions. This policy logic,
together with the logic of the male-breadwinner regime that upholds
the traditional family, produces similar contradictory results for mothers
and parents across these countries. The conservative regime rewards
women workers covered by insurance schemes in the event of childbirth,
and these mothers receive generous maternity benefits equivalent to
roughly 80–100 per cent of their earnings. But, since the policy logic of the
gender regime prescribes that a mother care for her infant child, the duration of benefits falls in the moderate category ranging from three and a
half to five months. As noted in Chapter 1, this generous treatment of
mothers as workers contrasts with the benefits of mothers or parents
as carers. Several of the countries provide long leave, but with meagre
benefits—or no benefits.

The conservative welfare states, including France, have been extremely
reluctant to equate care and domestic services with work or to set benefits
based on the principle of care at the same level as benefits based on
employment. Generally benefits related to caring for children are flat rate.
Overall there have been few policy innovations coupling work-related and
care-related benefits. Perhaps most telling is that these social-insurance
schemes, which confer lavish benefits on men by virtue of their support
obligations, largely fail to offer paternity leave, acknowledging men's
responsibilities for childcaring and child-rearing. When paternity leave is
provided, as in France and Belgium, it is only two or three days. Social provision, despite the formal availability of parental benefits, reflects and

reinforces a strict division of labour in the family based on traditional gender assumptions. It is the mother, not the father, who is the primary caregiver. To the extent that home care allowances and care credits in the
pension system have been introduced, the policies of some of these countries approximate a separate gender roles regime.

Likewise, the dynamics between the gender regime and welfare regime
affect women's situation with respect to care. The gendered consequences
of four interlocking features—the subsidiarity principle, the male-
breadwinner regime, continental family law, and the Bismarckian solution—are that women find themselves in a double bind. Women provide
care for others but are less likely to be eligible for benefits to pay for their
own care; or they are eligible only for means-tested benefits.

The principle of subsidiarity assigns major responsibilities for solving
social problems to the family and civil society, and the state is to intercede
only if they cannot manage. The principle simultaneously invests the state
with the moral responsibility to support families in their tasks. As distinct
from the liberal regime, the state adopts an interventionist position in supporting and protecting the traditional family—but primarily through
cash transfers to the head of the household. The paucity of public provision of welfare services in the conservative/corporatist welfare states
is often attributed to the principle of subsidiarity. It establishes the family
as the preferred site of care, and shapes the delivery of services outside
the family. Personal welfare services and care have usually been supplied
by private not-for-profit associations, with funding from the state. These
associations have been largely staffed by volunteer women workers,
backed up by publicly employed professionals. The male-breadwinner
policy regime, which accords high wages and generous social and tax
benefits to the family provider, enables married women to provide care in
the home and to engage in volunteer carework outside the home.

Equally important has been the influence of family law. It is not merely
that women are caregivers for members of the family, but also that family
obligations are more extensive. Parents are responsible for maintenance
and care of their children until they become self-supporting. Because of
these obligations, parents could qualify for child allowances until their off-
spring were nearly 30 years old. Family responsibilities also extend over
three generations, so that adults have the duty to support and care not only
for their children but also for their aged parents.

Compared to the liberal and social-democratic welfare states, women
are more likely to be out of the labour market providing care as unpaid
work for family members and as volunteer workers in the homes of others.
Since caring activities are not paid work, women are excluded from the
social-insurance schemes that form the backbone of social provision in

the conservative welfare states. Countries in this regime are experimenting with a Bismarckian solution to the costs of institutional care. In attempting to meet the challenge of an ageing population, policy-makers in Germany and Austria have introduced a new form of social insurance to cover expenses in old-age nursing homes (Evers *et al.* 1994). These insurance benefits are available to employees, who are more likely to be men. People outside the labour market, who are more likely to be women, have recourse to charitable provision (Munday 1996*a*, *b*). The introduction of care insurance signals the emergence of a new gender differentiation in social entitlements, wholly in accord with regime policy logics.

❖ The Liberal Regime and Gender

Distinctive for the policy logic of the liberal regime is the primacy of the market and the privacy of the family, resulting in a doctrine of minimal government intervention in the economy and family life. State intervention is mainly prescribed in the event of market and family breakdowns. Otherwise families and individuals are expected to support and care for themselves. The centrality of the market and a strong work ethic have also promoted the development of occupational and fiscal welfare. These two sorts of welfare reward persons with earnings and exclude those without financial means. For persons who do not succeed in the market or cannot provide for themselves, the state has guaranteed a minimum safety net comprised of means-tested benefits. The interplay between these distinctive features of the liberal regime—minimal state responsibility, heavy reliance on means-testing, and the prominence of occupational and fiscal welfare—and the logics of the male-breadwinner regime and the separate gender roles regime produces a different set of gender inequalities compared to the conservative regime.

The dictates of the doctrine of minimal intervention have generally kept cash benefits for families at low levels compared to the conservative and social-democratic regimes (Wennemo 1994: 132–66), although the UK has been an exception. Apart from health care in the UK, Canada, and Australia, and education, benefits in kind and social services have largely been associated with means-testing. Family services, and in particular day care, have been targeted to the needy. With the rise of neo-liberal politics, market solutions and for-profit organization of services have gained increased acceptability. So far it is chiefly in the USA that market solutions and for-profit organization of services account for the actual provision of childcare, medical services, and care of the elderly.

The liberal countries' heavy reliance upon means-tested programmes, which is clearly demonstrated in social expenditures and the proportion of the population receiving these benefits, stands out in an international perspective (Eardley *et al.* 1996). None the less, the liberal countries exhibit sharp differences in the accessibility of these benefits. Australia has lacked social-insurance schemes, and nearly all income-maintenance programmes are means-tested. These programmes are universal in the sense that they are available to all Australians with demonstrable need. At the other extreme, the USA is one of the few industrialized countries that denies assistance to the population as a whole. Instead, only a few categories of the poor—the aged, disabled, and dependent children—have been defined as worthy of aid.

In Australia the centrality of income-tested programmes has meant that benefits are overwhelmingly familialized. For the most part, the unit of benefit has been the family, putting married women at a disadvantage. Their husbands' incomes may disqualify them for unemployment benefits, disability benefits, etc. Although benefits have been familialized, the gender differentiation of entitlements that typically results from social-insurance schemes privileging male earners has been much less pronounced. Australian social provision recognizes need, irrespective of whether the claimant is a carer or an earner (O'Connor *et al.* 1999).

Social-insurance schemes and a gender differentiation of entitlements—where men enjoy benefits as earners and women as wives—are more important in the other three countries. The social provision of the USA has a bifurcated structure, with a tier of social insurance or 'social security' and a tier of means-tested benefits or 'welfare'. In the social-insurance tier, men's rights are attached to their status as workers, while many women receive pension benefits on the basis on their husband's entitlements. In the assistance tier, women have predominated as claimants for two reasons. First, definitions of the deserving poor have skewed women's and men's access to means-tested benefits. Family failures but not market failures have provided entitlement. Women as needy carers of dependent children can claim benefits, but able-bodied men who are impoverished earners lack the right to assistance. Secondly, compared to men, women are less likely to have social-security entitlements to protect them against disability or old age. They have no other recourse than public assistance (Sainsbury 1996).

A cornerstone of the post-war British welfare state has been the national-insurance scheme, which provides pensions, unemployment, disability, and sickness benefits. With the exception of pensions, men are disproportionately the beneficiaries of the scheme, basing their claims as earners who have paid contributions. Family men have been able to claim additional benefits for dependants. Women have less often claimed pension benefits on the basis of their own insurance, and there has been a deterioration in the benefits of women who do. As in the USA, many women have pension entitlements as wives (Sainsbury 1996). Like Australia, but unlike the USA, assistance covers both family and market failures. Still a larger proportion of women are assistance beneficiaries, largely because of their lack of occupational welfare benefits, poorer access to insurance benefits, and lower benefit levels.

The preference for market solutions has spurred the growth of occupational welfare—the provision of benefits by the firm or the employer. Occupational welfare replicates the reward structure of the market and job hierarchies of the firm. Benefits are based on long-term service and reflect pay differentials, while low-level employees are often excluded. Inequalities between the sexes in access and benefit levels are generally wider in occupational welfare schemes than in social-insurance schemes. Vertical segregation of the labour market and differences in pay adversely affect women's ability to claim these benefits. A stronger gender differentiation in entitlements among married persons also characterizes occupational benefits. Married men have the highest coverage and proportion of beneficiaries, while married women have the lowest coverage, and few are beneficiaries in their own right (Sainsbury 1996). Maternity benefits and parental leave are mainly provided as occupational welfare, which largely accounts for the low levels of provision in the liberal countries reported in Chapter 4.

Fiscal welfare (benefits distributed through the tax system) has become increasingly pronounced in the liberal welfare states. Tax expenditures for private pensions have grown in the UK; in addition to this trend, tax benefits are especially prominent for social and family policy purposes in the USA, Canada, and Australia. Tax credits compensate low-income groups, and they offset childcare expenses, or the costs of children or a handicapped child.

The growing prominence of fiscal welfare has two negative consequences for women. First, when qualifying conditions for tax benefits involve an income ceiling, it is usually family income that determines eligibility. Accordingly, this sort of tax benefit introduces familialism into systems of individual taxation. Refundable tax credits are also biased against a second earner, creating huge disincentives if the earnings convert a tax refund into a liability to pay taxes (McCaffery 1997: 81–3). Secondly, despite tax credits to benefit the working poor, fiscal welfare is often much more advantageous for the middle- and upper-income brackets—and has thus been aptly termed 'reverse targeting'. In contrast to means-tested programmes that are targeted to the needy, fiscal welfare is targeted to persons with earnings and often those who are well-off. The tax regime of liberal welfare states is plagued by a redistributional paradox.

❖ DIANE SAINSBURY

Progressive tax rates have been counterbalanced by 'reverse targeting' through pervasive fiscal welfare. The income disparities between women and men disadvantage women in their ability to reap the benefits of fiscal welfare.

As the strength of the breadwinner regime ebbs, the non-interventionist stance of the state with respect to the family in the liberal countries has entailed fewer obstacles to women's employment compared to the conservative countries, but also few measures to promote combining paid work and parenting. The lack of publicly provided childcare largely stems from restrictive notions of state responsibilities; and regime variability in the provision of childcare services—the greater commitment in Australia to work-related childcare—is related to differing visions of the appropriateness of state intervention across the liberal countries. The policy logics of the conservative and the liberal regime interact with the separate gender roles regime in different ways. In the conservative regime care-related benefits do not have the same status as work-related benefits, but most countries have introduced flat-rate care allowances. Of the liberal countries the UK and Australia offer more benefits based on the principle of care than the USA and Canada, but in the liberal regime care-related benefits are more likely to be means-tested. The preponderance of means-tested benefits in the liberal regime undermines the individual rights of many women and allows marital status to play a substantial role in determining women's entitlements. The heavy reliance on means-tested benefits is especially detrimental to the well-being of solo mothers, which is evident in their high poverty rates, as documented in Chapter 5.

❖ The Social-Democratic Regime and Gender

The policy logic of the social-democratic regime sanctions state intervention to modify the play of market forces in the attempt to achieve a greater measure of social equality. Four principal modifications can serve to exemplify this policy logic. Rather than accepting that market forces determine the level of employment, active labour-market policy was initiated to promote full employment. These measures were aimed at groups that had a weak position in the labour market to improve their job skills or remove obstacles to their employment. A second modification was the expansion of public services made available as a social right rather than as commodities to be purchased on the market. As distinct from the conservative regime, state responsibility for welfare services has not been confined to funding, but includes the production and delivery of services. Thirdly, social rights based on citizenship or residence rather than work performance have diluted the influence of the market on entitlements. Fourthly, funding benefits through general revenues rather than contributions by insured persons has a similar effect, and it sharply contrasts with the conservative regime where contributions have almost exclusively been the foundation of entitlement.

As we saw in Chapter 3, the gender policy regime in the Scandinavian countries has been distinctly different from most of the other countries. Historically, women have had strong entitlements as mothers rather than as wives—coinciding with a separate gender roles regime. In varying degrees across the Scandinavian countries, this regime has been replaced by the individual earner–carer regime and its policy logic. The logic is derived from a gender ideology that envisions greater equality between women and men and the transformation of the traditional division of labour between the sexes, so that each individual is involved in caring and earning. Social rights are granted to the individual—even to children—independently of family relationships. State responsibilities pertain to areas of reproductive work, formerly entirely in the sphere of the family.

This gender regime and the social-democratic regime have complementary logics. Social rights based on citizenship/residence simultaneously weaken the influence of the market and the family on entitlements. This principle of entitlement individualizes and thereby defamilializes social rights; it also combats a gender differentiation in entitlements, since it does not recognize a difference in the worth of unpaid and paid work. Active labour-market policy was introduced to help workers who were most vulnerable to seasonal unemployment, business-cycle fluctuations, and economic restructuring. Initially this policy benefited workers in the primary and secondary sectors—predominantly male blue-collar workers. Once active labour-market measures were directed to both sexes, they enhanced women's employment opportunities. Similarly the expansion of public services improved access for people with little means. At the same time, public services provided jobs, and provision of day care made it easier for mothers to work. Most importantly, the goal of equality underpins both logics. What is distinctive, especially compared to the liberal welfare states, is that the notion of equality is not limited to equal opportunities but also encompasses equality of outcomes. The emphasis on equality of outcomes has been transposed to gender relations. The official goal of gender-equality policies is the equal presence of women and men in all spheres of society—not merely equal opportunities in all spheres.

Regimes are ideal types—a conceptualization that assumes the co-occurrence of all its defining properties. In the real world this co-occurrence hardly ever exists; politics and political imagination combine these attributes in a variety of ways. The chapters in Part One identified several intra-regime differences that are significant in structuring gender relations in specific countries. Intra-regime variations and country-specific deviations are produced by politics. Decision-makers design policies in response to problems; not infrequently they find inspiration in solutions adopted in other countries.

❖ POLICY DESIGN AND STRATEGIES

Policy design deserves attention because policies vary in their capacity to reduce gender inequalities. The previous chapters provide lessons about the positive and negative aspects of certain policy frameworks. They also point to the politics and institutions that shape particular policies, allowing us to speculate about the opportunities for and obstacles to reducing the gendered impact of policies.

In summing up the lessons, I focus on three strategies to eliminate gender inequalities, based on Nancy Fraser's gender-equity models (1994, 1997), to which earlier chapters have referred. The first strategy is based on the universal-breadwinner model. As its name suggests, the goal of this strategy is that all women and all men should be earners enjoying a paid income and social benefits attached to work performance. The core policies of this strategy involve state provision of services to enable employment, such as education and training, day care, and care of the elderly. The second is the caregiver-parity model, which aims at equalizing the rewards tied to the role of carer and to the role of earner. It envisions social entitlements based on both the principle of care and the principle of work, with the two principles bestowing equal benefits. This strategy centres on informal care and its support through state provision of care allowances. The third is the universal-caregiver model, which calls for the redesigning of policies to break down the traditional gender division of labour so that men and women can combine caregiving and breadwinning. This strategy retains the emphasis on the employment-enabling services of the universal-breadwinner model, but policy measures supporting informal care are targeted at both men and women. In many respects the universal-caregiving model resembles the individual earner–carer gender policy regime presented in Chapter 3 and sketched out in the previous section. What are the lessons of the chapters as reflected in the strategies associated with the three models?

❖ *The Universal-Breadwinner Strategy*

At the heart of the universal-breadwinner strategy is the equal employment of women and men and policies to achieve this end. Chapter 2 compares equal-employment policies based on a legislative/individualist approach and those based on an industrial-relations/collectivist approach. Julia O'Connor identifies several difficulties inherent in the legislative approach to reduce gender pay differentials, especially when it is complaint based. This approach puts the onus on individual workers to demonstrate unfair wages—a task that is all the more difficult in the absence of collective resources or collective bargaining procedures. Legislation has covered only a small section of the workforce. Individual wage improvements, therefore, have not been translated into gains at the aggregate level. The experiences of the liberal countries also reveal that effective enforcement mechanisms are hard to design. The approach is essentially legalistic; positive discrimination and affirmative action are open to legal challenges and have generated intense political controversy, which has slowed implementation and led to reverses.

By contrast, the collective approach is characterized by the active involvement of the labour-market partners; it covers most employees and promotes adjustment in conflicts of interest. Of critical significance with respect to differences in policy design are measures actively promoting equality of opportunity in employment rather than confining measures to formal access to jobs. Among the measures to enable employment are training programmes and work-related childcare.

Together, Chapters 4 and 7 demonstrate precisely the importance of policies that expand labour-market opportunities. In quite diverse national contexts, policies supporting mothers' employment bolster their share of family earnings and reduce their dependency within the family. These sorts of policies are also decisive to the economic well-being of solo mothers. Across all countries, paid employment reduces solo mothers' risk of poverty, and the availability of good quality, flexible, and affordable childcare is a key factor in the employment of solo mothers. Interestingly, and contrary to the conventional wisdom, Chapter 5 found little evidence of a strong relationship between economic disincentives to enter employment or to increase working hours—such as generous social-assistance benefits and high marginal tax rates—and solo mothers' labour supply. Finnish policies, for example, provided powerful disincentives, but the proportion of employed solo mothers who were working full-time was the highest of all the countries examined. An additional lesson of several chapters is that policies improving the nature and quality of women's labour-market participation are vital. It is these aspects that determine earnings, providing financial independence and the basis of autonomy. For solo mothers they make the difference between poverty and a decent standard of living.

Equal access to labour-market earnings is a major goal of the universal-breadwinner model, but this goal is complemented by equal access to work-related benefits. Currently women's overall access to benefits based

❖ DIANE SAINSBURY

on labour-market participation is poorer than men's in all countries. Nowhere do women's utilization rates of benefits match their labour-market-participation rates, because female workers are excluded by additional qualifying conditions, such as minimum work requirements and/or earnings requirements.

Eligibility requirements differ in stringency and their potential to exclude workers. Among the most stringent are requirements of lifetime employment and continuous contributions. As we saw in Chapter 3, Norwegian workers have had to work for forty years to meet the requirements for an occupational old-age pension compared to thirty years for Swedish workers, and a much larger share of Swedish women received such a pension. Requirements of continuous contributions disqualify many workers and often result in wasted contributions. Even schemes with 'universal' coverage, such as Danish occupational pensions (ATP), do not assure women workers of benefits because of rigorous contributions requirements. These requirements are difficult for both sexes to meet, but women are hit especially hard. Men and women employees have had less difficulty in fulfilling Swedish conditions, which did not include contributions requirements.

Although the construction of eligibility requirements can make a difference in the availability of benefits, there is evidence that a strategy concentrating on measures to strengthen workers' attachment to the labour market offers the greatest pay-off (Sainsbury 1996: ch. 5). A two-prong strategy—(1) to eliminate short part-time work (under twenty hours per week) and (2) to secure pro-rata wages for part-timers—enables nearly all workers to meet minimum hours and earnings requirements. An alternative route has been to bring eligibility requirements in line with the new labour-market conditions, so that peripheral workers are eligible. A flaw of this strategy is that benefits remain meagre, because they are based on poor earnings. The inclusion of peripheral workers may, however, reduce or remove incentives for employers to create marginal jobs.

❖ The Caregiver-Parity Strategy

The strategy informing the caregiver-parity model focuses on measures to support care rather than to enable employment. The core measures consist of care allowances and care credits in social-insurance schemes. This strategy has called attention to care responsibilities as a major obstacle for women receiving benefits in work-related pension schemes. Several countries—Germany, the UK, Sweden, Norway, and France—have made arrangements to soften or eliminate loss of pension rights because of breaks in employment due to caring responsibilities. One common solution to this problem has been care credits; another has been that the calculation of benefits is based on best earnings during a specified number of years rather than on lifetime earnings. Most countries have only recently introduced care credits, so that it is not yet possible to evaluate their effects either in improving women's claims to pensions or in equalizing their claims in relation to men's.

Even without policy evaluations, a number of difficulties are apparent. The first is that long spells out of the labour market affect employability and earnings. Even short breaks may impair promotion, jeopardizing career advancement and lifetime earnings. Secondly, care credits safeguard the carer's entitlement, but they are pegged at a level lower than average earnings and are thus considerably lower than men's average earnings. Accordingly, care credits may equalize women's and men's pension claims in terms of access but not benefit levels. The third difficulty, which is fundamental to the caregiver-parity strategy, arises when care responsibilities end. This difficulty characterizes programmes, such as the Norwegian transitional benefit and the Australian sole parent's pension, that provide a minimum income to carers. These have been long-term benefits and, as we saw in Chapter 3, difficult to combine with part-time employment. When the period of benefits expires, the caregiver may have been out of the labour market a full decade or more, making entry or re-entry an enormous problem. Finally, the caregiver-parity model is individually oriented; it provides individual solutions that may undermine public provision of services. Care allowances can serve as an excuse not to expand day care or institutional care of the elderly. Alternatively, care allowances may be introduced to substitute for existing services, such childcare in Finland or services for the elderly in the UK.

❖ The Earner–Carer Strategy

If the next wave of woman-friendly welfare state development concerns policies to enable both women and men to be earners and carers, as Janet Gornick concludes in her chapter, lessons can be drawn from the experience of the Scandinavian countries. Their parental-leave reforms reveal the importance of not merely grafting fathers' rights on to maternity insurance schemes. In three of the countries, fathers' rights have been contingent upon mothers' rights—an interesting reversal of married women's rights via their husband's. The Norwegian and Danish schemes provide cash benefits for fathers only if the mother is entitled to earnings-related benefits. Both countries have high female labour-market participation rates, but one-quarter of all fathers were disqualified in the 1990s. If decision-makers in other countries, especially those of continental Europe, were to adopt this principle, it would exclude larger proportions of fathers. Even more detrimental is the principle that the mother's earnings determine the benefit levels of both parents, which has been applied in the Norwegian scheme. On the other hand, the Swedish parental insurance scheme has attached rights to the child, and parents can choose how to divide the leave among themselves. But mothers 'choose' leave, and fathers do not.

The rather discouraging outcomes of Scandinavian policies suggest that another design is required: *equal individualized rights for each parent.* As distinct from the Scandinavian schemes, this would mean each parent would be entitled to equal periods of leave to care for a child. In fact, Swedish temporary paid leave to care for a sick child uses this formula, and fathers have a higher utilization rate of this programme than of regular parental leave. In the 1990s legislation—the Norwegian 'daddy quota' and the Swedish 'daddy month'—has assigned a specific period of leave exclusively for fathers. In both countries, more fathers are claiming parental benefits, and the increase has been quite dramatic for Norwegian fathers.

To dismantle a gender differentiation in claiming parental benefits, it is essential that *benefits compensate the parent for the loss of his or her income.* In the Netherlands and Denmark, employees in the public sector receive more generous benefits than other workers. Dutch and Danish fathers working in the public sector have a better record in utilizing leave compared to other fathers. Conversely, when Sweden reduced replacement rates in its parental insurance scheme, the proportion of fathers taking paternity leave dropped by about 10 per cent. Flat-rate benefits virtually eliminate the possibility of fathers taking leave, as has been made clear from the German and French experiences. That German benefits are also income tested makes doubly sure that fathers will not participate.

It is also important *to link care-related and work-related benefits.* This sort of coupling represents an initial step in putting benefits related to care on a par with benefits related to work, especially when replacement rates and duration are the same. This construction marks the equal legitimacy of care and work; it makes possible interchangeable periods of work and care for all earners. The linking of benefits creates an incentive structure for women to engage in paid work and for men to provide care, which is not provided by the caregiver-parity model. Finally, this linkage counteracts the emergence of a new gender segregation in benefit levels that occurs when care-related benefits are flat rate and work-related benefits are earnings related.

Policies reflecting an earner–carer strategy are also suited to the needs of solo mothers who must fulfil the dual tasks of earner and carer (Kilkey and Bradshaw, Chapter 5, this volume). A universal-breadwinner strategy is likely to compel solo mothers to be full-time workers, even if they want to spend more time with their children. A caregiver-parity strategy is accompanied by transitional difficulties when care responsibilities cease and economic uncertainties. Few countries have provided benefits to care-givers that allow them a livelihood above the poverty line.

Although Nancy Fraser presents her gender-equity models as visions in an imagined future, she acknowledges that the models are implicit in cur-rent feminist political practice.[3] In fact, these strategies are very evident in the politics of women's movements. The chances of success are shaped by the political arrangements in specific national contexts as well as regime policy logics.

❖ POLICIES AND POLITICS: Changing Arenas of Women's Activism

A recurrent theme of this book has been the importance of the strategies of the women's movement in influencing legislation as a source of welfare state variation. Women's demands and how they are framed, potential allies and coalition building, institutional arrangements—all offer polit-ical opportunities and constraints in policy formation. Besides women's politics, the chapters have paid particular attention to the strength of the labour movement and the nature of industrial frameworks, political par-ties and the partisan composition of government, and state structures.

❖ Women's Movements

Women's movements represent diverse strands of feminism, and in each country a particular blend of feminism has configured organizational forms, strategies, and goals. A fundamental difference among movements has been the strength of a gender ideology that stresses differences between the sexes and women's special capacities versus one that emphas-izes gender equality and equal rights. These contrasting ideologies envi-sion different gender orders and prescribe the means and instruments to attained the preferred vision of gender relations. Historical analyses trac-ing the development of the women's movement in a specific country have documented shifts in the prominence of these ideological stances over time. The cross-national comparisons in this volume cast light on how they currently vary between countries. Frequently we have detected a rela-tionship between major ideological stances, agendas of reform, and policy formation.

In Germany, the UK, and Norway feminists pursuing a caregiver-parity strategy have figured more prominently in the women's movement com-pared to many other countries. They have demanded measures that recognize the value of women's caring activities in social provision. Legislation in these countries has accommodated or at least reflected these demands. The Germans, during a period of welfare state cutbacks, introduced care allowances for *all* mothers, formally all parents, and successively extended the duration of leave to three years. They also introduced care credits in the old-age and disability pension systems. In the UK there has been a long-term trend to improve care-related benefits from the late 1970s onwards (Sainsbury 1996). Behind this trend were British feminist objections to the injustices against married women in social provisions and campaigns for child-benefit reform and its defence. In Norway women from the centre-right and the far left supported policies that benefited women in the home. Maternity benefits not based on labour-market participation were upgraded, care credits in the pension system enacted, and care allowances were introduced, repealed, and reintroduced. This legislation suggests that these countries are evolving towards the separate gender roles regime, where the principle of care assumes a larger role in determining the social rights of women.

Equal-rights advocates have been influential in the women's movements in the USA, the Netherlands, and Sweden; and their demands have contributed to shaping the policy agenda. However, demands for equal rights have played themselves out differently. Movement demands in the USA come closer to the universal-breadwinner strategy, while feminists in the Netherlands and Sweden have put more emphasis on men and women sharing the tasks of breadwinning and caring. Dutch feminists have stressed that women's dependence on men's income and men's dependence on women's domestic services must be replaced by women's economic independence and men's care independence. In contrast to the other social-capitalist countries, the Netherlands has no home care allowances and undeveloped leave policies, which only recently were introduced. The Dutch women's movement and activists in the women's policy unit have directed their energies to measures enhancing women's financial independence. They have concentrated on social-security legislation, taxation, and improved provision of childcare.

❖ Industrial-Relations Frameworks and Unions

Chapters 2 and 7 point to the influence of corporatist industrial arrangements and strong unions on women's earnings and their access to work-related benefits. The full importance of these arrangements is not brought out in Esping-Andersen's typology, because he links corporatism exclusively with the conservative welfare state regime. Many feminists have been very critical of corporatist arrangements and unions, viewing them as a vehicle to advance men's interests (e.g. Hernes 1984; Bryson 1992). This view is challenged by the results in Chapters 2 and 7, which also reveal an unlikely clustering of countries. In countries with strong unions and/or collective bargaining covering most employees, male/female wage differentials are smaller for full-time workers. Powerful unions that promote wage equalization as a general policy produce less wage dispersion, diminishing pay differentials between women and men. In addition, strong unions and encompassing bargaining arrangements have often secured pro rata pay for part-timers, eliminating another source of wage differentials (Maier 1994).

Corporatist arrangements and unions, however, vary in the degree to which they promote women's interests. Besides earlier explanations emphasizing the degree to which unions are encompassing and the unions' positions on employment policy, these variations appear related to the extent of women's labour-market participation and their entry into the unions. The growth in union membership since the early 1970s has mainly come from women workers. In all the countries for which we have data, women's share of total union membership has grown. As more women join, the unions must respond; and large numbers of female members have brought about a reorientation in union policy. In the conservative countries women's membership has ranged from 15 to 30 per cent; in liberal countries women's share was slightly over one-third; while Finnish, Swedish, and Danish women currently account for roughly half of union membership. What appears more decisive than the female share of membership is the union density of women workers. Following the Scandinavian countries, Australian women workers had the highest union density (OECD 1991: 116–17). Women's entry into unions has been accompanied by their increasing visibility in union office, and in the 1990s women gained top leadership positions in the unions in Australia and Sweden. In other words, unions can be transformed into arenas of women's activism.

❖ Parties and Partisan Composition of Governments

Parties and the political complexion of governments matter. As evident in the earlier chapters, parties display very different degrees of political commitment to gender equality as a policy goal. Left parties have been positive, while parties on the right remain sceptical, if not hostile. This is markedly the case for equal-employment policies. Julia O'Connor suggests that the distinctiveness of Australian equal-employment policies and their approximation of the social-democratic approach are, in part, related to the organizational strength of the Labor Party. In the USA comparable-worth programmes were adopted at the local and state level where the Democrats controlled the state government. Conversely, at the national level the Republican administrations under Presidents Nixon, Reagan, and Bush did not support employment-equality legislation. Nor have conservative governments in the UK and Canada. The most progressive piece of Canadian legislation was quickly overturned once the conservatives returned to office (O'Connor, Chapter 2, this volume).

Among the obstacles to gender-equality reforms frequently cited in the literature is the strength of Christian Democratic parties and Catholicism as a political force. The Norwegian case and the experiences of the liberal welfare states cause us to question the emphasis on the Catholicism/Protestantism split in explaining cross-national variations of gender inequality and policies to combat inequalities (Schmidt 1993: 208; Siaroff 1994: 94–8; Gardiner 1997a: 13). Instead the cases of Norway and the USA indicate that the political mobilization of religious groups—irrespective of whether they consist of Catholics or Protestants—is crucial. Religious groups mobilized as political parties, influential factions, or a core constituency of political parties often work to influence policies so that they incorporate their traditional beliefs about the family and the inappropriateness of women's work outside the home. This is not to argue that Catholicism and Christian Democratic parties are unimportant. Rather, this position is too narrow. As shown in earlier chapters, the institutionalization of religious and traditionalist beliefs in the party system of Protestant countries has put a brake on the adoption of gender-equality policies. It also totally neglects the opposition of conservative and rural parties to these policy measures.

The implications of our analyses, along with evidence from earlier studies (e.g. Norris 1987; Wennemo 1994; Stetson and Mazur 1995), is that left parties offer a promising arena and target for feminist activism. To their credit, left parties are associated with the introduction of childcare services, equal taxation, women's policy machinery, and policies that reduce gender pay differentials and lower poverty rates among women and children. The chapters also indicate that women's entry into *all* parties can have an impact on policy proposals and party politics. In the USA a Republican congresswoman spearheaded a drive to change taxation for married women, going against prominent party spokesmen. Norwegian women increased their parliamentary representation in all parties, and the expansion of childcare services has been attributed to this increase. Women's presence in the parties puts pressure on them to adopt policy proposals that are advantageous to women, and that are formulated by women.

❖ The Importance of States

Irrespective of whether the state is conceived of as a structure or a terrain, the state is a crucial site in regulating and constructing gender relations. It is too important an arena not to enter because of ideological antipathy or fears of co-option. A variation of special significance is the strategic selectivity of the state (Mósesdóttir 1995; Mahon 1997), which is related to the openness or closeness of the policy process (both formation and implementation) and how policies allocate resources.

Policies create politics by affecting gender identities, interests, the goals, and resources of women and men. Social identities are theorized to be a condition for political mobilization and critical to the formation and articulation of interests and goals. State policies, especially social policies and education, enhance resources altering the capacities for political action. Policies are vital to the power resources of vying groups and collectivities and to the bias of mobilization. Certain women mobilize but others do not, and in turn mobilization shapes the policy agenda.

The growing literature of state feminism focuses on women as state actors and the position of women in the bureaucracy. Chapter 6 pointed to the importance of the placement of women's agencies in the administration: the department or sector, at the centre or on the periphery, and the level—local, regional, and national. However, state feminism defined so that special policy units are the main state arena of women's activism is too limited. Across countries public sectors and state bureaucracies differ in how they have institutionalized gender interests. The scope of the public sector and the nature of state activities affect women's entry into the state bureaucracy, the types of position they occupy, and their opportunities to exert influence.

❖ POLICY LOGICS AND FUTURE POLITICS

The policy logic of the conservative regime and other countries that have adopted the Bismarckian solution would seem to offer a favourable setting for a universal-breadwinner strategy because of the primacy of labour-market participation in determining social entitlements. This advantage is offset by the policy logic of the prevailing gender regime in the conservative countries, especially in those countries whose constitutions pledge protection of the traditional family. Instead the policy logic seems to favour a scenario of innovations in accord with the caregiver-parity strategy and a transition from the male-breadwinner regime to the separate gender roles regime. Sections of the women's movements in several of these countries have pursued a politics of difference and claims based on motherhood.

❖ DIANE SAINSBURY

An alternative scenario can emerge from the current predicament of social-capitalist welfare states, described by Jet Bussemaker and Kees van Kersbergen in Chapter 1. A key element of the predicament is deteriorating dependency ratios. An increasing share of the population is dependent upon social benefits, while the proportion of the economically active population is dwindling. One way to alter the imbalance is to bring women into the labour market and strengthen their attachment to paid work. Major impediments are the lack of childcare provision and passive labour-market policies. Bussemaker and van Kersbergen note, however, that it is precisely in these areas that policy change can be detected.

In the liberal countries the contradiction between policies that have been informed by the male-breadwinner regime and the prevalence of dual-earner couples creates pressures for change. A chief obstacle is a policy logic driven by the doctrine of minimal government responsibility combined with the privacy of the family. In the liberal countries political forces of varying strength are poised to mobilize in defence of the traditional family and 'family values'. The liberal heritage of these countries also seems to make them more susceptible to welfare state restructuring based on neo-liberal arguments and demands. The growth of means-testing and fiscal welfare measures directed to the working poor undermine the social rights of married women. These two trends re-establish the importance of family relationships in determining social rights, and they create employment disincentives. On the other hand, liberal tenets of equal opportunity and equity can provide necessary leverage for a strategy of change. As dual-breadwinner families grow more numerous, they form a political constituency whose needs must be addressed. The current move to eliminate the marriage penalty in US taxation and the Australian commitment to meet all work-related childcare needs by the year 2000/1 can be interpreted as responses to accommodate two-earner couples.

The social-democratic regime has been eroded by doubts about its future viability. A policy logic based on equality has produced a never-ending stream of demands for extended entitlements and upward adjustments in benefit levels to match groups enjoying the most generous benefits. Continuous reform has strained the public purse and the economy. The deep recessions in Finland and Sweden in the early 1990s brought an end to full employment and cast a serious shadow over social-democratic policies. In Esping-Andersen's view, full employment is the linchpin of the social-democratic regime, and others see it as a prerequisite for the equal right to work. Feminists have warned of reversals in the gains women have made during the past three decades. Threats to women's employment, especially in the public sector, and cuts in welfare state benefits and services loom large in this scenario. An additional challenge is the policy legacy of the separate gender roles regime, which thwarts the development of an individual earner–carer regime.

A regime policy logic rooted in the notion of equality also generates counter-trends. First, this policy logic has favoured sharing the burdens of cutbacks during periods of welfare state retrenchment, buttressing the legitimacy of the welfare state. Secondly, the logic has repercussions for unemployment, as revealed by the Danish experience. One of the most important lessons of Danish policies is that higher levels of unemployment do not necessarily lead to the abandonment of women's and men's equal right to work. Despite a troubled economy, high unemployment, and welfare state cutbacks in the 1970s, women's employment rate increased during the next decade and half. This suggests that economic crisis need not one-sidedly undermine women's employment opportunities, and that women's mobilization can prevent a major deterioration (Dahlerup 1993). Denmark also calls into question Esping-Andersen's reasoning about the necessity of full employment for the survival of the Scandinavian model. Thirdly, the logic has strengthened women's claims. Their increasing parity in many spheres of society—in the workplace, unions, parties, and central and local political institutions—put women in positions to influence future policies.

Across welfare state regimes women's activism has been a force in shaping policies historically and in contemporary times. A regime policy logic involves a set of constraints and opportunities affecting future politics. None the less, as we have seen, women's politics are a source of policy variations both across and within regimes because of differences in ideology, power resources, strategies, and sites of influence. In analysing welfare regime challenges of the twenty-first century, it is necessary to revamp comparative research so that it not only considers the gender division of welfare but also includes women's collectivities among the political agents relevant to the development and restructuring of welfare states.

❖ Notes

1 Italian solo mothers have fairly low poverty rates, and social policies combat their potential poverty. Benefits are very generous for widows, and the share of widows among Italian single mothers stands out, as does the small portion of never-married mothers. In addition, as brought out in Chapter 4, childcare provision enables mothers to enter employment.

2 As late as the mid-1960s French married women did not have an 'independent' right to work; their right to enter employment was conditional upon the consent of their husband. Paternal authority extended to children and was

not replaced by joint authority of the parents until 1970. Indeed, this is a pattern common to the conservative countries.

3 Nancy Fraser (1994: 593; 1997: 43) argues that the universal-breadwinner model is implicit in the current political practice of most US feminists and liberals, and the caregiver-parity model is implicit in the practice of most West European feminists and social democrats. This categorization is too general, and it is misleading, as I have documented in Chapter 3. She also omits any mention of the universal-caregiving model as a vision of Scandinavian feminists and social democrats or Dutch feminists.

❖ REFERENCES

ANTTONEN, A., AND SIPILÄ, J. (1996), 'European Social Care Services: Is It Possible to Identify Models?', *Journal of European Social Policy* 6/2: 87–100.

BRADSHAW, J. (1998), 'International Comparisons of Support for Lone Parents', in Ford and Millar (1998), 154–68.

BRYSON, L. (1992), *Welfare and the State* (Houndmills).

BUSSEMAKER, J. (1997), 'Citizenship, Welfare State Regimes, and Breadwinner Arrangements: Various Backgrounds of Equality Policy', in Gardiner (1997), 180–96.

CASTLES, F. G. (1993) (ed.), *Families of Nations: Patterns of Public Policy in Western Democracies* (Aldershot).

DAHLERUP, D. (1993), 'From Movement Protest to State Feminism: The Women's Liberation Movement and Unemployment Policy in Denmark', *NORA, Nordic Journal of Women's Studies*, 1: 4–20.

EARDLEY, T., BRADSHAW, J., DITCH, J., GOUGH, I., AND WHITEFORD, P. (1996), *Social Assistance in OECD Countries* (London).

EVANS, P. M. (1997), 'Divided Citizenship? Gender, Income Security, and the Welfare State', in Evans and Wekerle (1997), 91–116.

——AND WEKERLE, G. R. (1997) (eds.), *Women and the Canadian Welfare State* (Toronto).

EVERS, A., PIJL, M., AND UNGERSON, C. (1994) (eds.), *Payments for Care: A Comparative Overview* (Aldershot).

FORD, R., AND MILLAR, J. (1998) (eds.), *Private Lives and Public Responses* (London).

FRASER, N. (1994), 'After the Family Wage: Gender Equity and the Welfare State', *Political Theory*, 22/4: 591–618.

——(1997), *Justice Interruptus: Critical Reflections on the 'Postsocialist' Condition* (New York).

GARDINER, F. (1997*a*), 'Introduction: Welfare and Sex Equality Policy Regimes', in Gardiner (1997*b*), 1–21.

—— (1997b) (ed.), *Sex Equality Policy in Western Europe* (London).

HERNES, H. (1984), 'Women and the Welfare State: The Transition from Private to Public Dependence', in Holter (1984), 26–45.

HOLTER, H. (1984) (ed.), *Patriarchy in a Welfare Society* (Oslo).

LEWIS, J., AND OSTNER, I. (1991) , 'Gender and the Evolution of European Social Policies', paper presented at the CES Workshop 'Emergent Supranational Social Policy: The EC's Social Dimension in Comparative Perspective', Center for European Studies, Harvard 15–17 Nov.

MCCAFFERY, E. J. (1997), *Taxing Women* (Chicago).

MAHON, R. (1997), 'The Never-Ending Story Part I: Feminist Struggle to Reshape Canadian Day Care Policy in the 1970s', paper presented at the conference 'Gender, Citizenship and the Work of Caring', University of Illinois at Urbana-Champaign, 14–16 Nov.

MAIER, F. (1994), 'Institutional Regimes of Part-Time Working', in Schmid (1994), 151–82.

MILLAR, J., AND WARMAN, A. (1996), *Family Obligations in Europe* (London).

MITCHELL, D. (1991), *Income Transfers in Ten Welfare States* (Aldershot).

MÓSESDÓTTIR, L. (1995), 'The State and the Egalitarian, Ecclesiastical and Liberal Regimes of Gender Relations', *British Journal of Sociology*, 46/4: 623–42.

MUNDAY, B. (1996a), 'Introduction: Definitions and Comparisons in European Social Care', in Munday and Ely (1996), 1–20.

—— (1996b), 'Social Care in the Member States of the European Union: Contexts and Overview', in Munday and Ely (1996), 21–66.

—— AND ELY, P. (1996) (eds.), *Social Care in Europe* (London).

NORRIS, P. (1987), *Politics and Sexual Equality: The Comparative Position of Women in Western Democracies* (Brighton).

O'CONNOR, J., ORLOFF, A. S., AND SHAVER, S. (1999), *States, Markets, Families: Gender, Liberalism and Social Policy in Australia, Canada, Great Britain, and the United States* (Cambridge).

OECD (1991), Organization for Economic Cooperation and Development, *Employment Outlook* (Paris).

—— (1997a), *Employment Outlook* (Paris).

—— (1997b), *Family, Market and Community: Equity and Efficiency in Social Policy* (Paris).

SAINSBURY, D. (1994) (ed.), *Gendering Welfare States* (London).

—— (1996), *Gender, Equality and Welfare States* (Cambridge).

SCHMID, G. (1994) (ed.), *Labor Market Institutions in Europe* (Armonk, NY).

SCHMIDT, M. (1993), 'Gendered Labour Market Participation', in Castles (1993), 131–78.

✦ DIANE SAINSBURY

SIAROFF, A. (1994), 'Work, Welfare and Gender Equality: A New Typology', in Sainsbury (1994), 82–100.

STETSON, D., AND MAZUR, A. G. (1995) (eds.), *Comparative State Feminism* (Thousand Oaks, Calif.).

WENNEMO, I. (1994), *Sharing the Costs of Children: Studies on the Development of Family Support in the OECD Countries* (Stockholm).

❖ Index